Networking for
VMware Administrators

Stay snazzy!

VMware Press is the official publisher of VMware books and training materials, which provide guidance on the critical topics facing today's technology professionals and students. Enterprises, as well as small- and medium-sized organizations, adopt virtualization as a more agile way of scaling IT to meet business needs. VMware Press provides proven, technically accurate information that will help them meet their goals for customizing, building, and maintaining their virtual environment.

With books, certification and study guides, video training, and learning tools produced by world-class architects and IT experts, VMware Press helps IT professionals master a diverse range of topics on virtualization and cloud computing. It is the official source of reference materials for preparing for the VMware Certified Professional Examination.

VMware Press is also pleased to have localization partners that can publish its products into more than 42 languages, including Chinese (Simplified), Chinese (Traditional), French, German, Greek, Hindi, Japanese, Korean, Polish, Russian, and Spanish.

For more information about VMware Press, please visit **vmwarepress.com**.

Networking for VMware Administrators

Chris Wahl
Steve Pantol

vmware® PRESS

Upper Saddle River, NJ • Boston • Indianapolis • San Francisco
New York • Toronto • Montreal • London • Munich • Paris • Madrid
Capetown • Sydney • Tokyo • Singapore • Mexico City

Networking for VMware Administrators

Library of Congress Control Number: 2014901956

ISBN-13: 978-0-13-351108-6

ISBN-10: 0-13-351108-1

Text printed in the United States on recycled paper at RR Donnelley in Crawfordsville, Indiana.

Second Printing September 2014

All terms mentioned in this book that are known to be trademarks or service marks have been appropriately capitalized. The publisher cannot attest to the accuracy of this information. Use of a term in this book should not be regarded as affecting the validity of any trademark or service mark.

VMware terms are trademarks or registered trademarks of VMware in the United States, other countries, or both.

Warning and Disclaimer

Every effort has been made to make this book as complete and as accurate as possible, but no warranty or fitness is implied. The information provided is on an "as is" basis. The authors, VMware Press, VMware, and the publisher shall have neither liability nor responsibility to any person or entity with respect to any loss or damages arising from the information contained in this book.

The opinions expressed in this book belong to the authors and are not necessarily those of VMware.

Special Sales

For information about buying this title in bulk quantities, or for special sales opportunities (which may include electronic versions; custom cover designs; and content particular to your business, training goals, marketing focus, or branding interests), please contact our corporate sales department at corpsales@pearsoned.com or (800) 382-3419.

For government sales inquiries, please contact governmentsales@pearsoned.com.

For questions about sales outside the U.S., please contact international@pearsoned.com.

VMWARE PRESS PROGRAM MANAGER
Anand Sundaram

ASSOCIATE PUBLISHER
David Dusthimer

ACQUISITIONS EDITOR
Joan Murray

DEVELOPMENT EDITOR
Eleanor C. Bru

MANAGING EDITOR
Sandra Schroeder

PROJECT EDITOR
Seth Kerney

COPY EDITOR
Anne Goebel

PROOFREADER
Jess DeGabriele

INDEXER
Cheryl Lenser

EDITORIAL ASSISTANT
Vanessa Evans

BOOK DESIGNER
Gary Adair

COVER DESIGNER
Chuti Prasertsith

COMPOSITOR
Bumpy Design

To my wife Jennifer, for her steadfast patience and support
while I flailed around like a fish out of water trying to write this book.
—Chris Wahl

To my long-suffering wife, Kari. Sorry for the continued trouble.
—Steve Pantol

Contents

Foreword

Virtual networking has long been the Cinderella of server virtualization, as anyone reading VMware release notes can easily attest—with every new vSphere release, we get tons of new CPU/RAM optimization features, high availability improvements, better storage connectivity, and networking breadcrumbs.

The traditional jousting between networking and virtualization vendors and the corresponding lack of empathy between virtualization and networking teams in large IT shops definitely doesn't help. Virtualization vendors try to work around the traditional networking concepts (pretending, for example, that Spanning Tree Protocol [STP] and Link Aggregation Groups [LAG] don't exist), while routinely asking for mission-impossible feats such as long-distance bridging across multiple data centers. The resulting lack of cooperation from the networking team is hardly surprising, and unfamiliar concepts and terminology used by virtualization vendors definitely don't help, either.

The virtualization publishing ecosystem has adjusted to that mentality—we have great books on server virtualization management, troubleshooting, high availability, and DRS, but almost nothing on virtual networking and its interaction with the outside physical world. This glaring omission has finally been fixed—we've got a whole book dedicated solely to VMware networking.

Who should read this book? In my personal opinion, this book should be mandatory reading for anyone getting anywhere near a vSphere host. Server and virtualization administrators will get the baseline networking knowledge that will help them understand the intricacies and challenges their networking colleagues have to deal with on a daily basis, and networking engineers will finally have a fighting chance of understanding what goes on behind the scenes of point-and-click vCenter GUI. If nothing else, if you manage to persuade the virtualization *and* networking engineers in your company to read this book, they'll learn a common language they can use to discuss their needs, priorities, and challenges.

Although the book starts with rudimentary topics such as defining what a network is, it quickly dives into convoluted technical details of vSphere virtual networking, and I have to admit some of these details were new to me, even though I spent months reading vSphere documentation and researching actual ESXi behavior while creating my VMware Networking Technical Deep Dive webinar.

What will you get from the book? If you're a server or virtualization administrator and don't know much about networking, you'll learn the concepts you need to understand the data center networks and how vSphere virtual networking interacts with them. If you're a networking engineer, you'll get *the other perspective*—the view from the server side, and the details that will help you adjust the network edge to interact with vSphere hosts.

Finally, do keep in mind that *the other engineer* in your organization is not your enemy—she has a different perspective, different challenges, and different priorities and requirements. Statements such as "We must have this or we cannot do that" are rarely helpful in this context; it's way better to ask "Why would you need this?" or "What business problem are you trying to solve?"—and this book just might be a piece of the puzzle that will help you bridge the communication gap.

Ivan Pepelnjak

CCIE #1354 Emeritus

ipSpace.net

Introduction

In many organizations, there is still no Virtualization Team, or even a dedicated Virtualization Person. The care and feeding of a vSphere environment often falls under the "Perform other duties as assigned" bullet in the job description of existing server or storage administrators.

Virtualization is a complex subject, interdisciplinary by nature, and truly "getting it" requires a solid understanding of servers, storage, and networking. But because new technologies are often managed by whoever arrived to the meeting last, skill gaps are bound to come up. In the authors' experience, networking is the subject most foreign to admins that inherit a vSphere environment. Server and storage teams tend to work rather closely, with the network hiding behind a curtain of patch panels. This book is intended to help vSphere admins bridge that gap.

This book is not intended to be a study guide for any particular certification. If your goal is Network+, CCENT, or beyond, there are other, more comprehensive options available.

Part I, "Physical Networking 101," is intended to build a foundation of networking knowledge, starting with the very basics of connectivity and building up to routing and switching. It provides the background and jargon necessary for you to communicate effectively with your network team as you scale up your virtualization efforts.

In Part II, "Virtual Switching," we look at virtual networking, explaining how and where it differs from the physical world we built up in Part I. We go on a guided tour of building virtual networks, starting with real-world requirements, and review the virtual and physical network configuration steps necessary to meet them.

In Part III, "You Got Your Storage in My Networking: IP Storage," we add storage into the mix, using the same approach from Part II to look at iSCSI and NFS configurations.

Motivation for Writing This Book

Chris: Aside from a grandiose ambition to cross "write a book" off my bucket list, there is something inherently romantic about the idea of passing one's experiences down to the next generation of technical professionals. The field of networking is like sailing in dark and uncharted waters, with little islands of knowledge along the way. Having made the voyage, I felt it best to return as a guide and see if I could both help others through and learn more on the second go-round for myself.

Steve: What Chris said, but maybe less flowery. And it seemed like a good idea at the time.

Who Should Read This Book

This book is targeted at IT professionals who are involved in the care and feeding of a VMware vSphere environment. These administrators often have strong server or storage backgrounds but lack exposure to core networking concepts. As virtualization is interdisciplinary in nature, it is important for vSphere administrators to have a holistic understanding of the technologies supporting their environment.

How to Use This Book

This book is split into 19 chapters as described here:

- **Part I, "Physical Networking 101"**

  - **Chapter 1, "The Very Basics":** This chapter provides a high-level introduction to networking concepts.

  - **Chapter 2, "A Tale of Two Network Models":** This chapter describes the purpose of network models and describes the two major flavors.

  - **Chapter 3, "Ethernet Networks":** This chapter introduces the basics of Ethernet networks.

  - **Chapter 4, "Advanced Layer 2":** This chapter builds upon the previous chapter by diving into more advanced Ethernet concepts including VLANs, switch port types, Spanning Tree Protocol, and Link Aggregation.

  - **Chapter 5, "Layer 3":** This chapter describes the IP protocol, Layer 3 networking, and supporting applications.

  - **Chapter 6, "Converged Infrastructure (CI)":** This chapter provides a brief overview of converged infrastructure and describes example platforms.

- **Part II, "Virtual Switching"**

  - **Chapter 7, "How Virtual Switching Differs from Physical Switching":** This chapter highlights the differences in the mechanics and execution between physical switches as described in Part I and the virtual switches that are the focus of the rest of the book.

  - **Chapter 8, "vSphere Standard Switch":** This chapter covers the features available with the vSphere Standard Switch.

  - **Chapter 9, "vSphere Distributed Switch":** This chapter covers the features available with the vSphere Distributed Switch.

- **Chapter 10, "Third Party Switches—1000v":** This chapter covers the features available with the Cisco Nexus 1000v virtual switch.

- **Chapter 11, "Lab Scenario":** This chapter introduces the lab scenario that is used in Chapters 12 and 13, guiding the reader through a design exercise.

- **Chapter 12, "Standard vSwitch Design":** This chapter describes the configuration steps necessary to configure the Standard vSwitch to support the use case defined in Chapter 11.

- **Chapter 13, "Distributed vSwitch Design":** This chapter describes the configuration steps necessary to configure the Distributed vSwitch to support the use case defined in Chapter 11, with a focus on the feature differences between the Distributed and Standard vSwitches.

- **Part III, "You Got Your Storage in My Networking: IP Storage"**

  - **Chapter 14, "iSCSI General Use Cases":** This chapter introduces the concepts behind iSCSI and describes an example use case.

  - **Chapter 15, "iSCSI Design and Configuration":** This chapter describes the configuration steps necessary to configure iSCSI to support the use case defined in Chapter 14.

  - **Chapter 16, "NFS General Use Cases":** This chapter introduces the concepts behind NFS and describes an example use case.

  - **Chapter 17, "NFS Design and Configuration":** This chapter describes the configuration steps necessary to configure NFS to support the use case defined in Chapter 16.

- **Part IV, "Other Design Scenarios"**

  - **Chapter 18, "Additional vSwitch Design Scenarios":** This chapter describes different design options that could be considered for varying hardware configurations.

  - **Chapter 19, "Multi-NIC vMotion Architecture":** This chapter introduces the concepts behind Multi-NIC vMotion and describes the steps necessary to configure it for a sample use case.

- **Appendix A, "Networking for VMware Administrators: The VMware User Group":** This appendix is a call to action introducing the VMware User Group as a means of harnessing the power of the greater VMware community and encouraging the reader to get involved.

About the Authors

Chris Wahl has acquired more than a decade of IT experience in enterprise infrastructure design, implementation, and administration. He has provided architectural and engineering expertise in a variety of virtualization, data center, and private cloud-based engagements while working with high performance technical teams in tiered data center environments. He currently holds the title of Senior Technical Architect at Ahead, a consulting firm based out of Chicago.

Chris holds well over 30 active industry certifications, including the rare VMware Certified Design Expert (VCDX #104), and is a recognized VMware vExpert. He also works to give back to the community as both an active "Master" user and moderator of the VMware Technology Network (VMTN) and as a Leader of the Chicago VMware User Group (VMUG).

As an independent blogger for the award winning "Wahl Network," Chris focuses on creating content that revolves around virtualization, converged infrastructure, and evangelizing products and services that benefit the technology community. Over the past several years, he has published hundreds of articles and was voted the "Favorite Independent Blogger" by vSphere-Land for 2012. Chris also travels globally to speak at industry events, provide subject matter expertise, and offer perspectives as a technical analyst.

Steve Pantol has spent the last 14 years wearing various technical hats, with the last seven or so focused on assorted VMware technologies. He holds numerous technical certifications and is working toward VCDX—if only to stop Wahl from lording it over him. He is a Senior Technical Architect at Ahead, working to build better data centers and drive adoption of cloud technologies.

Acknowledgments

Chris would like to thank the people that helped him get to a point in his career where he could share knowledge around virtual networking with the technical community. It has taken years of trial and error, resulting in many successes and failures, to reach this point. While there were many people providing guidance and a leg up along the way, he would like to specifically thank his past mentors Wayne Balogh, Sean Murphy, Matt Lattanzio, and Pam Cox, along with his parents Dawn and Matt for their steadfast support towards a career in technology. Additionally, an immeasurable thank you to his supportive spouse Jennifer for providing positive energy and inspiration on a daily basis.

Steve would like to thank his wife, Kari, and their numerous children—Kurt, Avery, and Ben—for putting up with him, both in general and as it relates to this project. And his parents, Don and Betty, for spending so much early 90s money on computers, and not yelling when he took them apart. Also, a special thank you to Xfinity On-Demand, particularly the Sprout and Disney Junior networks, for shouldering much of the burden of parenting over the last several months.

We both would like to thank everyone at our employer, Ahead, including Mitch Northcutt, Eric Kaplan, Paul Bostjancic, and Mike Mills, for their technical and logistical support. Also our amazing technical reviewers, Doug Baer, Scott Winger, and Trevor Roberts, and the team at VMware Press, Joan Murray, Ellie Bru, and Seth Kerney, who have all been tireless in working and reworking the manuscript to make it perfect.

About the Reviewers

Doug Baer is an Infrastructure Architect on the Hands-on Labs team at VMware. His nearly 20 years in IT have spanned a variety of roles including consulting, software development, system administration, network and storage infrastructure solutions, training, and lab management. Doug earned a Bachelor of Science in Computer Science from the University of Arizona in Tucson, Arizona, and holds several top-level industry certifications, including VCDX #19 and HP's Master ASE Cloud and Datacenter Architect (#14).

You can find him working in the Hands-on labs at VMware's large events, presenting at VMware User Group events, writing on the VMware blogs (http://blogs.vmware.com/), or answering questions on the VMware Community forums. If you look hard enough, you might even find him as "Trevor" in videos on the Hands-on labs site. In his free time, Doug likes to get away from technology and spend time hiking with his family or running on the roads and trails all over Arizona.

Trevor Roberts Jr. is a Senior IT Architect with Cisco who enjoys helping customers achieve success with Virtualization and Cloud solutions. In his spare time, Trevor shares his insights on datacenter technologies at www.VMTrooper.com, via the Professional OpenStack and Professional VMware podcasts, and through Twitter @VMTrooper. Trevor is also currently authoring a manuscript on the topic of DevOps for VMware Administrators.

Scott Winger is an aspiring writer who has been a computing technologist for a large Midwest university since 1987. He has a degree in Mathematics and studied Computer Architecture, Operating Systems, Programming Languages and Compilers, Database Management Systems, Networking, and Numerical Methods at UW-Madison. He is a nationally recognized teacher of the sailor's arts and teaches various networking and computing classes at a nearby Cisco Academy and Technical College. Scott earned his most recent certification, VMware Certified Professional, in May 2013 and is in constant pursuit of additional certifications from Cisco, Microsoft, and VMware.

We Want to Hear from You!

As the reader of this book, *you* are our most important critic and commentator. We value your opinion and want to know what we're doing right, what we could do better, what areas you'd like to see us publish in, and any other words of wisdom you're willing to pass our way.

We welcome your comments. You can email or write us directly to let us know what you did or didn't like about this book—as well as what we can do to make our books better.

Please note that we cannot help you with technical problems related to the topic of this book.

When you write, please be sure to include this book's title and authors as well as your name, email address, and phone number. We will carefully review your comments and share them with the authors and editors who worked on the book.

Email: VMwarePress@vmware.com

Mail: VMware Press
        ATTN: Reader Feedback
        800 East 96th Street
        Indianapolis, IN 46240 USA

Reader Services

Visit our website and register this book at www.informit.com/title/9780133511086 for convenient access to any updates, downloads, or errata that might be available for this book.

Chapter 1

The Very Basics

Key Concepts

- Sneakernet
- Network Effect
- Access, Distribution, and Core

Introduction

If you have a tab-A-into-slot-B understanding of networking, or if your Visio diagrams show servers connected to a big black box labeled "Here Be Dragons," this chapter is the place to start. If you are a little more familiar with the fundamentals, and you're comfortable using terms like TCP/IP, Ethernet, and Switch in a sentence, feel free to skip ahead.

If you're a server admin, you must have some experience with networking—you have plugged in a network adapter; you've assigned an IP address. But often it is a very user-centric exposure to the topic, just going through the motions—someone else tells you what port to plug into; someone else assigns IP addresses. You go through the motions, but you have never needed to understand why. Besides, you have plenty of work to do already, and there just aren't enough hours in the day to know everything about everything. In an increasingly virtualized world, though, you will need to know at least a little to get by.

Reinventing the Wheel

To build our foundation, imagine a world much like our own, but where the concept of networking does not yet exist. Business is still done on computers, or something much like them, but no need has yet arisen that would require them to be connected to exchange data. On the rare occasions that data does need to be moved from one station to another, it is done by copying to removable media—some sort of wax cylinder, presumably—and walking it over to another party. After our post-connectivity enlightenment, this arrangement came to be called *Sneakernet*, as in your sneakers were the transport for the data.

Let's say you work in desktop support, so you are a bit more technically inclined than the rest of the business. In between break-fix type work, you and Bob, a coworker in accounting, like to exchange pictures of cats, sometimes festooned with silly captions. Not the highest-brow pursuit, but it helps the day go by. You and Bob have access to stations with scanners and printers, so you've been taking pictures at home and bringing them in to scan, edit, and print, and you exchange the print-outs via interoffice mail. One day, a new green initiative is issued from on high, strictly limiting your ability to use the printers for things that are not business-critical. You consider adjusting your workflow to use the wax cylinders, but this is not ideal—spare wax cylinders themselves are becoming harder and harder to come by. You think to yourself that there must be a better way.

You think back to a game you used to play as a kid, using two paper cups and a taut string to talk to a friend over a longish distance. You'd take turns talking into the cup, then moving it up to your ear to listen for a response. Then your much smarter friend pointed out that if you built two sets, you could talk and listen at the same time—you talk into one cup, connected to a cup your friend held up to his ear, he talked into a cup connected to a cup you held up to your ear. You know there's something to this concept you can use here, this idea of separate transmit and receive wires, crossed over to allow two parties to communicate. You set to work in your mad scientist basement laboratory.

The next morning, you bring in your results to show Bob. You install a card in each of your computers, connect them with a two-wire crossover cable, and install a new application that will allow you to send any file down the wire to the other station. You have brought along a few new cat pictures for testing, and they transfer from your computer to Bob's without a hitch. You've built the first two-person network.

Bob is blown away, and thrilled to have his work hobby back. Weeks go by with the two of you happily shifting files back and forth, until Paul from HR looks over your shoulder and catches what you're up to. He wants in, too. You pause to consider this. Even though Paul's a little weird—he prefers dog pictures—you can see the value of having more than just two people connected.

Metcalfe's Law

You probably know intuitively that when it comes to connecting people, two is more useful than one, and three is better than two, and so on. Robert Metcalfe, inventor of Ethernet, is credited with formalizing this concept of a "network effect" in Metcalfe's Law: The value of a network is proportional to the square of the number of connected compatible communicating devices. Compare this to the cost of a network, which typically grows linearly as users are added, and you'll see you quickly hit a critical mass where value drastically outpaces cost.

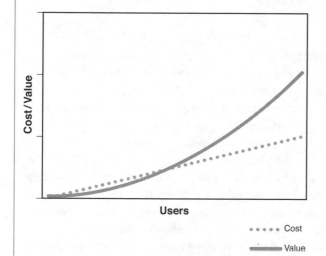

Over the years, "users" has come to replace "connected compatible communicating devices" in common usage, and Metcalfe's Law has been used to describe everything from fax machines to social network adoption.

Robert Metcalfe also predicted that the Internet would collapse under its own weight by the end of 1996—nobody bats a thousand.

But how do you add a third station to your two-person, single-link network? You consider the logistics of a three-ended cable for a moment, but you know this won't stop with Paul. Word will get out, so you need a solution that can scale. You envision a box with many network ports that sits between you, Bob, and Paul. Each of you connects to it by a cable, and the box receives everything each of you send, and repeats it out of all the other ports. And back to the lab you go. You add one more bit of smarts to the device—anything it receives on the first wire of each port, it will repeat out the second wire on the other ports. Now you don't need to worry about crossing over the send and receive wires when you make your cables. The box also helps you deal with distance limitations. Signal over your cables degrades over distance, but the box will repeat the signal at full strength, doubling your potential range. You decide to call this box a *hub*, naming it after a children's television channel you had on in the background while developing it.

The next morning, you bring in the hub, a card for Paul, and some new cables. By lunch time, you're up and running. Each picture you select is indiscriminately beamed to the other two parties. But Sharon in Legal noticed you stringing cable up in the drop ceiling, and she wants in, too. Sharon and Paul don't get along, though, and Sharon would like to be able to send pictures that might portray Paul in a less-than-flattering light. Obviously, she'd prefer Paul not receive these.

Back to the drawing board you go. To meet Sharon's needs, your transfer application needs to become targeted somehow. But your hub will mindlessly repeat anything it receives to all connected parties. Maybe, you reason, the problem isn't the hub, it's the computers connected to it. The cards in your, Sharon's, and Bob's machines are all identical. Maybe you could burn some sort of unique identifier into them, and then you could rewrite the transfer application to use that unique ID. You pull out your parts to get to work on the new cards, when it hits you—the hub will repeat everything it gets, so even if Sharon sends the picture directly to you, that data will still be repeated back to Paul. Well, since you're changing the cards anyway, you'll add a bit of programming to them so they will disregard any data they receive that is not intended for their specific ID. That should work. While you're down in the lab, you figure you'll make a bunch of cards. Since you don't know exactly who will get what card yet, you decide to assign them numbers. You figure only 15 or so people in the company would ever need them, so you can get away with a two-digit identifier, so 00-99. Just prior to setting the ID on the first card, you think you'd rather not paint yourself into a corner, and double the ID field instead. Now your network could support up to 10,000 devices—unthinkable, but go big or go home.

You bring in the new hardware the next morning and round up Bob, Paul, and Sharon to explain the new system. You'll get 0000, Bob gets 0001, Paul gets 0002, and Sharon gets 0003. This works well, for a while. Soon you have ten active users in your under-the-table network, and you start to feel the strain. Your users complain that it's hard to remember who's who, and Bob's been complaining that he hasn't gotten a single cat picture since you replaced his computer a few days prior. He thinks the rest of you are ignoring him.

The solution to Bob's problem hits you right away—when you replaced his computer, he got a new card from the pile. He's not 0001 anymore, he's 0010. You'll have to let everyone know this changed. But that will just further fuel the complaints that the numbering system is hard to use. What you need is a system that can accommodate friendly names, names people can remember. And if the hardware ID changes, that mapping of friendly names to hardware IDs needs to be able to be updated automatically, so you don't have to go bother everyone.

You create a lookup table, listing everyone's name, a friendly name—you'll ask everyone what they want to use for their computer name—and the network ID. You decide you will distribute this file to everyone each night, at least for now, until you can think of a better way to manage this issue of name resolution. The transfer application needs to be rewritten, again, to support sending files to friendly names in addition to network IDs. You make the necessary changes and distribute the new file and instructions. All is well, for a time.

Awareness of your little project has started to increase. Your CIO has heard rumblings and demands to know what you've been up to. After you explain your work to date, he asks if the transfer program can transfer any type of file, or if it's limited to just silly pictures. When you tell him data is data, and any file would work, you see the gears turning in his head. He thanks you for your time and walks off.

A few weeks later, he comes to you with a request to connect every computer in your building—500 stations spread across multiple floors. He asks you to think about this and get back to him with the details. There will be challenges. Your hub has 16 ports, so that's a problem right off the bat. You don't see any reason why you couldn't build a hub with 500 ports, but what if it failed? Everyone would be offline. And where would you put it? There's nowhere in the building where you could reach every station within the distance limits of your cables, and even if there was, creating and installing that many cables of such varied lengths would be expensive, in terms of both materials and time.

Well, if the request is coming from the CIO, maybe time and money aren't going to be a problem, so you start by attacking the first issue, distance. One 500-port hub won't work, but maybe two 250-port hubs would. Since the hubs are repeating everything they hear anyway, you figure you should be able to attach two together without a problem. Come to think of it, since everything is repeated out of every port, two computers should be able to transfer data whether they're attached to the same hub or chained many hubs away from each other. Smaller devices should be easier for you to build, and easier for you to replace in the case of failure. After some head scratching and doodling, you decide on a three-tiered model. At the first, or *core*, tier, a single hub will feed hubs in the second, or *distribution*, tier. You'll put one distribution hub on each floor, and these will feed a third tier of hubs, an *access* tier. End-user workstations will connect to access hubs distributed throughout the floor. This will allow you to keep cable runs short and structured, and provide a cookie-cutter approach for expanding or deploying to new buildings.

You run this by the CIO, and he approves. You get to work deploying the new infrastructure, and before you know it, connectivity is embraced throughout the company, and no one can remember how they ever got by without it.

Summary

Congratulations, you've built your first network. Go ahead and add "networking" as a skill in your LinkedIn profile. This has been an egregious oversimplification, sure, but it introduces the concepts we build on through these first few chapters. We introduced bits and pieces—applications, network cards, cables, and hubs—and we worked through some design challenges as we scaled. The next few chapters flesh out these initial concepts in greater detail.

Chapter 2

A Tale of Two Network Models

Key Concepts

- Network Model
- Network Architecture
- Layering
- Encapsulation
- OSI Model
- TCP/IP Model

Introduction

In the previous chapter, we worked through a thought experiment where we built a company-wide network from the ground up, from scratch. This approach is not recommended in the real world.

When building a real network, you have to consider availability of components, supportability of the systems, and interoperability with other systems. If every company in the world rolled their own network from the ground up, trying to exchange data between companies would be a nightmare, more so than usual.

Luckily, we don't have to do that. We can go out and buy off-the-shelf equipment that conforms to well-known networking models, allowing us to build networks in a predictable and supportable fashion.

A *network model* is a conceptual breakdown of networking functions, separating the communications process into layers and describing the interactions between them. A *network architecture* is a set of documents, each describing bite-sized pieces of the greater system conforming to the model. A given document might define a *protocol*, or a set of rules describing how devices communicate. Another document might describe a physical specification, such as connector type. Yet another might set the rules governing how two other components interact. The complete, comprehensive set of documents should describe every aspect necessary to build a working network. The only way to be sure that all devices in a system can properly communicate is if every component in that system follows the same set of rules.

Way back when, network architectures tended to be proprietary, with each major vendor doing their own thing. Later, open standards would be introduced that anyone could follow. There are two open standards models worth talking about—the classic reference model used for teaching networking concepts, and the other one that we actually use.

Back in 1977, the International Organization for Standardization began work on the Open Systems Interconnection (OSI) project. They had the best of intentions—bringing together representatives from all around the world to build a standards-based system that would allow every computer in the world to communicate. At the time, networking technologies were typically government-sponsored, like ARPANET, or vendor-driven and proprietary, like IBM's Systems Network Architecture (SNA) or DEC's DECnet. OSI was an attempt to bring technology vendors and other interested parties together to build a common framework that anyone could implement, allowing for interoperability. OSI had two major components, a seven-layer abstraction model and a suite of protocols designed around that model.

About the same time, researchers supporting the Defense Advanced Research Project Agency (DARPA) were working on an open-architecture method of interconnecting disparate networks. This grew into the Internet protocol suite, commonly referred to as TCP/IP after its two most important protocols, Transmission Control Protocol and Internet Protocol. It was quickly adopted. The US Department of Defense mandated TCP/IP as the standard for all military networks in March 1982, and the Unix TCP/IP stack was placed in the public domain in June 1989, allowing everyone access and effectively starving support for other protocol suites, including OSI.

So while the OSI never really took off in a productized sense, the OSI Model remains a vital and valuable tool used every day by people around the world for teaching networking concepts and describing troubleshooting and design issues. The TCP/IP Model, being the underpinnings of nearly every communications device in use today, is worth some attention, too.

Model Behavior

Before delving into the specifics of either model, let's run through a couple of concepts key to understanding how models work.

Layering

To better understand networking processes, we break them down into more manageable layers and define standard interfaces between them. This offers the following benefits:

- **Reduced complexity:** By breaking the process up into easier-to-consume chunks, we make the entire process easier to learn, use, support, and productize. And when troubleshooting, we can focus on the parts, not the whole.

- **Modularity and interoperability:** Vendors can write software that implements functions at one layer, and that software can coexist with other vendors' software running at other layers, so long as they respect the standardized interfaces between layers.

The phone system is an example of layering at work. All you need to know is how to work the phone. Dial the number, and the rest is someone else's problem. You don't need to know anything about circuit-switching, telephone lines, microwave transmissions, undersea cables, communications satellites, or cellular networks. Standard interfaces have been implemented between your phone and the rest of the telephony infrastructure such that your only concerns are whether the phone is working (do you have power, do you have a signal) or potential user error (did you dial correctly).

In layered models, each layer provides a service between a lower and/or a higher layer. In making a phone call, you're asking the infrastructure below you to route the call and ring the phone on the other end. The phone here is an endpoint—the device you the user interact with directly. When two endpoints communicate, the same layers are exchanging information, outsourcing the details of that exchange to lower layers. You make your call; you start talking to the person on the other end, or more often, their voicemail, but you get the idea.

Encapsulation

Encapsulation provides a mechanism for implementing the separation between layers. Each layer within a model has a corresponding Protocol Data Unit (PDU). All layers but the lowest layer will define a header, and the data from the next-highest layer is encapsulated as a payload behind that header. The header contains information used by the protocol operating at that layer. The PDU is made up of that layer-specific header and the payload of lower-layer data. Figure 2.1 illustrates the encapsulation process within the OSI model.

higher

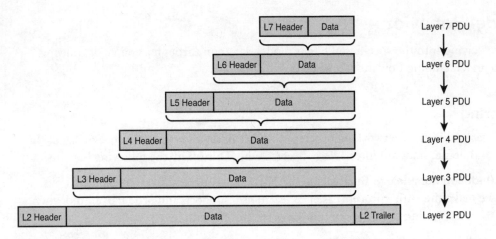

Figure 2.1   Encapsulation

The OSI Model

The OSI Model consists of seven layers and is depicted in Figure 2.2.

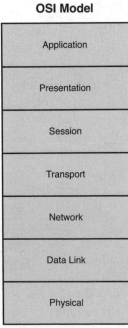

Figure 2.2   The OSI Model

From the bottom up:

- **Layer One, the Physical Layer:** This layer deals with the physical transmission medium as well as the injection of data onto the media. This includes cable types, connectors, pins, encoding, modulation, currents, and the process for activating and deactivating the transmission medium. This layer typically references other standards defining physical technologies.

- **Layer Two, the Data-Link Layer:** This layer handles logical access to the physical medium. A trailer containing a Frame Check Sequence field is added at this layer to facilitate error recovery. The OSI Model refers to the PDU at this layer with the generic term L2PDU. In the real world, we call them frames.

- **Layer Three, the Network Layer:** This layer defines logical addressing, routing and forwarding, and path determination. Logical addressing provides each device a unique identifier that can be used by the routing process. Routing determines how devices forward packets toward their final destination. Path determination is the process routers use to learn all possible routes to a given destination, and how to determine the optimal route to use. At this layer, we call the PDU a packet.

- **Layer Four, the Transport Layer:** This layer defines data delivery, including error recovery and flow control. At this layer, we call the PDU a segment.

- **Layer Five, the Session Layer:** This layer defines how communications sessions are started, managed, and ended.

- **Layer Six, the Presentation Layer:** This layer defines data formats and negotiates which will be used. Data compression and encryption are addressed here.

- **Layer Seven, the Application Layer:** This layer defines the interface between the communications driver and local user applications that need to communicate with the underlying network. This layer also defines authentication processes.

Layer Eight

You might have heard references to "Layer Eight Problems" at some point in your career. Layer Eight is often invoked in a sly, snarky sense to say that the root cause of an issue is not technical. In some cases, the implication can be that it's a PEBKAC error, one where the Problem Exists Between Keyboard And Chair. Layer Eight is often used in this sense to refer to people, management, politics, or money.

Layers Eight and Nine can also be used in a more constructive sense to refer to people and processes. This seems to fit the concepts of layering and encapsulation a bit better—processes define procedures for people to carry out by using applications, and so on down the stack.

Outside of a PearsonVue test center, you are unlikely to ever be forced to recite the seven layers in order, but should you feel the need to commit them to memory, a mnemonic device could come in handy.

A mnemonic device is any easily remembered trigger that can remind you of harder-to-remember information. Common mnemonics include "Righty-Tighty, Lefty-Loosey" for how to work a screwdriver, "Roy G. Biv" for the order of colors in a rainbow, and "King Philip Came Over From Great Spain" for remembering the taxonomy classifications.

Entering the term "OSI mnemonic" into your search engine of choice will return a website with a number of mnemonics to choose from, some of which are hilarious, obscene, or both—traits that make them all the more likely to stick. Of the G-rated ones, we prefer "Please Do Not Take Sales People's Advice," as it offers a practical life lesson as sort of a bonus.

The TCP/IP Model

Like the OSI Model, the TCP/IP Model uses a layering approach to break down and compartmentalize functions, but with four layers instead of seven. These are the Application Layer, Transport Layer, Internet Layer, and Network Interface Layer, as depicted in Figure 2.3.

As with the OSI Model, we review the layers from the bottom up.

The Network Interface Layer

The Network Interface Layer defines how a host connects to a network, covering the physical connection itself as well as the specifics of the physical media used for data transmission. It's somewhat confusing that Ethernet is both the key network interface protocol *and* the physical media we concern ourselves with here.

Ethernet will be covered in greater detail in Chapter 3, "Ethernet Networks."

TCP/IP Model

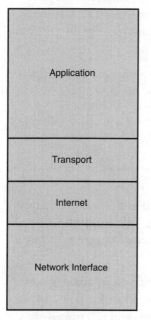

Figure 2.3   The TCP/IP Model

The Internet Layer

The Internet Layer defines mechanisms for addressing and delivering data throughout the network. Protocols operating at this layer include IP, ARP, ICMP, and IGMP.

Internet Protocol (IP) defines the logical addresses assigned to network devices. This address is made up of a network address and a host address. The network address is used to direct data to the proper destination network, and the host address uniquely identifies the host on that destination network. These addresses take the dot-decimal form such as 192.168.1.100 that you've likely encountered before and have assigned countless times to various devices. A subnet mask is defined for each IP address to allow the address to be parsed into its network and host portions.

Address Resolution Protocol (ARP) is used to translate an IP address to a hardware address for the delivery of frames to either the next hop device or to their final destination device. An ARP request is sent through the local network asking which network interface has a particular IP address. The network adapter with that IP address sends an ARP reply, containing its hardware address.

Internet Control Message Protocol (ICMP) is used to control the flow of data through the network, report errors, and perform diagnostics. The most commonly used ICMP commands are ping and tracert, which are used to verify connectivity and identify the pathways between hosts.

Internet Group Message Protocol (IGMP) allows one host to send data to many destination hosts at the same time. This is called multicasting and is so far beyond the scope of this book that we hesitate to even bring it up.

The Internet Layer is explored in greater depth in Chapter 5, "Layer 3."

The Transport Layer

The Transport Layer defines the type of connection between hosts and whether and how acknowledgements are sent. From a practical standpoint, there are only two protocol options at this layer: Transmission Control Protocol (TCP) and User Datagram Protocol (UDP).

TCP is a connection-oriented protocol, which establishes, manages, and terminates network connections. TCP guarantees delivery of data and includes support for flow control, error checking, and recovering lost data through acknowledgements and retransmissions.

UDP, by contrast, is a connectionless protocol. UDP data is assumed to not need error correction or flow control, and is thus blasted indiscriminately over the network without a true connection being established, and without any confirmation that the data has arrived at the intended destination. This sounds worse than it is, as UDP is very useful for applications such as streaming media where data loss is preferable to the delays incurred by retransmissions of lost packets, or in situations where error checking can be done more effectively by an upper layer application.

The Application Layer

The TCP/IP Model's *Application Layer* defines services used by software running on the endpoint. When applications need access to the underlying network, this layer processes their requests by converting them to a network-transportable format. In doing so, connections are made over the appropriate ports.

A port is a type of address assigned to an application or protocol. There are 65,536 possible TCP/UDP ports. Ports 1 to 1023 are reserved for well-known applications by the Internet Corporation for Assigned Names and Numbers (ICANN). Ports 1024 to 49151 are called *registered* ports, in that they are also registered with ICANN. Ports 49152 to 65535 are private, or *dynamic*, ports used as needed by various applications.

Port 0

If you were paying really close attention there, you might have noticed we said there were 65,536 possible ports and then categorized only 65,535 of them. Technically, the reserved port range is 0-1023, but Port 0 is set aside for a specific use and not used to pass traffic. Port 0 was intended as a shortcut in Unix socket programming. When port 0 is requested, the system assigns the next available dynamic port. This saves the programmer the trouble of having to hard-code a port number or write code to determine which dynamic ports are available before assigning one.

Protocols running at this layer include HTTP (Port 80) for requesting and serving web pages, FTP (Ports 20 and 21) for file transfer, and SMTP (Port 25) for e-mail. A complete list of ports and their assignments is available at www.iana.org/assignments/port-numbers.

Comparing OSI and TCP/IP Models

The OSI and TCP/IP Models have much in common, as they describe the same set of things, just differently. A comparison of the layers of each model, how they map to each other, and example protocols at each layer is shown in Figure 2.4.

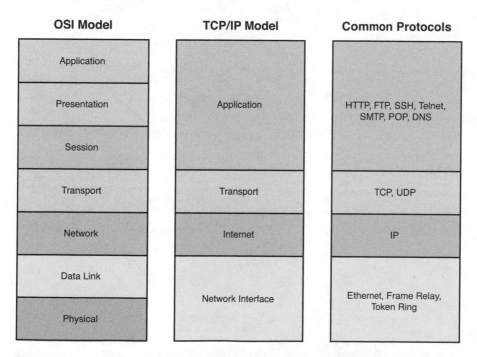

Figure 2.4   The OSI and TCP/IP Models compared side-by-side

Summary

This chapter described networking in theory, rather than in practice, focusing on introducing foundational concepts such as network models, layering, and encapsulation. Beginning with the next chapter and through the end of Part I, "Physical Networking 101," we get a bit more hands-on, dealing with the more practical aspects of networking.

Chapter 3

Ethernet Networks

Key Concepts

- Ethernet
- MAC Address
- Collision Domain
- Broadcast Domain
- Repeaters, Hubs, and Switches
- Switching Logic

Introduction

Now it's time to leave the classroom discussion and get into some nuts and bolts. While this book is mainly concerned with virtual networking, at some point your traffic needs to hit a physical link if you are going to get anything done. So an understanding of physical networking is essential. In this chapter, we discuss Ethernet and the related Layer 1 and Layer 2 technologies that you are likely to encounter in the data center. We start with a quick history lesson on Ethernet, then move on to cabling technologies, physical addressing, and the business of interconnecting devices and forwarding data between them.

Ethernet

When we talk about networking in the data center, we are usually talking about some flavor of Ethernet. The term *Ethernet* refers to a group of standards that describe the physical *and* data-link layers of the typical local area network (LAN), and the technologies that implement them.

History and Theory of Operation

Ethernet has been around a while—it's pushing 40. It was developed in the mid-1970s at Xerox PARC in an effort led by Robert Metcalfe, productized and introduced commercially in 1980, and formally standardized as IEEE 802.3 in 1985.

Ethernet was originally built around the idea of a shared medium—at the time, coaxial cable serving as a shared physical bus. The communications specifications were modeled after those used in a radio transmission system called AlohaNet developed by the University of Hawaii but with the shared physical cable treated as the "ether" through which communication was sent—hence the name, as IT people are nothing if not suckers for a good 19th century physics reference. Figure 3.1 shows a simple shared-bus LAN topology.

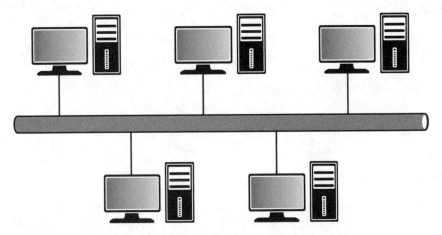

Figure 3.1   Devices on a shared-bus Ethernet network

A shared communications medium presents a challenge. Computers are attached to the shared physical bus. They transmit by sending an electrical signal across that bus. They receive by detecting said electrical signal. Well, what happens if two computers try to transmit at the same time? The two signals overlap, and become jumbled and incoherent to other devices on the bus. In Ethernet-speak, this is called a *collision*.

For successful communication over a shared link, you need to have some mechanism in place to ensure that only one device can transmit at a time. Ethernet accomplishes this through an algorithm called *Carrier Sense Multiple Access with Collision Detection (CSMA/CD)*.

As even the abbreviation is a mouthful, let's break it down further. "Carrier Sense" means to check the wire first. If another transmission is in progress, wait until the wire is idle before transmitting. "Multiple Access" means that more than one device is sharing the bus—collisions are possible. "Collision Detect" describes how to detect and react to a collision. As a collision involves multiple simultaneous signals, collisions can be spotted by looking for higher-than-expected signal amplitudes. When these are detected, the transmitting stations send a further jamming signal to ensure that all stations are aware of the collision, and then employ a back-off algorithm for each station to wait a random amount of time before attempting to retransmit.

Ethernet Standards and Cable Types

Ethernet is available in a number of speeds and form-factors. These days, in a modern data center, you are most likely to encounter gigabit and 10 gigabit Ethernet, carried over either copper or fiber. Outside of the data center, you might be dealing with 100Mbps connections, or even wireless, but we're going to focus the discussion on connectivity within the data center, where the magic really happens.

Fiber Versus Fibre

In the United States, discussions about fiber in the data center can get confusing quickly. Americans use "fiber" to refer to the fiber optic cables themselves. Sometimes, that fiber is used to plumb the storage area network (SAN), over which the Fibre Channel Protocol is used. So "fiber" is the medium and "Fibre Channel" is a protocol that can be run over that medium. Make sense? To complicate things further, Fibre Channel Protocol can be run over unshielded twisted pair (UTP) cable, too.

Outside of the United States, "fibre" is the preferred term for the medium as well, leading to all sorts of spellcheck frustration.

For more information on Fibre Channel, we direct you to *Storage Implementation in vSphere 5.0* by Mostafa Khalil.

Gigabit Ethernet over copper wire, and its 10 and 100 megabit ancestors, uses UTP cabling. These cables consist of four pairs of wires, twisted together down the length of the cable, terminating in RJ45 connectors on each end.

Everything You Know About Connectors Is a Lie

You might dismiss this as pedantry, but we just can't be part of the lie anymore. You know that thing at the end of your Cat5 cable? It's not an RJ45 connector. An RJ45 connector is keyed such that it wouldn't fit in a standard Ethernet NIC port. The connector used on standard UTP cables is an 8P8C (or 8-position, 8-contact) connector. The real RJ45 connector is an 8P2C (8-position, 2-contact) type. The standard for which the real RJ45 plug and socket were designed for never really took off, and the connectors for 8P8C and RJ45 look similar enough (minus the keying) that the name RJ45 stuck for both.

With Gigabit Ethernet over copper wire, all four pairs are used to transmit and receive simultaneously. This differs from the earlier 10 and 100 megabit standards which defined separate send and receive pairs.

Gigabit and 10 gigabit Ethernet over fiber involve two strands of fiber optic cabling, a transmit strand and a receive strand. The fiber can be multi-mode for relatively short distances, or single-mode for longer distances. Single-mode fiber carries only a single frequency of not-safe-for-the-eye laser-driven light, while multi-mode carries multiple LED-driven frequencies which are harmless if you happen to look at them. In data center applications, fiber cables typically terminate in either SC or LC connectors. SC connectors are squarish and use a push-on, pull-off attachment mechanism, with each transmit/receive pair typically held together with a plastic clip. LC connectors are a smaller form-factor option, and use a retaining tab attachment mechanism similar to an RJ45 connector.

Upstream fiber connections typically involve hot-pluggable transceivers. Gigabit interface converters (GBICs) or small form-factor pluggable transceivers (SFPs) are used to support gigabit Ethernet connections, and enhanced small form-factor pluggable transceivers (SPF+) are used for 10 gigabit connections.

SFP+

Ten gigabit Ethernet over copper is most commonly found in an SFP+ direct attach form-factor, in which twinaxial copper is terminated by SFP+ housings attached to the end of the cable. Some vendors refer to these as Direct Attach Copper (DAC) cables. These are used for fairly short runs, 1 to 7m for passive cables or up to 15m for active cables, with the latter drawing transmission power from the connected device. Ten gigabit copper over UTP (10GBase-T) is also available, but is less common at the moment, as upgrading infrastructure to support it tends to cost more than using existing SFP+ ports.

Table 3.1 lists a number of commonly used physical Ethernet standards.

twinaxial compatible w/ SFP+

Table 3.1 Common Ethernet Standards

Common Name	Speed	IEEE Standard	Cable Type and Max Length
Ethernet	10 Mbps		
10BASE5		802.3	Copper coaxial, 500m
10BASE2		802.3	Copper coaxial, 185m
10BASE-T		802.3	Copper UTP, 100m
Fast Ethernet	100 Mbps		
100BASE-TX		802.3u	Copper UTP, 100m
100BASE-FX		802.3u	Fiber, 2km
Gigabit Ethernet	1000 Mbps		
1000BASE-LX		802.3z	Fiber, 5km
1000BASE-SX		802.3z	Fiber, 500m
1000BASE-T		802.3ab	Copper UTP, 100m
10 Gigabit Ethernet	10 Gbps		
10GBASE-SR		802.3ae	Fiber, 400m
10GBASE-LR		802.3ae	Fiber 10km
10GBASE-CR		Pending	Copper twinaxial, 15m
10GBASE T		802.3an	Copper UTP, 100m

Table 3.2 shows a number of common cable connectors and types.

Table 3.2 Common Ethernet Cable Connectors and Types

Name	Image
UTP with RJ45 / 8P8C End	

Name	Image
Fibre LC Connector	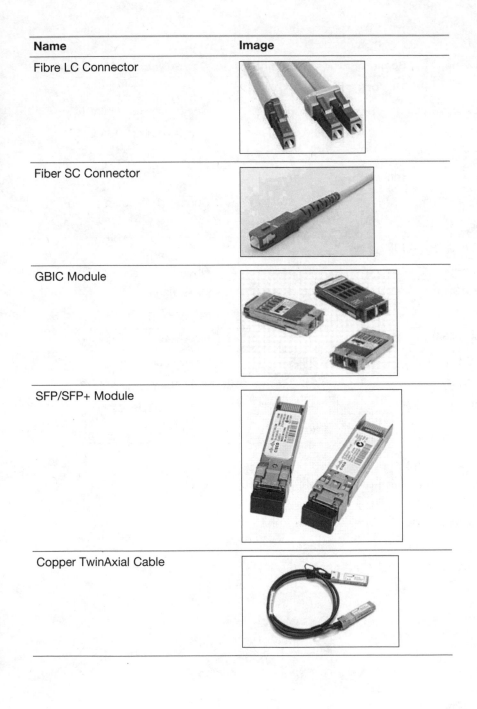
Fiber SC Connector	
GBIC Module	
SFP/SFP+ Module	
Copper TwinAxial Cable	

Ethernet Addressing

With a shared bus, all stations are aware of all transmissions. However, as we saw in Chapter 1, "The Very Basics," some messages are intended for only a single station, some for a subset of the stations, and some are intended to be received by all stations. So Ethernet defines an addressing scheme to allow for communication to be targeted to a single receiver, multiple receivers, or all receivers on the bus.

These Layer 2 addresses—dubbed *MAC (Media Access Control) addresses* in the IEEE 802.3 standard—are six bytes long and usually expressed as a string of twelve hexadecimal digits. Cisco devices typically separate each set of four digits with a period (1234.5678.90AB). Other vendors use a colon or dash between each set of two (12:34:56:78:90:AB or 12-34-56-78-90-AB). VMware uses the colon notation, so from here on out, we will, too.

These addresses come in three flavors. The first, and the type we spend the most time talking about, is a unicast address. Unicast addresses are used to identify a sender and the intended recipient of an Ethernet frame. When a network adapter observes a transmission on the shared bus, it checks to see if the destination MAC address matches its own. If it does, it processes the frame. If it does not, the frame is ignored.

Unicast MAC addresses are required to be globally unique. To support this, manufacturers of physical network adapters encode a MAC address into Ethernet adapters at the factory—this address is often referred to as a "burned-in address." The IEEE assigns each manufacturer an *organizationally unique identifier (OUI)*, which occupies the first half of each MAC address. The manufacturer then assigns the second half of the address. VMware has its own OUI (00:50:56) that is used to construct MAC addresses for virtual machine network adapters.

Globally Unique, Except When Not

The IEEE had the best of intentions in requiring that MAC addresses be globally unique, but manufacturers have not quite been able to live up to that requirement. Many people have had the experience of finding NICs with duplicate MACs, and modern NICs often allow you to change the MAC address to a custom-defined value. Global uniqueness has become more of a guideline, really. So as long as your MAC address is locally unique within your Layer 2 domain, you will be fine.

The two additional types of MAC addresses are used to identify multiple recipients. A broadcast destination address (MAC address FF:FF:FF:FF:FF:FF) is used to indicate that all network adapters on the shared bus should process the frame. And multicast destination addresses are used to target the frame to a group of network adapters on the bus. Multicast MAC addresses will use an OUI of 01:00:5e, with the remaining six bytes being user-definable.

Extending Ethernet Segments: Repeaters, Hubs, and Switches

We saw in Table 3.1 that each physical Ethernet standard has a maximum cable length. The reason for that length limit has to do with the way that electrical signals weaken as they traverse a medium. This is called *attenuation*. What do you do when you want to connect devices that are further apart than that? An early solution to this issue was the *repeater*, a device that connected two cable segments and would retransmit anything it heard on one side, out the other side. Repeaters were common in the 10BASE5 and 10BASE2 days, when an Ethernet segment was typically a single shared coaxial cable.

When UTP-based cabling was introduced, the repeater was replaced with the hub, as shown in Figure 3.2. A *hub* is effectively a multi-port repeater; each device on the segment is connected to the hub, and the hub repeats each transmission it receives on any given port to every other port. If an 8-port hub receives a transmission on Port 1, it will repeat that transmission on Ports 2 to 8. It does not retransmit out of the interface the transmission was received on. Each transmission from the hub is fresh and at full strength, resetting the distance counter.

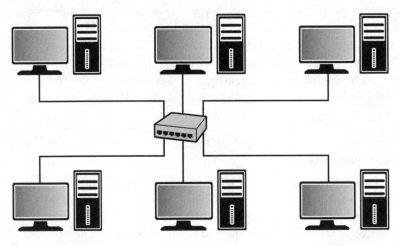

Figure 3.2   Devices connected to a hub

By cascading hubs together, you could support interconnecting a great many devices. However, because each hub is blindly repeating signals, the resulting network is still a single shared bus, prone to collisions. All devices in this network are said to be a part of the same *collision domain*. Further, CSMA/CD requires that only one device be transmitting at a time. So available bandwidth, then, is shared between all connected devices. Finally, in hub-based Ethernet, no device can transmit and receive simultaneously. This is referred to as *half-duplex* communication. As the number of devices on the shared bus increases, so do the chances for collisions. Eventually, sustained communication becomes impossible due to constant collisions.

Because of their propensity for collisions and poor use of bandwidth, a smarter class of interconnection devices, called *switches*, was developed. Switches do not create a single shared bus through mindless rebroadcasting. Instead, they examine the destination address of each frame to enable forwarding only to the relevant port. And if multiple frames are sent to the same destination at the same time, the switch can buffer the frames and send them one at a time to avoid collisions. So, in switches, although the bandwidth of the switches' backplane is shared, the bandwidth of each currently communicating link is *not* shared and the full-rated bandwidth, up to the limitations of the switches' backplane, is available to each set of communicating ports.

With these features, each switch port becomes its own collision domain. As long as there is only one device connected to each port, no collisions can occur. The CSMA/CD algorithm can be disabled, allowing both ends of the connection to send and receive simultaneously, effectively doubling performance. This is referred to as *full-duplex* communication.

While switches can make intelligent forwarding decisions for unicast traffic, they must still support broadcast and multicast traffic, allowing a sender to transmit to all or multiple connected devices. When a switch port receives a broadcast, it is retransmitted to all other ports, which is why a switch and its connected devices are said to be sharing a single *broadcast domain*. When a switch port receives a multicast, it is retransmitted only to the ports associated with that address.

Switching Logic

Let's dig a little deeper into how switches work their magic. The switch needs to examine each incoming frame and determine whether to forward it or ignore it. To accomplish this, the switch needs to learn what MAC address(es) should be associated with each of its ports. This mapping is built up over time by the switch by examining the source MAC address of each inbound frame. Knowing the source port and the source MAC address, it builds a lookup table in a special type of memory designed for super-fast searching called *Content Addressable Memory (CAM)*.

After examining the inbound frame's source address, the switch examines the frame's destination address and searches its MAC address table for a match. If no match is found, the switch floods the frame out of all other ports, the assumption being that the unknown destination address will reply and can then be added to the address table. If a match is found, and if that match is a port other than the port the frame arrived on, the switch forwards the frame out of the port corresponding to that destination address. If the match is the same port the frame arrived on, the frame is ignored. You might see this behavior if you have a hub attached to a switch port. The switch would associate all MAC addresses of devices attached to the hub with the same switch port, and the hub would repeat all signals received by its connected devices to the switch port.

Summary

In this chapter, we dove into Ethernet, discussing the theory of operation, the physical plumbing, and physical addressing. We also introduced the switch and covered how switches make forwarding decisions. The next chapter builds on these ideas, introducing advanced Layer Two concepts.

Chapter 4

Advanced Layer 2

Key Concepts

- Virtual LANs (VLANs)
- Trunk Ports
- Access Ports
- Spanning Tree Protocol (STP)
- Link Aggregation

Introduction

In the previous chapters, we've mostly discussed the ideas around creating identification for various network objects and have described various topologies for networks. This is great for simply getting traffic to traverse from one object to another, but there are a few advanced topics that are essential for transforming a basic network to one that's highly available and scalable.

In this chapter, you are introduced to three new concepts: a method in which physical local area networks (LANs) can be logically divided into virtual LANs (VLANs), techniques used to prevent Layer 2 loops that can seriously reduce a network's ability to carry useful traffic, and a discussion of link aggregation. These three topics are highly relevant in modern data centers, especially as they relate to the virtual networking concepts that will be deeply covered in Part 2, "Virtual Switching." The three major topics that are explored in this chapter are usually found in every network you'll ever encounter—and you'll see exactly why as you read on.

Concepts

A local area network is a shared resource consumed by each connected device. The goal is that each device can communicate effectively. However, sometimes a company might wish to separate parts of the network into different functional groups via smaller networks. The powers that be might wish to have each department isolated into its own network, or want to dedicate a network specifically to an application that drives revenue into the business.

There are significant performance and security advantages that can be realized by having multiple LANs. Imagine the scenario where people in the Human Resources (HR) department are sending and receiving sensitive personnel files to one another. An isolated HR LAN to ensure that no one can accidentally or maliciously view their network traffic might be justified in this case. An isolated LAN also ensures that the HR employees do not have to share a broadcast domain with other users on the network, which improves performance. Finally, a separate LAN limits the spread of certain types of malware.

Let's look at an example of two different LANs being utilized for a company that wishes to isolate the HR desktops from the sales and marketing desktops (see Figure 4.1). Notice how this requires two different switches.

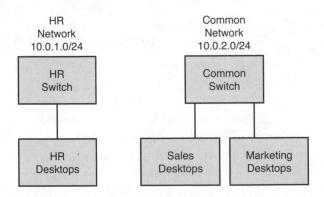

Figure 4.1   Two isolated physical LANs

However, purchasing an entire new set of networking gear to isolate the HR employees is not very cost effective. It would be similar to an airline buying a fleet of jumbo jet planes but only letting 10 people board each plane—there's a lot of wasted capacity and unnecessary overhead. Instead, the idea of a *virtual LAN*, or *VLAN*, was developed as the IEEE 802.1Q open standard to allow physical switches to be divided logically to provide separate, virtual LANs.

Figure 4.2 represents an Ethernet frame, with a focus on the 4 bytes that are normally left unused. Within these 4 bytes, 12 bits are reserved specifically for a VLAN ID. By populating the VLAN ID field with a value, we can effectively tag the frame and place it in a VLAN segment.

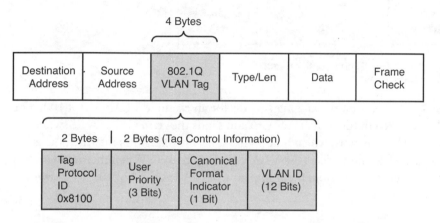

Figure 4.2   An Ethernet frame

A VLAN is defined by adding a 4-byte tag inside of a frame's header to let all the switches know which logical LAN it belongs to. The switches' ports are programmed to only forward frames with specified VLAN numbers and ignore the rest. This lets a network administrator control which ports belong to specific VLANs.

Revisiting the company that wants to isolate their HR desktops from the rest of the company, we now see that only one physical switch is required (see Figure 4.3). The VLAN tags are now handling the separation at a logical layer.

A port which allows only frames for a single VLAN is called an *access port*. Traffic that enters the port, which is an *ingress* action, will have the VLAN tag added to the frame by the switch itself. This allows the server attached to the port to be unaware of its VLAN membership, effectively letting the server send untagged frames toward the switch. On the flip side, traffic that is forwarded out of a port, which is an *egress*, will have the VLAN tag removed so that the server does not see the tag.

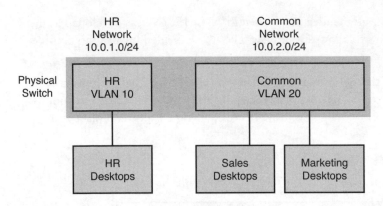

Figure 4.3   Two VLANs for HR and common use

Let's take a moment to focus on the tagging process for an example VLAN ID of 100. The server generates untagged traffic (no VLAN tag) and sends the frame toward the switch port. As the frame enters the port, which is an ingress, the switch knows that the port is configured for VLAN 100 and updates the VLAN ID field to 100. When the frame is later sent along to its next destination, the frame now has a VLAN ID of 100, as shown in Figure 4.4.

Figure 4.4   Ingress and egress VLAN ID state for an access port

Keep in mind that VLANs cannot talk to one another without the aid of a routing device. Each VLAN is its own Layer 2 networking domain. Even if two devices are physically plugged into ports that are side-by-side, using a different VLAN on each port effectively prohibits the two ports from talking unless there is a device to route the traffic.

Trunking

With a small number of VLANs or a small network topology, you can get away with using access ports for all your ports. This doesn't work out so well if you start to grow your network. If you had 100 VLANs, for example, you would need to configure at least 100 different access ports to forward traffic from one switch across to the next. But, what if we allowed a port to pass along multiple different VLANs? This is where the idea of *trunking* comes into play—it really is as simple as letting a port know that it can and should forward traffic for a range of specifically defined VLANs, or just "all VLANs" if you don't want to create a list.

Figure 4.5 shows four different VLANs—VLAN ID 100, 200, 300, and 400—all being assigned to a trunk port. This port now has the ability to pass along tagged traffic belonging to any of those four VLANs.

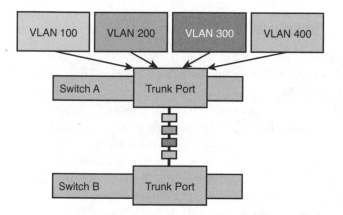

Figure 4.5   A trunking mode port with many VLANs

A *trunk port* is quite commonly used between switches to extend the VLAN. If two users are connected to two different switches in different parts of an office building and need to be part of the same VLAN, they have to be able to communicate with one another. The two switches can use a trunk port to pass along 802.1Q (VLAN-tagged) traffic from the two sites.

> **NOTE**
>
> While it is relatively common to attach servers to access ports, there are use cases where servers attach to trunk ports. We go over this in more detail in Part 2 when we start to talk about virtual networking, but just keep in mind that physical servers not running a virtualization hypervisor are almost always attached to an access port.

Native VLAN

Earlier, we stated that a server connected to an access port sends untagged frames toward the switch. The access port then adds the VLAN tag for the appropriate VLAN. But what happens if an untagged frame is received by a trunk port? Since a trunk port can belong to dozens of VLANs, how does the switch determine which VLAN tag to apply to the frame?

This is where the idea of a *native VLAN* enters the scene. This is a specially defined VLAN that will be used as a default for any traffic that is not tagged. When the switch sees an untagged frame enter its port, it looks up the native VLAN number and forwards the frame *without* tagging it with any VLAN information at all. The next hop switch has to agree on the VLAN number of the native VLAN.

why lookup at all?

Loop Avoidance and Spanning Tree

Single links between devices create single points of failure, so it's natural to want to add redundancy. Whenever budget allows, you will also want to introduce redundancy at the switch level, dual-connecting access switches to multiple upstream distribution switches, for example. This prevents the failure of any single network device causing an outage to the system as a whole. This is not without peril, however, as having redundant links between switches that carry broadcast traffic can expose a condition called a *broadcast storm* whereby a switch's ability to carry real traffic goes to near zero because it's instead carrying a growing and unending cycle of rebroadcasts of broadcast frames. Because Ethernet has no internal counter such as a time-to-live to expire traffic, frames that enter a loop do so indefinitely—or at least until the network administrator pulls the cable causing the loop, or turns on the Spanning Tree Protocol (STP) on each connected switch.

Spanning Tree Overview

Spanning Tree Protocol (STP) is a very deep topic that causes headaches for many professional network administrators. We spend the next portion of this chapter getting you up to speed on exactly what it is, how it works, and why it is so vital for the operation of a typical network.

What Is Spanning Tree?

STP, the IEEE 802.1D open standard, is designed to prevent looping behavior and allow network administrators to introduce redundant links without forming a traffic loop. STP learns the topology of the network and purposely blocks redundant links that could cause a loop. Should an active link fail, STP will unblock links as necessary to restore connectivity.

REAL WORLD EXAMPLE

It's easy to demonstrate this effect. If you have any cheap, consumer-grade network switch, you can plug two of the ports together, plug in your laptop or desktop, and ping some IP address to generate an ARP Request broadcast. Since low-end switches have no STP running to block the loop, you will observe incredible amounts of activity, that is, a broadcast storm on the switch, until you unplug the loop.

How Does Spanning Tree Work?

All the switches that are actively participating in STP first have to figure out which switch will be the *root bridge*. This is done by election, like picking a president or group leader, but with less politics involved. The root bridge is simply determined from the switch with the lowest bridge ID. The switches determine this by exchanging Bridge Protocol Data Units (BPDUs) containing their bridge IDs.

A bridge ID consists of two parts: the bridge priority and MAC address. By default, all switches have a bridge priority of 32,768. An administrator can change the bridge priority, increasing or decreasing it by multiples of 4,096, to forcefully determine which switch will be the root bridge. If all the switches are using the default 32,768 priority, then the tie is broken by finding the switch with the lowest MAC address value. It is prudent to set a lower bridge priority on the switch you specifically want to be the root bridge, as otherwise the root bridge role might change to an underpowered or over-utilized switch which happens to have the lowest MAC address.

When the root bridge has been identified, the remaining non-root bridge switches in the topology do some math homework to determine how they can best send traffic back to the root bridge. They exchange BPDUs to determine the network topology and track topology changes. Every path to the root bridge has an associated cost. Imagine that you wanted to drive from one city to the next and are given many different choices on how to get there. You might choose the interstate, which is more mileage but lets you drive at a fast speed, or the local roads, which is fewer total miles but a much slower speed.

Switches look at the speed of each link in each possible path back to the root bridge, in search of the lowest total path cost. The path cost is the sum of each link's cost value based on its data rate. For standard STP (802.1D), the cost values are shown in Table 4.1.

Table 4.1   STP Cost Values

Data Rate	Cost
10 Mbps	100
100 Mbps	19
1000 Mbps (1 Gbps)	4
10000 Mbps (10 Gbps)	2

Looking at the costs, you can see that if STP had to choose between a single 100 Mbps link (cost of 19) and four 1,000 Mbps links (cost of 4 * 4 = 16), it would choose the four 1,000 Mbps links. When the paths have been chosen, the switch ports which connect to other switches are assigned STP roles as follows:

- **Root Port (RP):** The switch port providing the least-cost path to the root bridge
- **Designated Port (DP):** An upstream switch port that is the next hop on the least-cost path to root bridge
- **Blocked Port (BLK):** Any port that isn't a root port or designated port is blocked from forwarding traffic

These connections are shown in Figure 4.6.

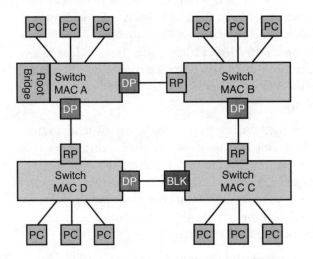

Figure 4.6 Spanning Tree roles in a sample topology

When a link fails, STP will go through a re-convergence process to determine which blocked port(s) to activate. The port will go through four states:

- **Blocking:** The starting state of any non-DP or RP port. No user data is sent or received, but BPDU frames will be sent and received.
- **Listening:** The port listens for BPDU frames but doesn't forward them and it doesn't update its MAC table. This allows outdated MAC addresses to expire, as they might no longer be valid following an STP topology change. The port continues to listen for any BPDUs that might cause it to return to the blocking state. Frames are not yet forwarded.
- **Learning:** The port does not yet forward frames, but it observes source addresses from frames received and populates the MAC table with them.
- **Forwarding:** Normal operation—the port is sending and receiving data.

PortFast

The default behavior of STP blocks a port until it has listened and learned the traffic on that port and determines that it can begin forwarding traffic without creating a loop. This is great for switch-to-switch links, but endpoint devices on your network—desktops, servers, printers, and so on—are usually not capable of creating a network loop. The act of blocking traffic for a period of time can cause some headaches and complications, particularly if the workstation or server is trying to use a Preboot Execution Environment (PXE) to boot, or requires a DHCP lease for its IP address. *ie. needs to communicate asap*

For these endpoint devices, an administrator can enable *PortFast* on a Cisco device, or designate a port as an *edge port* or "fast uplink" port with other switch vendors. PortFast is an extension to 802.1D that allows a port to skip the listening and learning states and transition directly to the forwarding state. You are effectively telling the switch to go ahead and trust the port immediately, and that it does not need to burn time proving that the port will not create a loop.

REAL WORLD EXAMPLE

It's very common, and often recommended by vendors, to enable PortFast for any ports connecting to your NICs on a server because they cannot form a loop. All the server NICs should be allowed to actively forward traffic.

Of course, exercise caution when enabling PortFast on a switch port, and ensure that no network device will be plugged into that port. There is the possibility that someone could plug in a rogue network device with an improperly configured STP bridge priority, and become the root bridge for your network topology. Though they are out of scope for this book, tools such as BPDU Filtering and BPDU Guard can provide a safeguard against this sort of risk.

Rapid Spanning Tree

Although STP does work as advertised, it's rather slow to converge. If the network topology changes, STP can take anywhere from 30 to 50 seconds to transition ports from blocking to forwarding traffic. Most environments consider this an unacceptable outage length. In today's hyper-connected world of always-on technology, can you imagine having your entire network down for almost a full minute?

> **NOTE**
>
> The vast majority of networks do not run the traditional 802.1D STP. It's become a blanket term that refers to any variation of STP that exists today and is easier to say when talking to your colleagues about the idea of blocking and forwarding traffic on switch ports.

Rapid Spanning Tree Protocol (RSTP), the IEEE 802.1W open standard, was introduced to allow faster network convergence. This protocol requires about 6 seconds to converge and uses fewer port states than STP. This is due to a variety of reasons, but mainly the fact that the protocol uses proposals and agreements instead of timers and a decoupling of port states from port roles. The three port states used are:

- **Discarding:** The port state replaces the STP disabled, blocking, and listening states. The port is dropping frames just like with an STP blocking port.

- **Learning:** At this point, the port is learning the MAC addresses by examining the traffic on the port, but is not forwarding or receiving data traffic.

- **Forwarding:** The switch port is forwarding and receiving data traffic.

RTSP also introduces two additional port roles:

- **Alternate Port:** This is a blocked port that provides an alternate path to the root bridge by means of a different peer switch than the active root port.

- **Backup Port:** This is a blocked port that provides a backup path to the root bridge by means of a redundant port to the same peer switch.

Link Aggregation

Not all redundant links between devices are bad things that invoke the wrath of STP. In fact, there is an entire set of protocols at your disposal that specifically address some of the needs for redundant links, which we cover here.

What Is Link Aggregation?

While something like STP is necessary to prevent network loops, it sure seems like a shame to have perfectly good network connections sit idle, just biding their time waiting for a link failure that might never come. We can make these links useful without angering STP by using link aggregation.

Link aggregation is the act of bundling multiple physical ports into a single logical grouping. This prevents any one member of the group from being blocked, as the group appears as one logical port to STP.

Link aggregation offers a couple of advantages over discrete links managed by STP:

- **Increased Bandwidth and Load Sharing:** Because multiple links are active within a logical group, additional bandwidth is available among unique sessions of traffic. Per Figure 4.7, no single traffic session, such as a single client talking to a single server, can use more than one physical link. Think of it like making a large highway with multiple lanes: You can fit more cars on the highway, but each car can only take up one lane at a time.

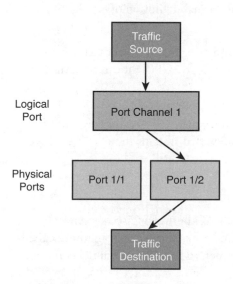

Figure 4.7   A data flow with link aggregation from a single source to a single destination travels through only one aggregated port.

- **Improved Redundancy and Availability:** If a single link in the group fails, other links continue to pass traffic and the group does not go down. There is no need for the STP topology to reconfigure itself or for STP to transition a new link from blocking to active.

One of the challenges with link aggregation is that it comes in a number of names, shapes, and standards. Terminology varies between vendor implementations, even when implementing the same standards. To un-muddle this, we try to use the generic term *Link Aggregation Group*, or *LAG*, to describe the general concept, and use vendor-specific terms when talking about their specific implementations.

Implementation Methods

There are many different ways to build a LAG, as each vendor decided to use a slightly different name or method in order to accomplish a logical link grouping. This can cause confusion and frustration to networking newcomers, so we cover the more common terms and technologies used.

802.3ad and 802.1ax – IEEE Open Standard

The IEEE LAN/MAN Standards Committee sponsored link aggregation in their 802.3ad open standard. The idea was to meet a long list of goals for link aggregation through nonproprietary means. Later, the standard was formally transferred and published as 802.1ax to avoid some confusion with other 802.1 layers. The formal definition of 802.1ax is as follows:

> Link aggregation allows one or more links to be aggregated together to form a link aggregation group, such that a media access control (MAC) client can treat the link aggregation group as if it were a single link.[1]

Within the 802.1ax open standard, the IEEE also defines the *Link Aggregation Control Protocol (LACP)*. The purpose of this protocol is to allow two systems to negotiate a LAG using a standard, nonproprietary protocol.

EtherChannel – Cisco

EtherChannel is a Cisco proprietary way of building a LAG between Cisco switches. It can consist of up to 8 active ports to forward traffic and 8 inactive ports, sometimes called *failover ports*, to take over for any active ports that happen to fail. EtherChannel comes in two flavors:

- A *Static EtherChannel*, or "mode on" in Cisco IOS-speak, is manually configured and will not use a negotiation protocol to build the LAG. If the network administrator inputs the wrong information in the switch, the LAG might still appear to be active but might not forward traffic properly.

- A *Dynamic EtherChannel* can use one of two protocols to automatically create a LAG: *Port Aggregation Protocol (PAgP)* or LACP. When a dynamic EtherChannel is created, both network switches involved negotiate to form the LAG. If the negotiation fails, the LAG is not established.

Etherchannel Versus Port Channel

Further complicating any discussion on link aggregation, the terms *EtherChannel* and *Port Channel* are often used interchangeably. There is a subtle difference, though. When configuring an EtherChannel between two switches, you create a Port Channel interface on each switch, bundling the physical interfaces together. An EtherChannel, then, is the logical pipe between switches consisting of a bundle of cables, while a Port Channel is the logical interface terminating the EtherChannel at each end consisting of a bundle of interfaces. Put another way, when you make a configuration change to EtherChannel, you do so via the Port Channel's interface. And when these changes are committed, they are automatically applied to each of the interfaces from which the EtherChannel has been constructed.

Other Vendor Terminology

Here is some additional terminology you are likely to encounter when discussing link aggregation:

- **Trunk (HP):** Some documentation for HP network equipment (and many network engineers that used to support said equipment) refers to a LAG as a trunk. This can cause confusion between LAGs and links carrying 802.1Q VLAN tags, as the latter is termed a trunk by just about everyone else. The HP "trunk" implementation conforms to the 802.1ad standard which is what *non*-HP engineers would call a LAG.

- **Multi-Chassis Link Aggregation (Various) or Cross-Stack EtherChannel (Cisco):** A multi-chassis LAG has terminating interfaces on two different nodes. This is a more highly available implementation, as the LAG can sustain the loss of a connected target. Implementation details are vendor-specific and outside the scope of this book, but you should know that MC-LAG exists and that it is more robust because the loss of a single switch chassis doesn't mean the loss of the aggregated link. Examples include virtual port channel (Cisco) and distributed trunking (HP).

- **NIC Teaming:** Many endpoint operating systems and hypervisors are capable of logically bundling network connections. This is typically referred to as *NIC teaming* or *NIC bonding*. In these configurations, a software driver must determine how to distribute traffic across the uplinks, as the connected physical switches are usually unaware of the teamed configuration.

Dynamic Link Aggregation

As mentioned, both the 802.3ad and Cisco implementations of link aggregation support two methods of building a LAG—static and dynamic. They really are as simple as they sound. A *static LAG* is manually configured by an administrator and shows an "up" state immediately after being created, even if the partner ports on the other end of the wire are not properly configured. A *dynamic LAG* uses a specific protocol to chat with its partner ports to discuss whether or not they are configured properly to form a LAG.

REAL WORLD EXAMPLE

In reality, the major choice of which method to use boils down to what the network equipment supports. The VMware vSphere Standard Switch (vSwitch), for example, cannot form a dynamic LAG and requires a static LAG if link aggregation is required. Other hardware and virtual switches, such as HP ProCurve, Cisco Nexus, and even the VMware vSphere Virtual Distributed Switch (version 5.1 and later), support dynamic LAGs using LACP. Most network administrators tend to prefer using a dynamic LAG when possible, as it helps ensure that the LAG is properly configured.

In today's modern switching world, there's really only one choice for dynamic LAG protocol: LACP. It's supported by everything you'd ever want to use. That said, it's not unusual to find devices using Cisco's PAgP in the wild.

Link Aggregation Control Protocol (LACP)

LACP is defined in the IEEE 802.3ad open standard and later as 802.1ax. It's not incredibly important that you understand all the finer details of exactly how the protocol works, but you should be aware of the general process used:

1. A networking device configured to use LACP will generate special LACPDU (LACP Data Unit) frames on all the ports that are part of the LAG.

2. The peer device will receive these special frames and, if also configured for LACP, will respond with its own LACPDU frames.

3. The networking devices will form a dynamic LAG.

Pretty simple!

REAL WORLD EXAMPLE

When working with someone using a Cisco networking device, he or she may refer to LACP as "mode active." That's because the actual CLI command to create an Ether-Channel for Cisco requires setting the mode. The choices for LACP modes are "active" and "passive." An *active* device will actively seek out a peer device to form a LAG, while a *passive* device will only listen for requests. At least one of the two devices must be active, or else both will only listen. It's common to set both devices as active to avoid worrying about which device will be set which way.

Port Aggregation Protocol (PAgP)

The other, increasingly irrelevant LAG protocol is Port Aggregation Protocol (PAgP). This protocol was developed by Cisco as their own method of dynamically forming LAGs. Modern Cisco gear no longer supports PAgP, as the rest of the world has settled on LACP.

Load Distribution Types

When using LAGs, a method for selecting what traffic will go down what physical port must be selected. Each session created between one device and another can only use one single port inside the LAG. It is a common misconception to think of traffic being sprayed across multiple ports—going back to the car on a highway example, you can't slice up your car and drive in four lanes at the same time. And even if you could, the pieces couldn't get to your destination any faster—and who would insure you?

Every LAG, static or dynamic, uses a load distribution method to determine which traffic session maps to which specific port. A LAG is capable of examining the header of frames and packets for three types of information:

- Source information (src)

- Destination information (dst)

- Source and destination information (src-dst)

The load distribution logic can extract the following information:

- IP Address (ip)

- MAC Address (mac)

- TCP/UDP Port (port)

You can choose what to look at based on what will best distribute your specific traffic load. The typical default method is to use source and destination MAC addresses, or src-dst-mac. This method is used when you simply do not know if there would be a benefit to source-based or destination-based distribution. Packets from host A to host B, host A to host C, and host C to host B could all use different ports in the LAG.

Here are some example use cases and load distribution methods:

- Traffic headed for a collection of web servers might benefit from using source IP address, or src-ip. With this method, packets from different IP addresses will potentially use different ports in the LAG, but packets from the same IP address will use the same port in the LAG.

- Streaming file transfers to an office building of PC workstations might benefit from destination MAC address, or dst-mac. With this method, packets to the same destination MAC are forwarded over the same port in the LAG, and packets to a different destination are sent on a different port in the LAG.

- Application servers that must pass traffic among each other might benefit from source and destination port, or src-dst-port. With this method, packets sent between hosts using different port numbers could be forwarded on different ports in the LAG, while packets sent between hosts on the same port number would be forwarded over the same port in the LAG.

PITFALL

Prior to vSphere 5.5, the VMware vSphere Distributed Switch only supports src-dst-ip load distribution. Make sure to tell your network administrator to use this method and set the load distribution algorithm on the VMware virtual switch to "Route based on IP hash."

Summary

Now that you've been down the road of advanced Layer 2 topics, you might be thinking that most of what we're trying to accomplish here involves the removal of logical loops. But keep in mind that a vast amount of effort has been put into creative ways to trick the network into thinking that one path exists when, in actuality, there might be multiple physical paths along the topology. Fortunately, most of what you'll deal with on the vSphere side of the network is completely unable to be looped—this is covered in much greater detail in Part 2.

Of much greater importance for your future career as a high-performance networking ninja will revolve around the understanding, consumption, and configuration of VLANs. Most of your vSphere environment will depend on the correct numbering and presentation of VLANs so that the guest virtual machines (VMs) can properly communicate with one another. Additionally, there are many performance benefits to be realized by using VLANs to isolate various types of traffic. Finally, link aggregation increases reliability and capacity for critical high volume loads such as vMotion and IP storage. Have no fear: We go very deep into these exact topics later on, with real, working examples of the physical and logical configuration.

Reference

1. IEEE Standards Association. 2013. 802.1AX 2008 - IEEE Standard for Local and Metropolitan Area Networks—Link Aggregation. Available at: *http://standards.ieee.org/findstds/standard/802.1AX-2008.html*.

Chapter 5

Layer 3

Key Concepts

- Router
- IP Address
- Subnet
- Default Gateway
- DHCP
- DNS
- ARP
- Ping

Introduction

With Layers 1 and 2 behind us, we can move on to Layer 3, the Network layer. There comes a time when every packet needs to leave its local segment and go off into the world to seek its fortune, while we look on with a single tear in our eye and wish it well. In this chapter, we describe the process of routing data from one device to another, between networks. We start with an overview of the Network layer functions, then move on to logical addressing at the Network layer, talk through routing mechanics, and close with describing a few of the tools supporting the functions at this layer.

The Network Layer

You might recall from Chapter 2, "A Tale of Two Network Models," that the OSI Layer 3 function is to schlep packets from a sender to a recipient, potentially navigating numerous hops along the way. To accomplish this, Network layer protocols support the process of forwarding packets, the logical addressing of devices, and methods of learning about connected networks and how to reach them.

Routing and Forwarding

Each host on a network uses a simple two-step process when determining where to send a packet. If the destination address is in the same subnet as the host, the source host simply sends the packet directly to that destination host. If the destination address is on a different subnet, the host sends the packet to the router on the subnet. The router examines the packet, comparing the packet's destination address to the routing table, looking for a match. If a match is found, the router resends the packet out of the corresponding interface.

Connected, Static, and Dynamic Routes

The router compares each packet's destination address to its routing table. That routing table can be populated in three different ways. The first concerns *connected routes*. The router will automatically add a route to its routing table for subnets it is directly connected to, so long as the interface is online and has an Internet protocol (IP) address assigned to it. If the router has an interface with the IP address 192.168.1.1 / 24, it will add the 192.168.1.0 / 24 network to its table, with that interface as the next hop.

The second method is *static routes*. For networks that are not directly connected, an administrator can manually enter a route statement directing a certain network to a certain interface. While this works just fine in a small or steady-state environment, it becomes difficult to manage at scale, or when new networks are added regularly.

The third method, *dynamic routes*, allows routers to learn routes by way of a routing protocol. Each router advertises the routes it knows about to other routers in a topology. When a router hears an update with new routes in it, it adds them to its routing table. Routing protocols include some mechanism to prevent routing loops from being added to tables, and include some sort of metric that routers use to compare learned routes, ensuring that the best route to a location is added.

The Gateway of Last Resort

Earlier, we said that if a match in the routing table is found, the router sends the packet out of the appropriate interface. Well, what if a match is not found? Often, a router will be configured with a *gateway of last resort*, also called a *default route* or *default gateway*. These terms can be used interchangeably, but "gateway of last resort" has a bit more flair to it. This is a special wildcard static route that says if the packet doesn't match anything in my routing table, shoot it over to *this* guy, and he'll know what to do with it.

> **NOTE**
>
> The previous statement holds unless you're working with a Cisco router on which the `no ip classless` command has been issued. In such a configuration, the gateway of last resort can be set, but will be ignored. If a match is not found in the routing table, the packet is dropped.

This concept extends to hosts on the network, too—each host will have its default gateway configured to be the router on its subnet. Note that because the default gateway is a wildcard route for any non-local network, you can only have one per host. Even if your host is multi-homed—that is, connected to multiple networks—there can only be one default gateway.

IP Addressing and Subnetting

Each device communicating on the network needs a unique IP address. The IP address is a 32-bit number, which we shorten into dotted-decimal notation, translating each byte of the 32-bit sequence into a decimal value, and separating those numbers with periods. So the IP address 204.248.52.7 is really the 32-bit sequence 11001100 11111000 00110100 00000111. You will often hear each of those decimal chunks referred to as *octets*, that is, a group of eight values.

IP addresses are grouped into sets of contiguous addresses, each of which is an IP network or subnet. The addresses within a single subnet will have a common string of values in the first part of the address. The full IP address consists of two parts—a network prefix defining the network and a host address identifying the host on that network. All hosts that share the same network prefix must be local to each other—there cannot be any routers between them. Likewise, hosts that have different network prefixes must be separated by a router.

Classful Addressing

So, given a value like 204.248.52.7, how do you tell where the network address ends and the host address begins? Back when IP was still just a twinkle in Defense Advanced Research Projects Agency's (DARPA's) eye, the Internet Engineering Task Force (IETF) created request for comments (RFC) 791 to describe different classes of networks usable by hosts as unicast addresses. Three classes were defined—Classes A, B, and C. Each class has a different length for its network prefix. Class A networks use the first byte of the address as the network prefix. Class B networks use the first two bytes, and Class C networks use the first three. When describing the network prefix, the convention is to write out the numbers in the prefix, and use zeroes for the host portion. Examples would be 4.0.0.0 for a Class A network, 128.123.0.0 for a Class B network, and 192.123.321.0 for a Class C network.

Each class of network can support a set number of hosts. A Class A network reserves the first byte for the network prefix, leaving three bytes (or 24 bits) available for host identification. The total number of available hosts is then 2^{24}, minus two reserved addresses per network, for a total of sixteen million and change. The last address in the range is reserved as a broadcast address. The first address in the range was historically reserved to refer only to the network prefix, though modern routing and switching hardware allows the use of that address. Class B networks support 2^{16} minus two or 65,534 hosts. For Class C, it's 2^8 minus two or 254 hosts. Table 5.1 lists the octet ranges, network numbers, total number of networks, and number of hosts per network for each class.

Table 5.1 Classful Network Descriptions

Class	First Octet	Valid Networks	Number of Networks	Number of Hosts
A	1 – 126	1.0.0.0 – 126.0.0.0	128 (2^7)	16,777,214 (2^{24} – 2)
B	128 – 191	128.0.0.0 – 192.255.0.0	16,384 (2^{14})	65,534 (2^{16} – 2)
C	192 – 223	192.0.0.0 – 223.255.255.0	2,097,152 (2^{21})	254 (2^8 – 2)

Classless Addressing

This system of classful addressing was not without its limitations. The supply of classful networks was rapidly depleted, and routing tables were becoming difficult to manage. The IETF devised a new system for describing networks in RFCs 1518 and 1519, called Classless Inter-Domain Routing or CIDR.

As with classful addressing, the IP address would be made up of a network prefix and a host identifier. But instead of restricting that network prefix to the bit boundary of an octet, CIDR allowed the network prefix to be an arbitrary length, through variable-length subnet masking (VLSM).

CIDR introduces the concept of the subnet mask, another 32-bit binary number that, when paired with an IP address, allows for the network and host portions of the IP address to be determined. The binary representation of a subnet mask is always a sequence of contiguous 1s followed by a sequence of 0s. A router performs a logical AND operation on the binary values of the IP address and the subnet mask to determine the network portion. Another way of looking at this is that the network portion of the IP address is the set of bits that correspond to the 1s in the subnet mask.

Let's work through a couple of examples. Let's say we have a host IP address of 10.20.30.40 and a Class A subnet mask of 255.0.0.0. What is our network address?

Well, the binary representation of 10.20.30.40 is 00001010 00010100 00011110 00101000. The binary representation of 255.0.0.0 is 11111111 00000000 00000000 00000000. Let's compare them:

```
IP:      00001010 00010100 00011110 00101000
Mask:    11111111 00000000 00000000 00000000
Network: 00001010 00000000 00000000 00000000
```

We can write out the network address by seeing which bits of the IP address map to a 1 in the subnet address, and then entering zeroes for bits that map to zeroes. Here, that becomes 00001010 00000000 00000000 00000000. Converting that to decimal, we get 10.0.0.0. Often, you'll see the subnet mask expressed as the number of 1s in the mask—this is called CIDR notation. Our network in CIDR notation is 10.0.0.0/8.

Now let's try one a little more complicated. We'll use the same IP address, 10.20.30.40, but this time our subnet mask will be 255.255.255.224.

Again, the binary representation of 10.20.30.40 is 00001010 00010100 00011110 00101000. The binary representation of 255.255.255.224 is 11111111 11111111 11111111 11100000. Let's compare them:

```
IP:      00001010 00010100 00011110 00101000
Mask:    11111111 11111111 11111111 11100000
Network: 00001010 00010100 00011110 00100000
```

This time, our network address came out to 00001010 00010100 00011110 00100000. Converting that to decimal and CIDR notation, we get 10.20.30.32/27.

> **TIP**
>
> There's a handy online calculator for translating IPs and subnet masks into their network address and network range at www.subnet-calculator.com/cidr.php.

Reserved Addresses

Some IP addresses are best avoided, as they are reserved for specific purposes. These include the smallest and largest IP address in each subnet. The smallest IP address is reserved for use as the network address, and the largest is the broadcast address for the segment. Other common reserved blocks are 0.0.0.0/8 reserved for wildcard source IP addresses, 127.0.0.0/8 reserved for loopback addresses, 169.254.0.0/16 reserved for link local addresses (you might recognize these as Automatic Private IP Addresses [APIPA] in Windows), and Class D (first octet 224-239) and Class E (first octet 240-255) are reserved for multicast and experimental addresses, respectively.

Other ranges are set aside for use as private IP space. These include 10.0.0.0/8, 172.16.0.0/12, and 192.168.0.0/16. Private addresses are typically used inside an organization where public IP addresses are not needed. Privately addressed devices can still access external resources by way of Network Address Translation (NAT). A complete list of reserved address ranges can be found in RFC 6890, "Special Purpose IP Address Registries."

Network Layer Supporting Applications

Having covered addressing and forwarding mechanics, let's turn to common tools that assist Network layer function, care, and feeding.

DHCP

Every device on the network needs an IP address, but manually configuring an address for each and every device presents logistical challenges as the network grows. Certain important devices—routers, switches, and servers, for example—should be configured manually, with static IP addresses that do not ever change. This ensures that these devices are always reachable at the expected address. Other devices, typically end-user devices, might have more transient connections and as such not need permanent, manually assigned addresses. For these devices, Dynamic Host Configuration Protocol (DHCP) can be used to allow the device to temporarily borrow, or lease, an IP address. DHCP also allows an administrator to configure other information including the default gateway address, DNS server addresses (more on that in a bit), and domain names.

When DHCP is used, a DHCP server maintains a list of various pools of IP addresses that can be used for each subnet. Devices configured to use DHCP issue a broadcast DHCP Discover message on their subnet. A DHCP server earmarks an IP address in its pool and responds with a broadcast DHCP Offer message directed to the client, which includes a proposed IP address, subnet mask, lease duration, and the IP of the DHCP server. The client then responds to the server via broadcast with a DHCP Request, indicating that the client has accepted the offer. A client might receive offers from multiple DHCP servers, but will respond with a request to only one. Any other DHCP servers that had sent offers will see the broadcast request and return their offered address to their pools. The DHCP server then issues a DHCP Acknowledgement to the client, confirming the reservation. The acknowledgment includes any additional configuration parameters that might be specified.

DNS

While some of us are cursed with being able to recall IP addresses they used 20 years ago (but not what their wife asked them to do this morning), this is not a fair expectation of your end users.

Domain Name Service (DNS) is a centralized mechanism for mapping user-friendly names to IP addresses. When a host is configured to use a DNS server, it will send DNS requests to the specified server, asking for translation. The DNS server will then reply with the IP address matching the friendly name. Multiple DNS servers can be specified, so if the client cannot reach the first server listed, it will try the next server in the list until a response is received.

ARP

Remember that each IP packet must be encapsulated in a Layer 2 frame before it can be sent to the next hop. The Address Resolution Protocol (ARP) is used to determine the destination media access control (MAC) address for that frame.

After a client has resolved a name to an IP address, it determines whether that IP address is on its local subnet. If it is, it issues an ARP broadcast on the segment asking for the holder of that IP address to respond with its MAC address. If the destination host is not on the local subnet, the client issues an ARP request for the default gateway IP address.

ARP requests are not issued for every bit of communication. As a client makes requests, the replies are remembered in the ARP cache. Each time a client needs to encapsulate a packet in a frame, it checks the ARP cache to see if it has a MAC match for the destination IP.

Ping

The ping command allows you to test basic IP connectivity between hosts. It uses the Internet Control Message Protocol (ICMP) to send an ICMP echo request to the destination host. The host is then expected to reply with an ICMP echo reply. When successful, you have confirmed that the network can deliver a packet from the source to the destination and back again.

Ping was named after the sound sonar makes, as the echo request and echo reply function is similar to the process of active sonar.

Summary

In this chapter, we reviewed the functions of Layer 3, the Network layer. We described the Network layer functions, Network layer addressing, the routing and forwarding processes, and some utilities that function at and support this layer. In the next chapter, we break away from networking theory to investigate a relatively new infrastructure consumption model.

Chapter 6

Converged Infrastructure

Key Concepts

- Converged Infrastructure
- Cisco UCS
- HP BladeSystem
- Nutanix Virtual Computing Platform

Introduction

Let's take a quick detour before we get into virtual networking. Think of it as a quick breather, an opportunity to come up for air after the networking concepts we just threw at you. So far, we've gone over a good bit of networking fundamentals, at some length. It's easy to get lost here, to get so caught up in the particulars of interconnecting devices to the point where you forget that those devices are the reason for the network to be there in the first place. Something similar often happens with server people, storage people, desktop people—everyone with a specialization. When these technologies are treated as discrete islands, staffed and procured separately, silos develop and inefficiencies abound.

Converged infrastructure is one approach to solving this problem. A converged infrastructure solution packages or otherwise integrates compute, networking, and storage technologies into a solution that is (ideally) easier to consume, deploy, and manage. In this chapter, we go over the basic concepts and provide a few examples of converged solutions that we often run into.

Concepts

To begin, let's look at a typical IT shop that has the traditional set of datacenter components: rack-mount servers tethered to network switches and a storage array. The personnel that manage and maintain this equipment are grouped into teams—the storage team, network team, and server team—and together they make up the Infrastructure Team.

When a new server needs to be added to the datacenter, quite a bit of activity needs to take place. Barring any political or procurement shenanigans, the three teams must work in harmony in order to get the new server into a production state.

The Server Team has to "rack and stack" the server. This is the process of unloading the server into the datacenter, removing it from the packaging, and then finding a rack location and mounting it to the rack. They can also be tasked with assigning the server name, applying an IP address, and working to complete any other personality attributes of the server.

The Network Team might cable the server into the nearby switch and ask the Server Team exactly how to configure the port for this server. They often ask questions about the VLAN configuration, number of cables needed, and the Maximum Transition Unit (MTU) settings to ensure that the port will correctly talk back and forth with the server. They might also want to investigate the Network Interface Cards (NICs) to verify what MAC addresses will be discovered by the switch for security purposes.

And finally, the Storage Team might need to examine the Host Bus Adapters (HBAs) to identify the World Wide Port Names (WWPNs) for building a Storage Area Network (SAN) and corresponding zoning configuration. They would then be able to build storage constructs, such as Logical Unit Numbers (LUNs) or Volumes, and present them to the server.

Sounds exhausting, doesn't it? Lots of hands are involved, and there are many opportunities for errors even if everything is communicating perfectly. And while no single set of tasks takes too terribly long, the logistics of coordinating the work and conforming to change control policies can compound delays, stretching delivery time to crazy lengths. We've worked with companies that consider a 90-day turnaround from delivery to production to be a job well done.

Converged Infrastructure Advantages

This model has been around for many years. And it works, mostly. So why change? Well, if you are only adding one or two servers a month, it's not a big deal to go through the multi-team goat rodeo. But what if you want to add 10, 100, or even 1,000 servers a month? You'd need an entire army of engineers to do nothing but add servers. It doesn't scale well and is extremely prone to error.

Converged infrastructure looks to remove large chunks of the human element. It aims to combine multiple types of resources into one logical management and control plane. Networking is certainly core to this idea, and is typically coupled with both compute and storage. Rather than having silos of IT infrastructure, converged infrastructure supports the collapsing of those silos into one team.

Here are some pretty slick advantages to converging the infrastructure:

- **Wire once:** Much of the networking tasks that were performed by the Networking Team are completed during the initial configuration of the solution. As additional servers are brought into the datacenter, the physical network remains untouched.

- **Agility and flexibility:** The majority of configuration is done through automation and templates, removing much of the risk associated with human configuration.

- **Visibility:** The entire solution can be analyzed and configured from a central management panel, rather than having to log into multiple portals across a wide variety of disciplines.

Examples

Over the past several years, the number of converged infrastructure offerings has soared. The market has reacted favorably to the idea of having simplified management and increased flexibility in their datacenter. Each offering has a different twist on exactly how they operate, what market segment they are focusing on, and how scalable the solution is. We provide a few examples of solutions that we run into in the datacenter. This is not an exhaustive list and is only meant to serve as examples of types of converged infrastructure.

Cisco UCS

Cisco's Unified Computing System (UCS) was a bit of a blank-slate approach to computing, trying to answer the question of what a compute platform should look like in a post-virtualization world. Cisco's approach unifies network and storage fabrics within an enclosure, reduces the number of points of management, and provides a policy and pool-based approach to server provisioning. It also allows you your choice of blade or rack-mount form-factors.

The smarts of UCS are housed in a pair of fabric interconnects, which run the UCS Manager software to control and manage the entire compute domain. Each fabric interconnect has upstream connections to external network and, optionally, SAN, and downstream "server port" connections to fabric extenders, implemented as either IO modules housed in blade enclosures, or top-of-rack style Nexus 2000-series devices. Each fabric extender functions as a remote line card of the fabric interconnect. The fabric extenders are completely dependent on the fabric interconnects; they cannot themselves forward traffic. Traffic flows into a fabric interconnect via an Uplink Port, then down through a Server Port to a fabric extender, and ultimately to the blade server or rack-mount server.

To be clear, this is a rather unique offering in the converged space—typically, converged infrastructure limits the design to either blades or a "blade-like" enclosure and does not allow you to use a rack-mount server.

Why is this relevant? Not all workloads can fit in a blade form-factor. One example is Apache Hadoop—it is a big data analytic cluster that can benefit from having many slow, local hard drives to use the inside of each server, more than can fit into a single blade.

Figure 6.1 shows a UCS chassis, with its IO modules connected to a pair of fabric interconnects.

The fabric interconnects function as *end-host* devices—they act like switches on the server-facing side, but like server NICs on the network-facing side. This eliminates some of the caveats of traditional switches. An end-host device cannot form a loop, and as such, there is no spanning tree to concern yourself with. This means that every uplink from the fabric interconnect to the upstream switches can be active. Multiple connections from each IO module to its fabric interconnect can also be made without worrying about loops—depending on your configuration, the links between each IO module and the fabric interconnect are treated as a port-channel bundle, or blades are pinned to a particular uplink. This ensures that traffic can flow up all uplinks. The fabric interconnects do not learn about any of the MAC addresses for entities not within their control. When switching traffic, any destination MAC address that is unknown is forwarded out an uplink port and is expected to be handled by a fully featured switch upstream.

All network configuration necessary for the servers is performed in UCS Manager. You define the VLANs, Quality of Service policies, MTU size, and number of NICs each server will have. Servers are usually configured to be stateless—a service profile containing MAC address and World Wide Name (WWN) identity information pulled from pools, network, and SAN configuration, and boot from SAN or LAN configuration details is associated with the physical blade. This allows for quick and easy replacement in the event of a failure—you replace the failed blade and re-associate the service profile to the replacement.

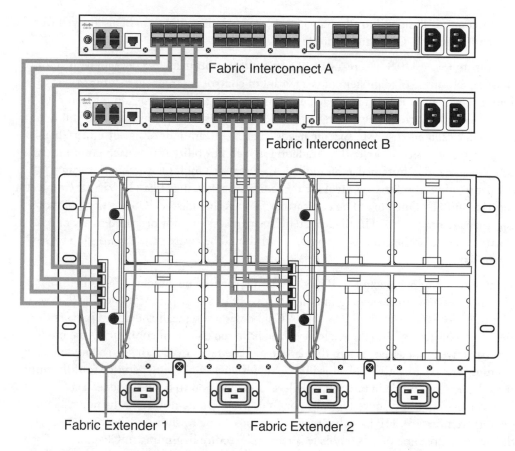

Figure 6.1 Cisco UCS architecture

Cisco offers two additional products to extend management capabilities. UCS Central provides centralized management for multiple UCS domains—that is, multiple pairs of fabric interconnects and their connected servers. UCS Director provides comprehensive administration and orchestration for not only Cisco UCS hardware but also other Cisco switch devices and multivendor storage devices.

HP BladeSystem

HP BladeSystem has been in the top spot for overall deployments of x86 blade architectures for many years. BladeSystem is fully focused on blade offerings and does not have any rack-mount server choices. However, BladeSystem offers a wide variety of special purpose blades—such as storage blades, PCIe slot blades, desktop blades, and so on. Additionally, the architecture is designed to allow a wide variety of blade switches to be used, even from other vendors such as Cisco and Brocade.

In contrast to Cisco UCS, where a pair of fabric interconnects form a domain with all of the blade enclosures, BladeSystem puts a fair bit of control and management into each individual blade enclosure. In fact, each enclosure houses an Onboard Administrator (OA) and eight slots for various networking modules. This gives the administrator flexibility to custom tailor each enclosure to specific needs (such as the amount or use of Fiber Channel, Ethernet, or a mix of both). The tradeoff for such flexibility is that each point needs to be managed and maintained as an individual entity, although management software does exist to allow combined control for the entities via offerings like HP Virtual Connect Enterprise and HP OneView. The contrasting point is that Cisco UCS has one point of logical management, while HP BladeSystem has many. We're not prepared to say one is any better than the other; this is just a point you should be aware of when working with either system.

From a networking perspective, HP BladeSystem is focused on a technology called *Virtual Connect (VC)*. These are switching modules that work in a transparent mode, which is very similar to end-host mode with UCS. The VC modules are typically deployed in pairs that sit next to each other within the enclosure. You have the choice of configuring the modules to be active and passive, where the passive module takes over if the active module fails, or running active and active and allowing the underlying vSphere hypervisor to shift traffic over to the active module in the case of failure. The decision to choose between active and passive versus active and active typically comes down to traffic flows and the north-bound switching architecture. HP has what they call a Cook Book to show you how to build both—we go into some details on blade server architecture beginning in Chapter 11, "Lab Scenario."

HP BladeSytem gives you the ability to define VLANs, virtual NICs, NIC speeds, and so on from within the VC manager. Configuration is done once with a VC Domain (be that a single enclosure or multiple enclosures with VC Enterprise Manager) and can then be used repeatedly for each current and additional blade. You can also use VLANs that exist only within BladeSystem for local traffic, such as vMotion or Fault Tolerance, if that would be optimal for your architecture or design. Additional automation and self-service features are available when BladeSystem is deployed as part of an HP CloudSystem Matrix solution.

Figure 6.2 shows the business end of an HP BladeSystem c7000 enclosure.

Figure 6.2   HP BladeSystem rear view

Nutanix Virtual Computing Platform

Nutanix offers a fresh look at converging the various resource food groups—compute, storage, and network—into a single *"hyper-converged"* platform. Nutanix's convergence goes to 11, as no remote storage array is involved—everything is baked into a Virtual Computing Cluster chassis.

This makes for an interesting experience when focusing on the networking construction, because the entire focus is the presentation of traffic into and out of the Nutanix cluster. The Ethernet connections that tie into the system are there to give the virtual machines a path out of the cluster to communicate with other entities. Each Nutanix node in the cluster provides a series of network adapters that can plug into an upstream switching system, making expansion of bandwidth a simple factor of the number of nodes. This is somewhat similar to the concept expressed in the "Cisco UCS" section, with the difference being that instead of wiring a UCS chassis to a UCS fabric interconnect, you just wire Nutanix nodes into an upstream switch that provides both clustering and access to the nodes. The remaining node-to-node communication is handled by the system. Other than assigning IP addresses, this node-to-node communication is transparent to the administrator.

Figure 6.3 shows the architecture of the Nutanix Virtual Computing Platform.

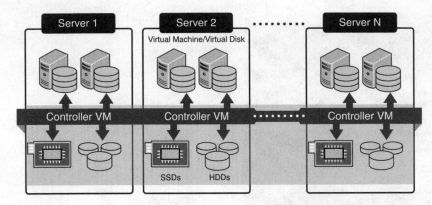

Figure 6.3   Nutanix Virtual Computing Platform architecture

Summary

In this chapter, we introduced the concept of converged infrastructure, made a case for why it has advantages over the traditional deployment model, and described the three vendor implementations that we come across most often. This ends our physical infrastructure discussion; in the next chapter, we explore virtual networking concepts.

Chapter 7

How Virtual Switching Differs from Physical Switching

Key Concepts

- Host Uplinks
- Virtual Ports
- External Switch Tagging (EST)
- Virtual Switch Tagging (VST)
- Virtual Guest Tagging (VGT)

Introduction

Although it's easy to point to the obvious difference between physical and virtual switching—one is hardware and the other is software—there is a bit more to it than that. There are differences both in the process by which traffic is switched, and in the advanced services and features offered. In this chapter, we look at how a virtual switch operates on a VMware vSphere host running ESXi, along with some of the terminology of logical objects represented by the virtual switch.

Physical and Virtual Switch Comparison

So your first question might be—what exactly is a virtual switch? After all, the previous section of this book focused entirely on the theory and practice of switching, along with some routing, and most of it focused on plugging wires into fancy boxes so that data could move around.

To begin, let's start by covering some basic functionality similarities and differences between physical and virtual switches. You might be surprised at how alike these two types of switches are; the differences can be subtle but have a profound impact on the design and configuration of a well-tuned virtual environment.

Similarities

It's important to note that a VMware virtual switch, or vSwitch as it is known, doesn't use any special or proprietary type of modification on the traffic. All the frames that flow into a vSwitch follow the exact same standards as outlined by the Institute of Electrical and Electronics Engineers (IEEE) 802.3 protocol, following the conceptual framework of the OSI Model's Data-Link Layer, and the practical application of the TCP/IP Network Interface layer. If you think about it, this makes a lot of sense—as otherwise you'd need special equipment just to pass traffic into or out of an ESXi host and its vSwitch.

Figure 7.1 shows the layout of an IEEE 802.3 frame.

Preamble	Start of Frame Delimiter	MAC Destination	MAC Source	802.1Q VLAN Tag	Type	Data (Payload)	Frame Check Sequence	Interface Gap
7	1	6	6	4	2	1500	4	12

bytes

Figure 7.1   An IEEE 802.3 frame layout

Additionally, ESXi hosts have the ability to use a wide variety of off-the-shelf network adapters (NICs) from the likes of Qlogic, Emulex, Intel, and others—consult the Hardware Compatibility List for an authoritative list. These use the standard connector types, RJ45/8p8c for copper or any of the standard fiber connector types, just as you would find in any other server that was running any other operating system or hypervisor. A vSwitch then begins using these network adapters and attached cables to switch traffic.

Differences

Because a vSwitch isn't a physical device, you have some flexibility in configuration. If you need a larger number of virtual ports on your vSwitch, you can just edit its properties and adjust as needed. With physical switches, this could require a forklift switch upgrade, adding new switches, or adding line cards to a chassis-based switch.

Switching Decisions

Another major difference is how a vSwitch handles Layer 2 switching. That is, the knowledge and movement of data to MAC addresses on the network. A physical switch has a large table of MAC addresses that it keeps in memory to quickly figure out where a frame needs to be sent. The addresses that are remembered are for nodes that are both directly and remotely attached to the switch—that is, nodes directly plugged into a switch port and also nodes that are connected to another switch's port.

Figure 7.2 shows the MAC addresses of devices connected to a virtual switch, as found in the vSphere Web Client.

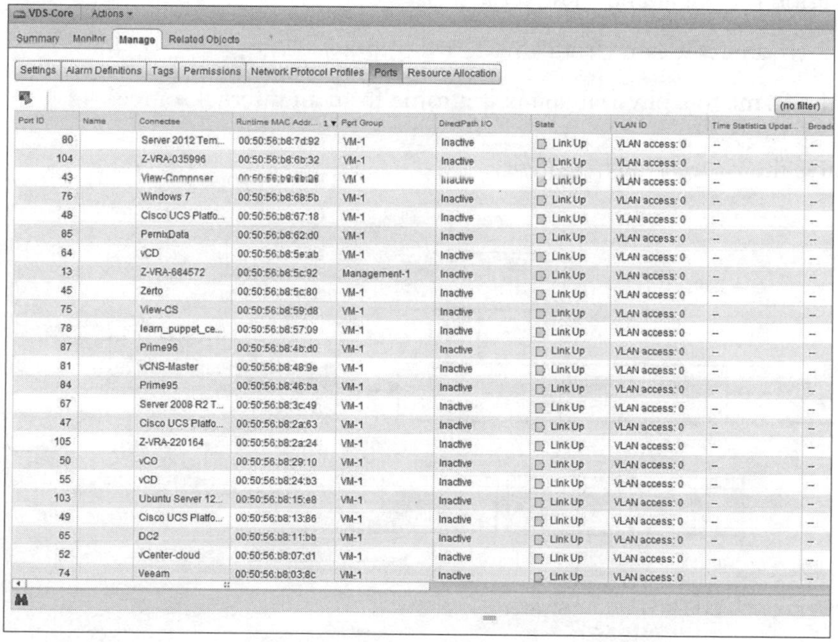

Figure 7.2   A virtual switch only tracks MAC addresses on its ports

A vSwitch does not concern itself with MAC addresses for nodes that are not directly attached to it. It only needs to know the MAC addresses for the virtual machines (VMs) and VMkernel port devices (covered further in this chapter) that are consuming virtual ports on the vSwitch. Beyond that, the vSwitch has no clue where other devices live. If a frame enters the vSwitch from the outside world destined for an unknown MAC address, it is ignored by the vSwitch. This is an important distinction—a physical switch will flood unknown frames out of all ports except the one the frame was received on, as part of the mechanism it uses to learn MAC addresses. A software vSwitch does not need to go through a learning process, and therefore knows which MAC addresses do and don't belong. Similarly, if a frame enters the vSwitch from one of its virtual ports, such as from a VM destined for an unknown MAC address, it is given over to an Uplink port to handle. This makes Layer 2 switching very simple and lightweight for a vSwitch. To sum it up, the switching logic looks like this:

1. Ethernet Frame enters the vSwitch.

2. If the destination is to a known MAC address, switch the frame to the virtual port that owns that MAC address.

3. If the destination is to an unknown MAC address:

    a. Drop the frame if it came from an external source.

    b. Send the frame to a physical uplink if it came from an internal source.

Figure 7.3 illustrates the virtual switching logic.

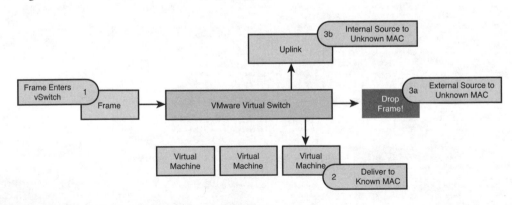

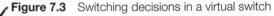

Figure 7.3   Switching decisions in a virtual switch

Keep in mind that the vSwitch is only able to do Layer 2 switching. If a frame is trying to reach a MAC address on another VLAN, Layer 3 switching is required and the frame will be sent to the physical uplink with the hopes that a higher level switch can perform the inter-VLAN routing.

Physical Uplinks

But not all ports on a vSwitch are virtual—after all, there has to be some way to get the traffic out of the host! This is where those physical network adapters (NICs) come in to play as uplinks into the physical network. Each uplink provides a traffic path northbound to the upstream physical switch so that data can enter and leave the virtual environment.

Host Network Interface Card (NIC)

An ESXi host's NICs act as uplinks for a virtual switch. That is, they are the means by which traffic can enter and leave a vSphere host. If desired, you can configure a large number of NICs—up to 32 1GbE NICs in vSphere 5.1—or as few as one. We tend to think that you shouldn't ever have less than two of anything to avoid creating a single point of failure, so shoot for two NICs at a minimum. If you don't want your traffic to go anywhere beyond the ESXi host, you can even create a vSwitch with no uplinks.

You're also given the choice of speeds for your NICs. This is usually a speed of 1 gigabit per second (1 Gbps) or 10 gigabits per second (10 Gbps). You might even notice these values expressed as "1GbE" and "10GbE"—the capital E denotes Ethernet.

Not all traffic will use the physical uplinks. Sometimes a VM (or even the host) wants to communicate with another VM on the same VLAN inside of the same virtual switch on the same host. In this case, there's no need for the traffic to leave the virtual switch and use an uplink—the switch knows that both entities are attached to it, and it will simply switch the frames locally. In the past, this was sometimes called "dark traffic" because it was difficult to track and monitor before more modern virtualization-aware tools and monitoring software were developed.

Figure 7.4 illustrates this concept of local vSwitch dark traffic.

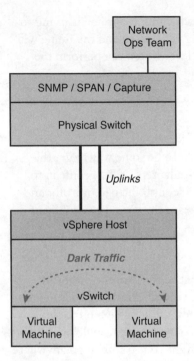

Figure 7.4   Locally switched traffic or "dark traffic"

Virtual Ports

Now that we've covered the physical side of a virtual switch—which are the physical uplinks provided by the NICs—let's move on to the virtual side.

A virtual switch has a dynamically defined quantity of virtual ports available to the VMs and the host itself. The fact that the virtual port count is dynamic is pretty important, because it allows the switch to be agile and meet the needs of newly created VMs and host ports, along with removing unused ports to keep the amount of host RAM consumed reasonable.

TIP

vSphere 4-distributed virtual switches used a static quantity of virtual ports. When you ran out of virtual ports, you'd have to increase the quantity using the graphical user interface (GUI) or a script. It was not fun!

With version 5.x of vSphere, however, the distributed virtual ports are now *elastic ports* by default. Elastic means that the virtual switch will manage the quantity of virtual ports automatically—creating and deleting them as needed—without user intervention.

The virtual ports are connected to three different types of ports: VM NICs, VMkernel ports, and service console ports.

Virtual Machine NICs

Every virtual network adapter that is created, connected, and active within a VM uses up a single virtual port on a vSwitch. This is actually how the connection is made between a VM NIC and the virtual switch—the virtual port is the bridge to the physical network.

VMkernel Ports

VMkernel ports are special ports that connect the vSphere host's VMkernel to the virtual switch. After all, the host also needs to talk with other hosts, the vCenter server, and whatever else that is important on your network, and that traffic has to be sent out of the virtual switch just like all the rest.

VMkernel ports can serve a few different purposes and carry various types of traffic:

1. Management
2. vMotion
3. Fault tolerance logging
4. iSCSI storage traffic
5. NFS storage traffic

Service Console

Prior to vSphere 5, you actually had two choices of ESX to choose from: ESX and ESXi. With vSphere 5, the only choice is ESXi. What's the difference? ESX, sometimes called the "classic" hypervisor, actually ran both the virtualization kernel (the VMkernel) along with a Console Operating System (COS). ESX was a comparably larger installation leading to a larger attack surface, and so VMware ultimately shelved the classic ESX architecture and now only offers the slim, VMkernel-only version of ESXi.

However, it is important to understand that classic ESX does not use a Management VMkernel port. Instead, it has a special interface called the Service Console for management; the COS rather than the VMkernel owned this interface. While it is out of scope to go any deeper for this book, it is good to be aware of the legacy architecture if you run into it.

VLANs

One final, but major, component of a virtual switch is VLAN tagging. You might remember IEEE 802.1q from back in Chapter 4, "Advanced Layer 2." Virtual switches support three different ways to determine how VLANs are handled and where.

External Switch Tagging (EST)

Much like it sounds, *External Switch Tagging (EST)* is a configuration where the virtual switch is completely ignorant of the VLAN tags. Instead, the external switch that the physical uplinks are connected to handles all of the VLANs and removes the tags before they ever reach the virtual switch.

This is accomplished by setting the physical switch ports on the upstream switch into Access mode. When traffic enters an Access port inside the northbound switch, the VLAN tag is inspected and removed before the port sends the traffic down to the virtual switch. Because of this, the virtual switch will only handle untagged traffic.

Also, because there are no VLAN tags making their way into the virtual switch, the VM NIC or VMkernel port are unaware of what VLAN they belong to and never see an 802.1Q VLAN tag. Everything on that vSwitch then must use that same VLAN—the one configured on the access port on the upstream switch.

Virtual Switch Tagging (VST)

Virtual Switch Tagging (VST) occurs when the virtual switch itself is inspecting and adding or removing the VLAN tags. In order for this to occur, the upstream switch port that is connected to the physical uplink must be configured as a trunk port. This allows the port to pass along a defined number of VLAN-tagged traffic down to the virtual switch with the tag intact.

When the frame arrives at the virtual switch, it inspects the VLAN tag to see what VLAN it belongs to and the destination MAC address. Assuming it finds a VM NIC or VMkernel port that matches the VLAN and MAC address, the frame is delivered with the VLAN

<u>tag removed</u>. Otherwise, the frame is discarded. When traffic is sent from a VM NIC or VMkernel port, the virtual switch makes sure to add the VLAN tag before sending the frame to a physical uplink.

VST is similar to EST in that the VM NIC or VMkernel port is unaware of the 802.1Q VLAN tag because the virtual switch has removed the tag before delivery.

> **NOTE**
>
> VST is the most popular and common method used by virtualization administrators for many reasons. VST is very simple to manage and maintain because the upstream switch port is configured as a trunk and requires little to no effort from a network administrator to maintain. Also, it grants additional visibility into how the VLANs are laid out for the virtualization administrator as you can easily see the tag numbers from the vSphere Client. And finally, it allows greater flexibility in the amount of VLANs that can be used on a virtual switch over EST, which only allows you to use a single VLAN per physical uplink. Oh, and it's also the method recommended and preferred by VMware.

Virtual Guest Tagging (VGT)

The final type of tagging is *Virtual Guest Tagging (VGT)*. In this configuration, the northbound switch port is configured as a trunk and passes VLAN tags down to the virtual switch. The virtual switch will inspect the VLAN tags to ensure they match the correct destination virtual port but will keep the tags intact. The tagged frames are passed along in an unaltered state to the VM or VMkernel port. In order for this configuration to work properly, the VM must be able to read and understand VLAN tags, as well as tag its own traffic that is being sent out.

Figure 7.5 illustrates how the VLAN tag can be added to a NIC from within a Windows VM.

VGT is a unique type of configuration and typically reserved for VMs that monitor or "sniff" traffic, provide routing services, or have some other need for seeing the frame with VLAN tags intact.

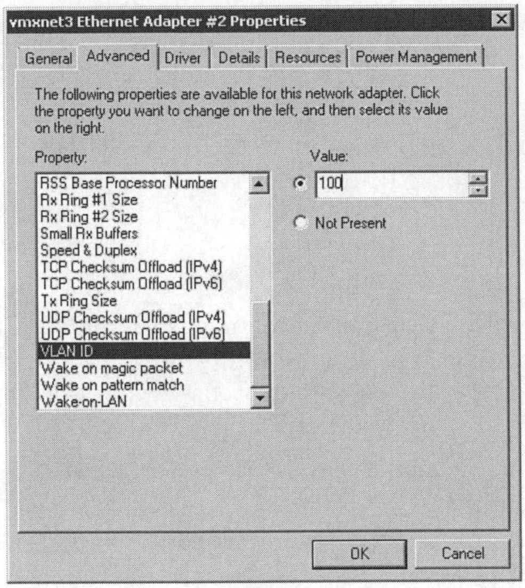

Figure 7.5 Configuring the VLAN in a Windows guest VM

Summary

In this chapter, we went over some of the key differences between physical and virtual switches. We covered the different ways they process traffic, the different types of virtual ports, and the different ways VLANs are handled. In the next chapter, we build on these distinctions and get more hands-on as we explore the configuration options available in the vSphere Standard Switch.

Chapter 8

vSphere Standard Switch

Key Concepts

- Control and Data Planes
- Virtual Ports
- vSwitch Security
- Traffic Shaping
- NIC Teaming and Failover
- VMkernel Ports
- Port Groups

Introduction

A VMware ESXi server cannot do much of anything worthwhile without some means of getting network traffic to and from the VMs it hosts. Fortunately, VMware realized this and has thoughtfully provided two solutions to this problem, the vSphere Standard Switch and the vSphere Distributed Switch. This chapter focuses on the former, the original recipe vSwitch that is included with every license level. Don't let the "standard" part of the Standard Switch fool you—it includes a bunch of great features to help you shuffle traffic around your network. With that said, let's look at what makes a VMware Standard Switch tick.

The vSphere Standard Switch

The goal of VMware's Standard Switch is to allow network traffic to flow in any scenario. This could mean that the ESXi host is not connected to a vCenter server at all, which is typically referred to as a "standalone" or "vSphere Hypervisor" install of vSphere. In this case, there's no higher level of management than the host itself, so the standard level switch needs to be able to function with nothing more than the host telling it what to do.

TIP

If you think about it deeper, when you first install VMware ESXi onto a server, it is a blank slate—it has no name, IP, or DNS information. While there are ways to script the install to auto-assign these identities, no assumptions can be made. This is another reason why the standard vSwitch must be able to operate with nothing more fancy than a standalone installation of ESXi.

Plane English

Before getting too far into how the Standard Switch works, we need to introduce a bit of terminology. When describing switch functions, we often use the terms "control plane" and "data plane." Control plane traffic and functions can best be thought of as traffic *to* the switch, and data plane traffic is traffic *through* the switch. Management, monitoring, and configuration traffic concerning the switch is control plane traffic. Frames passing from a virtual machine (VM) out to the rest of the world would be data plane traffic.

In your typical physical, top-of-rack style switch, control and data planes live within the same piece of equipment. With virtual switches, these functions can be separated.

Control Plane

The *control plane* of a standard vSwitch resides on the VMware host. That is, any manipulation of the vSwitch configuration, number of ports, and the way that traffic is moved around are all part of the host's responsibilities. More specifically, it's the job of the hypervisor kernel (called the VMkernel) to make sure that the vSwitch is configured and operational.

As such, even when you cluster a bunch of VMware hosts together, each host is responsible for its own standard vSwitches. In the case of a vCenter failure, every host's standard vSwitch would still be configurable by connecting the vSphere client directly to the host.

Data Plane

Every Standard vSwitch on a host is responsible for switching frames, which means that the *data plane* is a host's responsibility. As data enters the host NICs, which form the uplinks for a standard vSwitch, the VMkernel makes sure that the frames get to the appropriate destination. Sometimes this means that the traffic gets ignored, especially in the case of external traffic that enters the vSwitch with an unknown destination MAC address.

vSwitch Properties

Every vSwitch has two basic properties that can be configured in order to meet the requirements of your design and network's maximum transmission size.

Ports

Ports indicate the number of virtual ports that will be kept in memory, tracked, and made available to VMs, VMkernel ports, and uplinks that reside on the host. One weakness of a standard vSwitch is the requirement that the ESXi host be restarted if you change the number of ports. Prior to vSphere 4.1, the default number of vSwitch ports was only 56, leading many a green VMware administrator to hit that limit before realizing it was something that could be changed. Over time, VMware listened to the woes of virtualization administrators and, in vSphere 4.1, the default number of ports assigned to a standard vSwitch has been changed to 128, allowing some breathing room. An administrator can adjust the number of ports by powers of 2, from 128 to 256 and so on, all the way up to 4,096 possible ports.

Figure 8.1 shows the default vSwitch properties dialog in the vSphere Web Client.

REAL WORLD EXAMPLE

If you look at the port count on the classic vSphere client, you might notice that it shows 8 fewer ports (120) for the default. Hey, who stole my ports? Don't worry, this is the expected behavior. The hypervisor always reserves 8 ports for overhead activities such as network discovery, Cisco Discovery Protocol (CDP) traffic, and physical uplinks. On the newer vSphere web client, the actual port counts are shown.

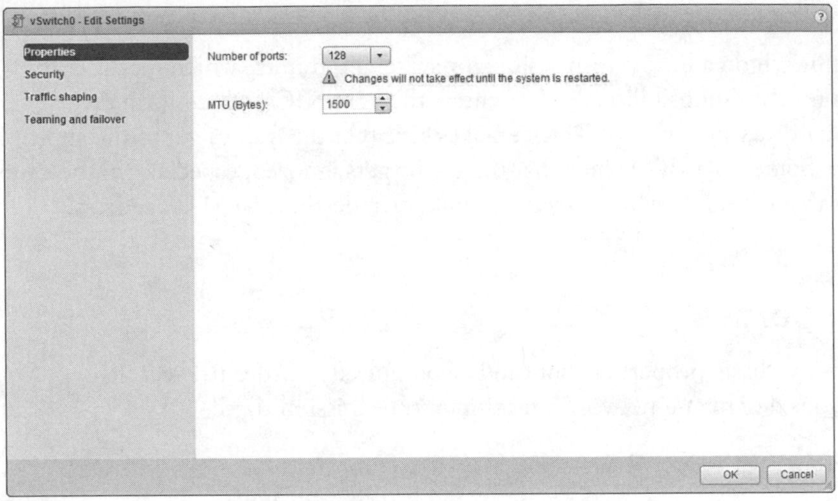

Figure 8.1   The default vSwitch properties

Maximum Transmission Unit (MTU)

The other item that you can configure is the MTU, which is the maximum amount of data that can be crammed into a frame's payload segment. By default, this is 1,500 bytes, which is the default for just about any networking device you can buy. You can safely assume that all of the physical equipment that runs northbound of the vSwitch will support a 1,500 MTU or larger, which avoids unnecessary packet fragmentation.

There's also an option to increase this size and set it to a "jumbo" size. We do love our silly names in this industry. Jumbo frames are just frames larger than the default size of 1,500. Even setting an MTU of 1,501 is technically enabling jumbo frames. Tremble before the mighty, slightly larger frame.

Most of the time, though, the term *jumbo frame* refers to a frame with an MTU of 9,000 or higher, though 9,000 is the maximum MTU ESXi will support. If you are talking to a network engineer and want to get an idea of what MTU size to set on your vSwitch, ask specifically what the MTU value is—don't just ask if he or she is running jumbo frames. This avoids any confusion.

REAL WORLD EXAMPLE

We've done a lot of work with people who want to enable jumbo frames thinking that a larger number is by default going to increase performance. This is not always true, and in some cases, enabling jumbo frames can actually hurt performance. It's also incredibly difficult to make sure that all of the physical networking equipment is properly configured for a jumbo frame size. Make sure that you have a solid technical reason, with performance testing, before you worry about increasing your MTU size on your infrastructure.

Security

The security settings on a vSwitch are probably one of the most misunderstood portions of a vSwitch configuration. There are three settings available for tuning: promiscuous mode, MAC address changes, and forged transmits, as shown in Figure 8.2.

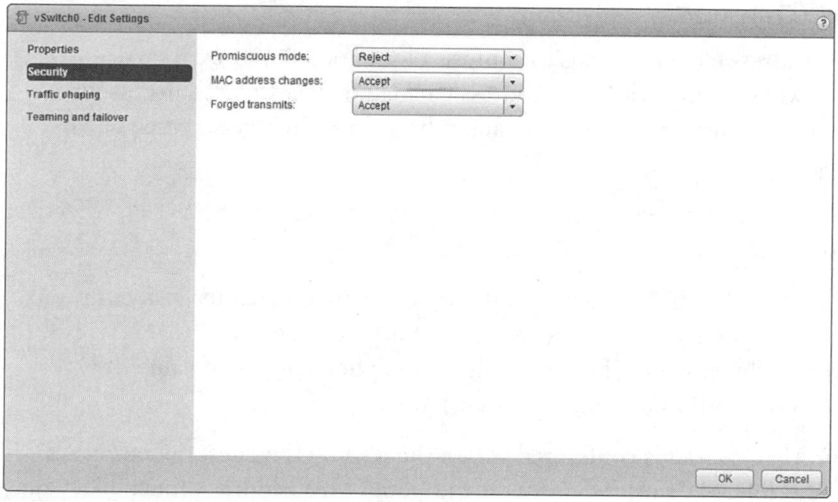

Figure 8.2 Security settings on a vSwitch

Promiscuous Mode

If you think back to when we covered physical switching, you'll probably recall that one major advantage to it is that we have the ability to switch traffic directly to a single destination MAC address. Unless the traffic is being flooded, broadcast, or specifically intended for a destination, devices on the network do not "see" the other traffic floating across the switch. This is great for most use cases as it provides for greater scalability and improved performance of the network, and is the default behavior on a standard vSwitch.

There are some situations where we really do want a VM to see traffic that is intended for another device. Imagine having some sort of network monitoring VM that needs to sniff traffic. This is where Promiscuous Mode comes in handy. By setting it to Accept, we are ordering the vSwitch to share traffic on each VLAN among other VMs on the same VLAN.

> **PITFALL**
>
> Promiscuous mode does not allow a VM to see traffic on VLANs that aren't specified by the port group. It can still only see traffic for the VLAN(s) that it belongs to. This is a very common misconception.

MAC Address Changes

The idea of MAC Address Changes tends to confuse a lot of people, so we'll go deep into this one. First, what exactly is a MAC Address Change from a vSwitch perspective? To understand this, you must first know more about how the switch keeps track of MAC addresses for VMs.

To begin with, every VM has three different types of MAC addresses: the Initial, Effective, and Runtime MAC addresses:

- The *Initial MAC address* is configured on the virtual network adapter inside the VM. This is something you either let vSphere decide for you when the virtual NIC is created or manually set yourself by changing that vSphere-provided value. It is very similar to a physical NIC's burned-in address (BIA).

- The *Effective MAC address* is configured within the VM by the guest operating system (OS). Typically, the guest OS just uses the Initial MAC address, much like your PC will by default use the BIA or your NIC.

- The *Runtime MAC address* is the actual live address that is being seen by the vSwitch port.

Figure 8.3 shows the Runtime MAC address of a VM in the vSphere Web Client.

So, now that you're a MAC address expert, let's go back in and discuss how the vSwitch polices MAC Address Changes.

When set to "Accept," the vSwitch allows the Initial MAC address to differ from the Effective MAC address, meaning the guest OS has been allowed to change the MAC address for itself. Typically, we don't want this to happen as a malicious user could try to impersonate another VM by using the same MAC address, but there are use cases, such as with Microsoft Network Load Balancing (NLB) where it makes sense.

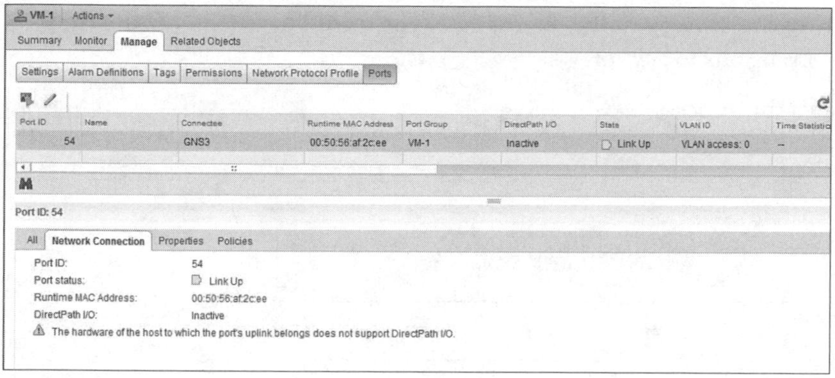

Figure 8.3 The Runtime MAC address of a VM

When set to "Reject," the vSwitch will disable the port if it sees that the guest OS is trying to change the Effective MAC address to something other than the Initial MAC address. The port will no longer receive traffic until you either change the security policy or make sure that the Effective MAC address is the same value as the Initial MAC address.

To sum it up, the MAC Address Changes policy is focused entirely on whether or not a VM (or even a VMkernel port) is allowed to change the MAC address it uses for receiving traffic. The next section covers sending traffic.

Forged Transmits

Very similar to the MAC Address Changes policy, the Forged Transmits policy is concerned with MAC Address Changes, but only as it concerns transmitting traffic.

If set to "Accept," the VM can put in any MAC address it wishes into the "source address" field of a Layer 2 frame. The vSwitch port will just happily let those frames move along to their destination.

If the policy is set to "Reject," the port will interrogate all the traffic that is generated by the VM. The policy will check to see if the source MAC address field has been tampered with. As long as the source MAC field is the same as the Effective MAC address, the frame is allowed by the port. However, if it finds a non-matching MAC address, the frame is dropped.

It's very common to see issues with the Forged Transmit policy when doing nested virtualization. *Nesting* is the term used to describe running the ESXi hypervisor inside a VM, which then runs other nested VMs with their own unique MAC addresses. The many different MAC addresses will be seen by the port used by the nested hypervisor VM because the nested guest VMs are sending traffic. In this case, you would have to configure the policy for Forged Transmits to Accept.

Figure 8.4 illustrates this process.

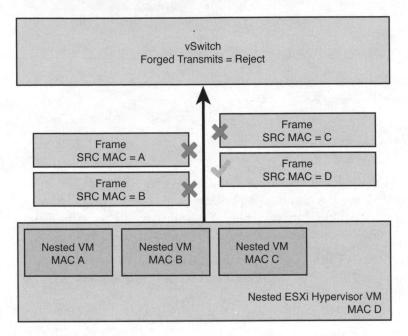

Figure 8.4   Nested VMs cannot send traffic without accepting forged transmits

Discovery

When you have a working vSwitch in your environment, chances are you're going to want to make sure that you can participate in one of a few different monitoring methods to determine the complex topology of switches. We sometimes refer to this as the "neighborhood" of switching.

Most switches are connected to at least one other switch, forming a web of switches that can all talk to one another. Using a discovery protocol, we can allow these switches, both physical and virtual, to understand who their neighbors are.

> **NOTE**
>
> An easy way to make friends with your networking department is to enable discovery on your vSwitches. We find that many have either never heard of the feature or are hesitant to

enable it. Make sure your security team is okay with you using a discovery protocol before turning it on, but once on, it makes understanding the neighborhood of physical and virtual switches dramatically easier for everyone!

Cisco Discovery Protocol (CDP)

The VMware standard vSwitch supports only one single protocol for discovery, the Cisco Discovery Protocol. Can you guess which switch manufacturer uses this protocol? We'll give you a hint—it's not Brocade.

CDP is a proprietary way to allow switches to chat with one another to figure out who they are plugged into. It's not required for traffic to flow, but it does give administrators and engineers a great way to see what device is at the end of a plugged-in port. It also updates itself in real time, meaning it has a lot more value than trying to keep your configuration in a spreadsheet or some other manual method. CDP is enabled by default on Standard Switches. Figure 8.5 shows the output of the `show cdp neighbors` command on a 3550 switch to which a Standard Switch has been connected.

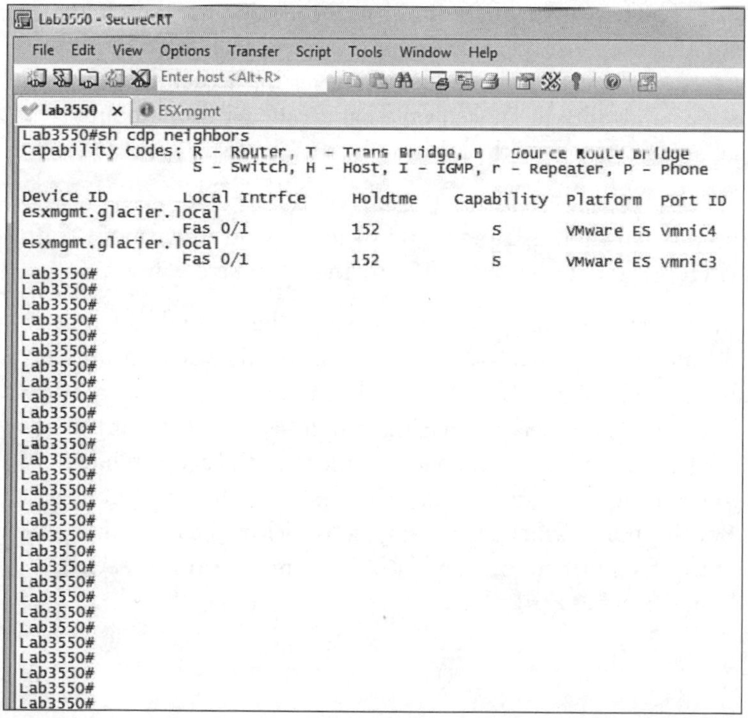

Figure 8.5 CDP information on a Cisco 3550 switch connected to two vSwitch uplink ports

Traffic Shaping

Traffic shaping is the ability to control the quantity of traffic that is allowed to flow across a link. That is, rather than letting the traffic go as fast as it possibly can, you can set limits to how much traffic can be sent.

Within a standard vSwitch, you can only enforce traffic shaping on outbound traffic that is being sent out of an object—such as a VM or VMkernel port—toward another object. This is referred to by VMware as "ingress traffic" and refers to the fact that data is coming into the vSwitch by way of the virtual ports. Later, we cover how to set "egress traffic" shaping, which is the control of traffic being received by a port group headed toward a VM or VMkernel port, when we start talking about the distributed switch in the next chapter.

Traffic shaping consists of three different control points, as shown in Figure 8.6.

- **Average bandwidth (Kbps)**: The average amount of bandwidth, measured in kilobits per second (Kbps), that you allow the switch to send. There might be short periods where the traffic slightly exceeds this value, since it is an average over time, but for the most part, it will be enforced and traffic will go no faster than the defined speed limit set here.

- **Peak bandwidth (Kbps)**: The maximum amount of bandwidth that the switch is allowed to let through. The use of the peak bandwidth value is determined by how often we've hit the average bandwidth limitation. Whenever the actual traffic volume is lower than the average bandwidth limit, we gain what is called a "burst bonus" which can be any number of bytes up to the limit set by the burst size value (covered next).

  This bonus can be used when there is a pent-up traffic demand to let more traffic flow through the switch using data sizes dictated by the burst size value.

- **Burst size (KB)**: This is an often misunderstood value, so we'll go into detail. The burst size is the actual amount of "burstable" data that is allowed to be transmitted at the peak bandwidth rate in kilobytes. Think of the burst bonus as a network traffic savings account. And the burst size is the maximum number of bytes that can go into that account. So, when you need to send more traffic than the average bandwidth value allows, you transmit a burst of traffic, which is more than the allowed average bandwidth. But this burst, which always stays at or below the allowable peak bandwidth, will be forced to end when the number of bytes in your traffic savings account, your burst bonus, reaches zero.

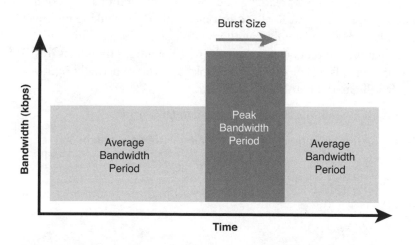

Figure 8.6 shows a window titled "vSwitch0 - Edit Settings" with the following options:

Properties
Security
Traffic shaping
Teaming and failover

Status: Enabled
Average bandwidth (kbit/s): 100000
Peak bandwidth (kbit/s): 100000
Burst size (KB): 102400

OK   Cancel

Figure 8.6 A look at the traffic-shaping controls

Figure 8.7 is an example showing a period of average traffic with a burst of peak bandwidth in the middle. You can determine how long the traffic will be able to burst by taking the burst size (KB) amount divided by the peak bandwidth (kbps).

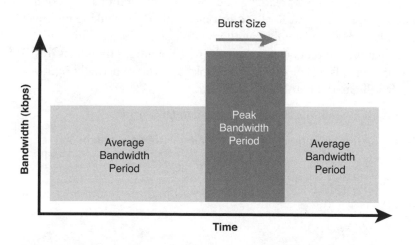

Figure 8.7 A traffic-shaping graph showing average and peak bandwidth

Making changes to the traffic-shaping values will instantly begin enforcing the limitations on the switch—there is no restart or warm-up period.

Traffic Shaping Math

Here's a concrete example showing how to calculate how long traffic will peak in a "best case" scenario:

- Let's assume, for easy math, that you set the average bandwidth value to 1,000 Kbps.

- You also set the peak bandwidth to 2,000 Kbps, which is twice the value of the average bandwidth.

- Finally, you configure the burst size to 1,000 kilobytes (KB). Hint—don't forget that there are 8 bits in a byte, which means that 1,000 KB is 8,000 Kb. Big "B" is for bytes and little "b" is for bits.

If the burst bonus is completely full, which would mean that it's the full value of the burst size (8,000 Kb), then you could peak for 4 seconds:

8,000 Kb burst size / 2,000 Kbps peak bandwidth = 8 / 2 = 4 seconds

NIC Teaming

Let's take a well-deserved break from networking math for a moment and shift into the fun world of NIC teaming. The concept of teaming goes by many different names: bonding, grouping, and trunking to name a few. Really, it just means that we're taking multiple physical NICs on a given ESXi host and combining them into a single logical link that provides bandwidth aggregation and redundancy to a vSwitch. You might think that this sounds a little bit like port channels from earlier in the book. And you're partially right—the goal is very similar, but the methods are vastly different.

Figure 8.8 shows all the configuration options for teaming and failover.

Let's go over all of the configuration options for NIC teaming within a vSwitch. These options are a bit more relevant when your vSwitch is using multiple uplinks but are still valid configuration points no matter the quantity of uplinks.

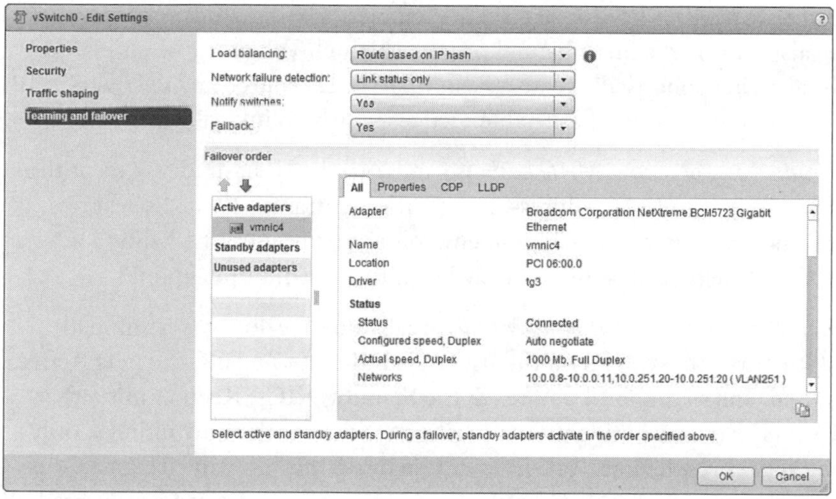

Figure 8.8 Configuration options for teaming and failover, as viewed from the vSphere Web Client

Load Balancing

The first point of interest is the *load-balancing policy*. This is basically how we tell the vSwitch to handle outbound traffic, and there are four choices on a standard vSwitch:

1. Route based on the originating virtual port

2. Route based on IP hash

3. Route based on source MAC hash

4. Use explicit failover order

Keep in mind that we're not concerned with the inbound traffic because that's not within our control. Traffic arrives on whatever uplink the upstream switch decided to put it on, and the vSwitch is only responsible for making sure it reaches its destination.

The first option, *route based on the originating virtual port*, is the default selection for a new vSwitch. Every VM and VMkernel port on a vSwitch is connected to a virtual port. When the vSwitch receives traffic from either of these objects, it assigns the virtual port an uplink and uses it for traffic. The chosen uplink will typically not change unless there is an uplink failure, the VM changes power state, or the VM is migrated around via vMotion.

The second option, *route based on IP hash*, is used in conjunction with a link aggregation group (LAG), also called an EtherChannel or port channel. When traffic enters the vSwitch, the load-balancing policy will create a hash value of the source and destination IP addresses in the packet. The resulting hash value dictates which uplink will be used.

The third option, *route based on source MAC hash*, is similar to the IP hash idea, except the policy examines only the source MAC address in the Ethernet frame. To be honest, we have rarely seen this policy used in a production environment, but it can be handy for a nested hypervisor VM to help balance its nested VM traffic over multiple uplinks.

The fourth and final option, *use explicit failover order*, really doesn't do any sort of load balancing. Instead, the first Active NIC on the list is used. If that one fails, the next Active NIC on the list is used, and so on, until you reach the Standby NICs. Keep in mind that if you select the Explicit Failover option and you have a vSwitch with many uplinks, only one of them will be actively used at any given time. Use this policy only in circumstances where using only one link rather than load balancing over all links is desired or required.

> **NOTE**
>
> In almost all cases, the route based on the originating virtual port is more than adequate. Don't try to get fancy with an exotic load-balancing policy unless you see an issue where the majority of traffic is being sent down the same uplink and other uplinks are relatively quiet. Remember our motto—the simplest designs are almost always the best designs.
>
> A single VM will not be able to take advantage of more than a single uplink in most circumstances. If you provide a pair of 1 Gb Ethernet uplinks to your vSwitch, a VM will still only use one of those uplinks at a time. There are exceptions to this concept, such as when a VM has multiple virtual NICs attached on a vSwitch with IP hash, but are relatively rare to see in production environments.

Network Failure Detection

When a network link fails (and they definitely do), the vSwitch is aware of the failure because the link status reports the link as being down. This can usually be verified by seeing if anyone tripped over the cable or mistakenly unplugged the wrong one. In most cases, this is good enough to satisfy your needs and the default configuration of "link status only" for the network failure detection is good enough.

But what if you want to determine a failure further up the network, such as a failure beyond your upstream connected switch? This is where beacon probing might be able to help you out. *Beacon probing* is actually a great term because it does roughly what it sounds like it should do. A beacon is regularly sent out from the vSwitch through its uplinks to see if the other uplinks can "hear" it.

Figure 8.9 shows an example of a vSwitch with three uplinks. When Uplink1 sends out a beacon that Uplink2 receives but Uplink3 does not, this is because the upstream aggregation switch 2 is down, and therefore, the traffic is unable to reach Uplink3.

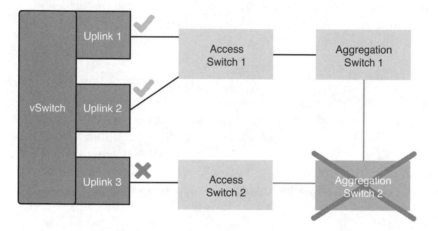

Figure 8.9   An example where beacon probing finds upstream switch failures

Are you curious why we use an example with three uplinks? Imagine you only had two uplinks and sent out a beacon that the other uplink did not hear. Does the sending uplink have a failure, or does the receiving uplink have a failure? It's impossible to know who is at fault. Therefore, you need at least three uplinks in order for beacon probing to work.

> **NOTE**
>
> Beacon probing has become less and less valuable in most environments, especially with the advent of converged infrastructure and the use of 10 GbE-enabled blades with only two NICs or mezzanine cards. Most modern datacenters connect all their servers and switches in a redundant fashion, where an upstream switch failure would have no effect on network traffic. This isn't to say that there aren't use cases remaining for beacon probing, but it's relatively rare. Also, never turn on beacon probing when the uplinks are connected to a LAG, as the hashing algorithm might divert your beacons to the wrong uplink and trigger a false positive failure.

Notify Switches

The Notify Switches configuration is a bit mystifying at first. Notify the switches about what, exactly? By default, it's set to "Yes," and as we cover here, that's almost always a good thing.

Remember that all of your upstream physical switches have a MAC address table that they use to map ports to MAC addresses. This avoids the need to flood their ports—which means sending frames to all ports except the port they arrived on (which is the required action when a frame's destination MAC address doesn't appear in the switch's MAC address table).

But what happens when one of your uplinks in a vSwitch fails and all of the VMs begin using a new uplink? The upstream physical switch would have no idea which port the VM is now using and would have to resort to flooding the ports or wait for the VM to send some traffic so it can re-learn the new port. Instead, the Notify Switches option speeds things along by sending Reverse Address Resolution Protocol (RARP) frames to the upstream physical switch on behalf of the VM or VMs so that upstream switch updates its MAC address table. This is all done before frames start arriving from the newly vMotioned VM, the newly powered-on VM, or from the VMs that are behind the uplink port that failed and was replaced.

These RARP announcements are just a fancy way of saying that the ESXi host will send out a special update letting the upstream physical switch know that the MAC address is now on a new uplink so that the switch will update its MAC address table before actually needing to send frames to that MAC address. It's sort of like ESXi is shouting to the upstream physical switch and saying, "Hey! This VM is over here now!"

Failback

Since we're already on the topic of an uplink failure, let's talk about Failback. If you have a Standby NIC in your NIC Team, it will become Active if there are no more Active NICs in the team. Basically, it will provide some hardware redundancy while you go figure out what went wrong with the failed NIC. When you fix the problem with the failed Active NIC, the Failback setting determines if the previously failed Active NIC should now be returned to Active duty.

If you set this value to Yes, the now-operational NIC will immediately go back to being Active again, and the Standby NIC returns to being Standby. Things are returned back to the way they were before the failure.

If you choose the No value, the replaced NIC will simply remain inactive until either another NIC fails or you return it to Active status.

Failover Order

The final section in a NIC team configuration is the failover order. It consists of three different adapter states:

- **Active adapters**: Adapters that are Actively used to pass along traffic.

- **Standby adapters**: These adapters will only become Active if the defined Active adapters have failed.

- **Unused adapters**: Adapters that will never be used by the vSwitch, even if all the Active and Standby adapters have failed.

While the Standby and Unused statuses do have value for some specific configurations, such as with balancing vMotion and management traffic on a specific pair of uplinks, it's common to just set all the adapters to Active and let the load-balancing policy do the rest. We get more into the weeds on adapter states later on in the book, especially when we start talking about iSCSI design and configuration in Part 3, "You Got Your Storage in My Networking: IP Storage."

Hierarchy Overrides

One really great feature of a vSwitch is the ability to leverage overrides where necessary. You won't see any override information on the vSwitch itself, but they are available on the VMkernel ports and VM port groups, which are covered next in this chapter. Overrides are simply ways that you can deviate from the vSwitch configuration on a granular level. An override example is shown in Figure 8.10.

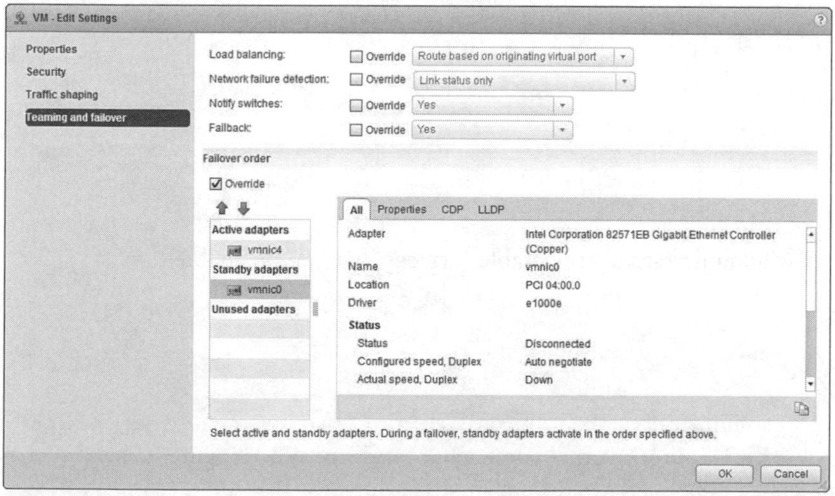

Figure 8.10   An example override on a failover order

For example, let's say that you have a pair of adapters being used as uplinks on a vSwitch. Within the vSwitch, you also have two VMkernel ports configured: one for management traffic and another for vMotion traffic. You can use overrides to set specific teaming and failover policies for each of those VMkernel ports. This allows you to separate management and vMotion traffic during steady-state operation, but still allow both to function in the event of a NIC Failure.

VMkernel Ports

The VMkernel ports, which are also referred to as "VMkernel networking interfaces" or even "virtual adapters" in various places, are special constructs used by the vSphere host to communicate with the outside world. You might recognize these ports due to their naming structure of vmk## with the "vmk" portion being a shorthand for VMkernel.

The goal of a VMkernel port is to provide some sort of Layer 2 or Layer 3 services to the vSphere host. Although a VM can talk to a VMkernel port, they do not consume them directly.

Port Properties and Services

VMkernel ports have important jobs to do and are vital for making sure that the vSphere host can be useful to the VMs. In fact, every VMkernel port can provide any combination of the following six services:

- vMotion traffic
- Fault tolerance (FT) logging
- Management traffic
- vSphere replication traffic
- iSCSI traffic
- NFS traffic

Figure 8.11 shows the administratively selectable services that can be enabled on a VMkernel port.

> **NOTE**
>
> While you can enable multiple services on a given VMkernel port, it is often preferable to split functions between multiple VMkernel ports. Fault tolerance (FT) logging, in particular, is strongly recommended to be segregated from any other function.

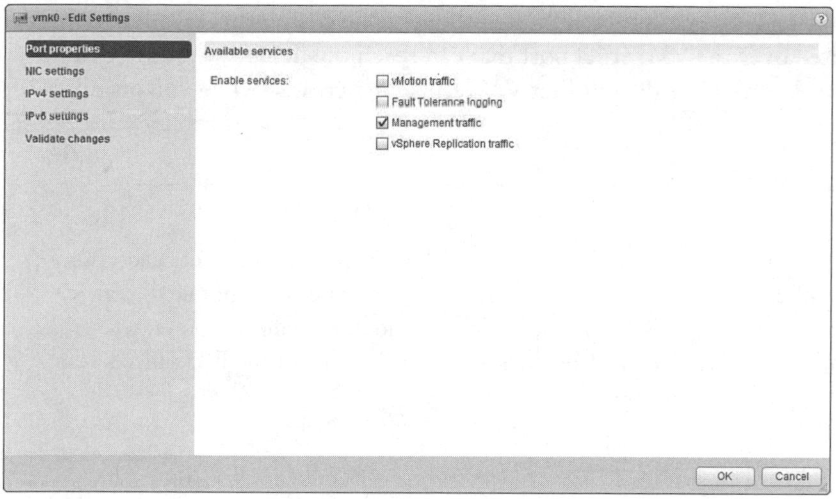

Figure 8.11 Services that can be enabled on a VMkernel port

You might notice that two of the services mentioned aren't shown as services that can be enabled: iSCSI traffic and NFS traffic. The reason is simple—there is no need to tell a VMkernel port that it can talk to iSCSI or NFS storage. All VMkernel ports can do this natively, and we typically just need to make sure that the IP address assigned to the appropriate VMkernel port is on the same subnet as the storage array.

> **NOTE**
>
> There are a lot of interesting design concepts around the use of VMkernel ports for iSCSI and NFS storage—feel free to skip ahead to Part 3 of this book if you want to learn more. For now, we'll just accept the fact that a VMkernel port doesn't need a service enabled to be useful for IP storage traffic.

IP Addresses

Every VMkernel port will have either an IPv4 or IPv6 address assigned, along with an MTU value. You have the choice of using a DHCP server for your IP address—which is not recommended for any serious production deployment—or assigning a static IP address.

Note that the default gateway and DNS server addresses are not definable by a VMkernel port. These values are input into the vSphere host directly. If the subnet you use for the

VMkernel port's IP address does not match the subnet of the destination IP address, the traffic will be routed over the VMkernel port that can reach the default gateway. Often, but not always, this is vmk0 (the default first VMkernel port created when you install ESXi).

TIP

Look carefully at the MAC address assigned to the vmk0 VMkernel port. Notice anything different about it when compared to other VMkernel ports? You should notice that vmk0 uses the real, burned-in address of the physical NIC instead of a randomly generated VMware MAC address. This MAC address is "seeded" at the time of the ESXi installation.

VM Port Groups

The final topic to touch on is VM port groups, which can be a bit of a struggle to understand at first. Let's imagine that you have a huge, unconfigured virtual switch with hundreds of ports on it. Chances are, you don't want all of the ports to be configured the same way—some of them will be used by your production VMs, others by your developers' VMs, and even more might be for the engineering VMs.

VM port groups are a way that we can create logical rules around the virtual ports that are made available to VMs. It's common to create a port group for each VLAN and network subnet that you want to present to your VMs. VM port groups do not provide vSphere services or require IP addresses—they are just ways to configure policy for a group of virtual ports on your vSwitch.

Figure 8.12 shows an example from our lab showing a vSwitch with a VM port group named "VM"—not very creative, sure, but it gets the point across. This is where we place our VMs, which are SQL, vCenter, and DC in this example. We've also disconnected one of the network adapters to show what that looks like.

You can also see our VMkernel port named "Management" just below the VM port group. It looks a lot like a VM port group, and that might be confusing at first. Don't worry, though—vCenter won't let you put a VM onto the "Management" VMkernel port.

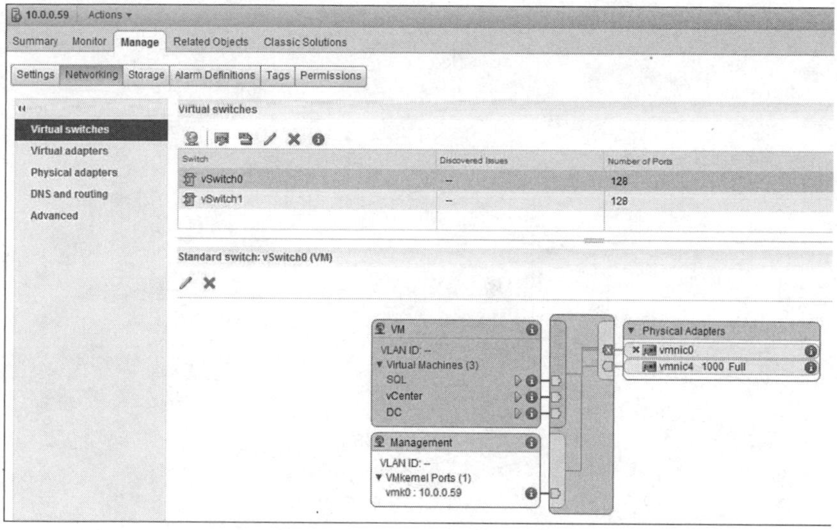

Figure 8.12   An example vSwitch with a VM port group named "VM"

Summary

We covered a lot of ground here, digging into every nook and cranny of the vSphere Standard Switch. You should now feel more knowledgeable about virtual switch configuration options, security settings, discovery settings, traffic-shaping policies, load-balancing methods, VMkernel ports, and port group configuration. In the next chapter, we take a close look at the options available with the vSphere Distributed Switch, highlighting the features that go above and beyond what is available with the Standard Switch.

Chapter 9

vSphere Distributed Switch

Key Concepts

- dvUplinks
- LLDP
- NetFlow
- Port Mirroring
- Private VLANs
- Egress Shaping
- Load-based Teaming
- Network I/O Control

Introduction to the vSphere Distributed Switch

The vSphere Distributed Switch (VDS) provides two major benefits to you, the customer. First, the VDS offers a centralized control plane for management of your virtual switching, taking much of the manual grunt work out of day-to-day administration. Second, the VDS offers advanced services and features over the standard switch.

The VDS sits in the middle of the feature scale, offering more capabilities than the standard switch, but leaving some room at the table for third-party switches such as the Cisco Nexus 1000V. We go further into third-party vSwitches in the next chapter. For now, we focus more on the VDS, how it is different from the standard switch, and some of the neat buttons and gizmos that it comes loaded with.

Control Plane

The control plane of the VDS sits at the vCenter layer of the stack. That is, vCenter is the vehicle used to create, modify, and remove a VDS and its related virtual port groups. This means that you can create your VDS one time and then choose which hosts will use it. It's a similar concept to the vSphere cluster. On its own, a cluster doesn't really do anything. You can set up the cluster's High Availability (HA) and Distributed Resource Scheduler (DRS) options, but until you actually add some hosts to the cluster, it just sits there looking pretty. A VDS is useless until hosts are added to it, and only then does the magic happen.

Each VDS has a quantity of uplinks defined. These are named *dvUplinks* with a number after them by default, but you can change the name. From a control plane perspective, giving your uplinks a custom name helps define the role of various uplinks each host will use to move traffic into and out of the VDS. When adding a host to the VDS, you map physical uplink ports to the logical dvUplink ports. Figure 9.1 shows the dvUplinks in a VDS using a custom name of "Core 1" and "Core 2" for the pair of dvUplinks.

TIP

Name your uplinks something descriptive to help with troubleshooting. I like to label mine based on the VDS's purpose, such as "Core-##" or "Storage-##." You could also call out the physical switching infrastructure, such as "TOR-A" or "TOR-B," to distinguish which top of rack (TOR) switch you are connecting to. Avoid using specific switch names or IPs, as that information is tracked by CDP or LLDP anyway. More on LLDP in a later section.

Handling vCenter Failure

That VDSes are managed through vCenter might be causing you some heartburn, as it seems to imply a dependency on vCenter availability. You might be wondering what happens when vCenter goes down—will virtual switching just stop?

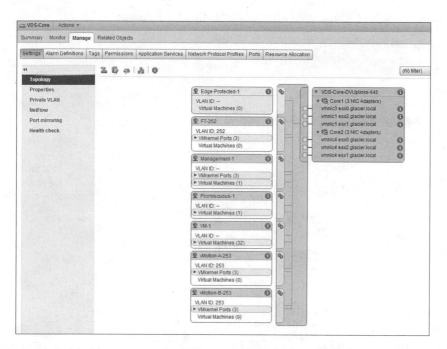

Figure 9.1 The dvUplinks in a VDS

The short answer is no, switching will continue without interruption. But, hey, we have a couple hundred pages to go, so let's get into the long answer. While it's true that the brains of a VDS lay with the vCenter server, there is a cached copy of the VDS configuration kept on every vSphere host and updated every five minutes. If vCenter fails, the host continues to use this cached copy of the VDS configuration. You can log into your vSphere host via Secure Shell (SSH) and see the file if you browse to /etc/vmware/dvsdata.db. The cached database is shown in Figure 9.2.

When the vCenter server comes back online, you might see a few errors appear stating that the VDS configuration is not synchronized to some of your hosts. This will clear up shortly as the vCenter VDS configuration is pushed down to the vSphere host during the regular five-minute update interval.

```
The time and date of this login have been sent to the system logs.

VMware offers supported, powerful system administration tools.  Please
see www.vmware.com/go/sysadmintools for details.

The ESXi Shell can be disabled by an administrative user. See the
vSphere Security documentation for more information.
~ # cd /etc/vmware
/etc/vmware # ls -l
-r--r--r--   1 root      root          3041 May  1 02:54 BootbankFunctions.sh
-rw-r--r--   1 root      root          1167 Jun 30 09:15 config
-rw-r--r-T   1 root      root          7699 May  1 02:54 configrules
drw-------   1 root      root           512 May 28 03:30 driver.map.d
-rw-r--r--   1 root      root         95744 Sep  4 02:08 dvsdata.db
-rw-------   1 root      root         26170 Sep  3 16:55 esx.conf
drwxr-xr-x   1 root      root           512 May 28 03:30 firewall
-r--r--r-T   1 root      root            59 May  1 02:54 ft-vmk-version
-r--r--r--   1 root      root            60 May  1 02:54 ft-vmx-version
drwxr-xr-x   1 root      root           512 Aug 29 12:31 hostd
drwxr-xr-x   1 root      root           512 May 28 03:30 icu
drwxr-xr-x   1 root      root           512 May 28 03:30 ike
-rw-r--r-T   1 root      root            50 May  1 02:55 ima_plugin.conf
-rw-r--r--   1 root      root           310 Jul 27 01:06 license.cfg
-rw-r--r-T   1 root      root           440 May  1 02:55 localsas
-rw-r--r-T   1 root      root             0 May  1 02:55 lockdown
-rw-r--r--   1 root      root             0 May 28 03:31 locker.conf
drwxr-xr-x   1 root      root           512 May 28 03:30 microcode
-rw-r--r-T   1 root      root           825 May  1 02:55 passthru.map
-r--r--r--   1 root      root        782492 Mar 23 17:58 pci.ids
drwxr-xr-x   1 root      root           512 May  1 02:55 pciid
drwxr-xr-x   1 root      root           512 May 28 03:30 rhttpproxy
drwxr-xr-x   1 root      root           512 May 28 03:30 secpolicy
drwxr-xr-x   1 root      root           512 May 28 03:30 service
-rw-r--r-T   1 root      root            64 Aug 19 16:43 settings
-rw-r--r-T   1 root      root             0 May  1 02:55 smart_plugin.conf
-rw-r--r-T   1 root      root           200 May  1 02:55 snmp.xml
drwxr-xr-x   1 root      root           512 May 28 03:30 ssl
-rw-r--r-T   1 root      root           480 May  1 02:55 support
-rw-r--r-T   1 root      root        380961 May  1 02:55 usb.ids
drwxr-xr-x   1 root      root           512 May 28 03:30 vm-support
drwxr-xr-x   1 root      root           512 Aug 21 21:41 vmkiscsid
-rw-------   1 root      root            29 Aug 19 16:00 vmware.lic
drwxr-xr-x   1 root      root           512 May 28 03:30 vmwauth
drwxr-xr-x   1 root      root           512 Aug 19 02:32 vpxa
drwxr-xr-x   1 root      root           512 May 28 03:30 weasel
-rw-r--r-T   1 root      root             0 May  1 02:55 welcome
-rw-r--r--   1 root      root           923 Jul 22 16:03 zloadmod.txt
/etc/vmware # ▮
```

Figure 9.2   The local cache copy of the VDS database

Data Plane

Just as with the Standard Switch, all data plane activity continues to occur down at the
Host layer. By design, no data is routed through the vCenter server, since it is simply a
control point. All switching decisions continue to occur on the host itself, following the
same Layer 2 rules as established in Chapter 3, "Ethernet Networks."

Monitoring

The VDS supports both Cisco Discovery Protocol (CDP) and Link Layer Discovery
Protocol (LLDP).

Cisco Discovery Protocol (CDP)

You might recall that the standard vSwitch supports CDP, but configuring and managing that feature requires using some ESXCLI, PowerCLI, or other command-line methods. With the VDS, in addition to enabling CDP or LLDP, you can also set the mode of either of these protocols to Listen, Advertise, or Both, directly from the vSphere Client or vSphere Web Client. In fact, it's just a dropdown box in the Discovery Protocol section. Neat, huh? This dropdown box is shown in Figure 9.3.

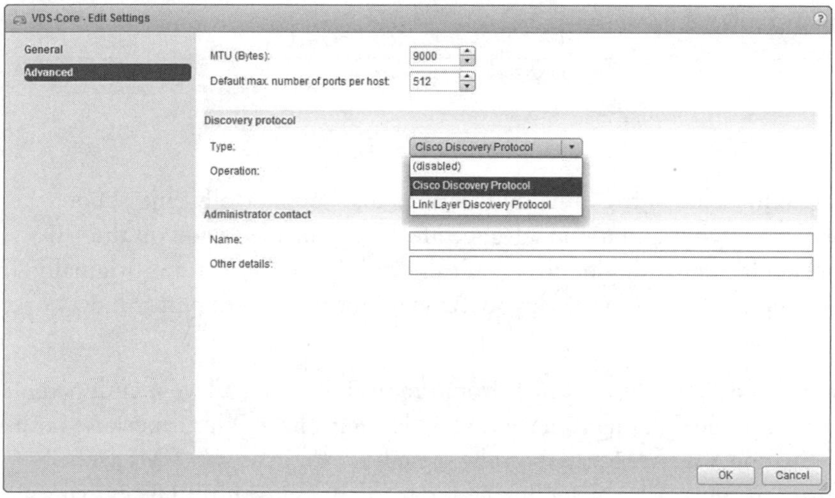

Figure 9.3 Enabling CDP on a VDS with a simple dropdown box

Link Layer Discovery Protocol (LLDP)

For those without a Cisco switching environment, you're in luck. The VDS supports the open standards equivalent of CDP, called Link Layer Discovery Protocol (LLDP). For all intents and purposes, LLDP will provide anything you would expect from CDP, but works across a variety of vendor platforms. Interestingly, more and more Cisco switches are also supporting LLDP these days, which helps in a heterogeneous switching environment.

As shown in Figure 9.3, the option to enable LLDP can be found with the same dropdown box used for CDP. You can also configure all three different operational modes: Listen, Advertise, or Both.

TIP

One question that commonly pops up revolves around the desire to set LLDP (or even CDP for that matter) into an Advertise or Both mode and what the down side might be. We have yet to encounter any environments where having additional information about the environment—from a perspective of server or networking—is a bad thing. While some organizations will have a policy preventing LLDP or CDP from being enabled in specific, compliance-related environments, most are okay with having it on. Check with your security and/or networking team first, but chances are high that they will appreciate having visibility into the virtual networking environment.

NetFlow

Now we're starting to hit some of the value-add features that people really enjoy about the VDS. The first one is NetFlow, and it's an advanced feature available to you on the VDS. NetFlow doesn't really have anything to do specifically with VMware, but was originally developed by Cisco and has become a reasonably standard mechanism to perform network analysis.

In Chapter 7, "How Virtual Switching Differs from Physical Switching," we mentioned the idea of dark traffic: traffic that might never end up leaving a host. This is because both the source and destination VMs are located on the same host. Perhaps two VMs are talking to one another on the same VLAN and happen to be on the same host. Heck, that's sometimes done on purpose to avoid putting additional stress on the physical network and because dark traffic gets switched at a host's much faster processor/RAM speeds rather than at physical networking speeds. NetFlow is a way to monitor and sample IP traffic that occurs within your VDS. The configuration is controllable down to the port group level. The traffic data is sent to a NetFlow collector running elsewhere on the network. NetFlow is commonly used in the physical world to help gain visibility into traffic and understanding just who is sending what and to where.

NetFlow comes in a variety of versions, from v1 to v10. VMware uses the IPFIX version of NetFlow, which is version 10, and stands for "Internet Protocol Flow Information eXport." IPFIX is actually a melding of NetFlow version 9 with some Internet Engineering Task Force (IETF) standards, and is sometimes referred to as the "IETF Standardized NetFlow 9." If you find it confusing that version 10 is sometimes called IPFIX 9, you're not alone. To keep things simple, it's often best to just call it IPFIX and folks will know what you mean.

> **TIP**
>
> vSphere 5.0 uses NetFlow version 5, while vSphere 5.1 and beyond uses IPFIX (version 10). If you are using software that requires version 5, or doesn't support IPFIX, you might want to avoid upgrading your vSphere hosts until you can figure out a workaround. vSphere 5.1 does not support NetFlow version 5.

In order to take advantage of NetFlow, you need to perform two steps. The first is to configure the NetFlow settings on your VDS itself, which we go into deeper here.

VDS NetFlow configuration is defined by the following items:

- **IP Address**: This is the IP of the NetFlow Collector where the traffic information is sent.

- **Port**: This is the port used by the NetFlow Collector. It is typically UDP port 2055 but can vary depending on the vendor collecting the data.

- **Switch IP Address**: This one can be confusing at first. In a typical hardware environment, every switch has some sort of IP identifier for management. By assigning an IP address here, the NetFlow Collector will treat the VDS as one single entity. It does not need to be a valid, routable IP, but is merely used as an identifier. For example, "1.1.1.1" is a valid entry.

These options are shown in Figure 9.4.

Figure 9.4   NetFlow options on a VDS

There are also a number of advanced settings that can be tweaked if desired:

- **Active flow export timeout in seconds**: The amount of time that must pass before the switch fragments the flow and ships it off to the collector. This avoids sending a large quantity of data after a particularly long flow occurs.

- **Idle flow export timeout in seconds**: Similar to the active flow timeout, but for flows that have entered an idle state. Think of this as the cleanup necessary to ensure that an idle flow gets shipped off to the collector in a timely fashion.

- **Sampling rate**: This determines the Nth packet to collect. By default, the value is 0, meaning to collect all packets. If you set the value to something other than 0, it will collect every Nth packet. For example, 3 would only collect every third packet.

- **Process internal flows only**: Your choices here are enabled or disabled (default). Enabling ensures that the only flows collected are ones that occur between VMs on the same host. This can be helpful if you are only looking to collect the dark traffic flows, already have NetFlow configured on your physical infrastructure, and wish to avoid sampling traffic twice (once at the Virtual layer and again at the Physical layer).

The second step is to enable Monitoring on any port groups you need to monitor. You'll quickly figure this out when you set up NetFlow but do not see any traffic flow information—and we've done that more than once. The related dialog is shown in Figure 9.5.

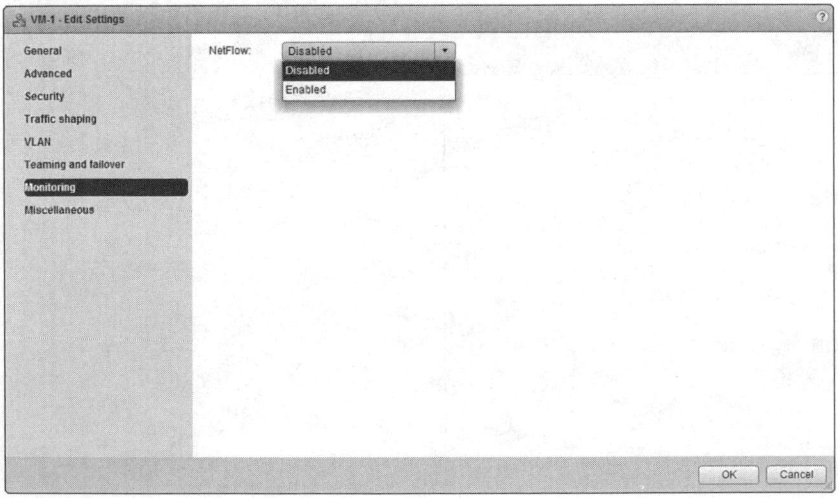

Figure 9.5   Enabling NetFlow on a port group

Port Mirroring

Occasionally, you'll come upon the need to clone traffic on a particular port to another port. This goes beyond just monitoring a port—a port mirror actually clones all the traffic to a configured destination. There are two main use cases for this: monitoring and capture. The two use cases are closely related to one another, but tend to have different end goals in mind. For *monitoring*, you might have a need, be it compliance or some sort of service level agreement (SLA), to know exactly what traffic is being sent from one specific device to another. The other need, *capturing*, is commonly found when doing telephony work for call recording compliance. For example: capturing voice-over IP (VoIP) traffic so that you can have a recording of a phone call in your call center.

This is relatively simple to do in the physical world, and goes by many names: SPAN (Switched Port ANalyzer) ports, port mirroring, and port monitoring to name a few. A specific source port or VLAN is selected for the configuration, and any traffic that flows through that port is cloned to a destination port. The cloning process is usually "dumb" to the actual traffic, and just makes an exact copy of the traffic for the destination port. This worked well when each port on a switch carried traffic for a single connected server or workstation.

The addition of virtual environments created a headache for port mirroring. A single switch port connected to a vSphere host could now carry traffic for tens or even hundreds of virtual servers. It became difficult to mirror traffic for a single virtual server outside of some very clunky networking topologies, such as connecting a VM to a specifically dedicated host uplink port. This was wasteful and also limited VM mobility. Other technologies, such as inclusion of a third party Nexus 1000V switch, could help with this issue, but were traditionally reliant upon special networking skills and a higher purchase price.

Starting with vSphere 5.0, the distributed switch began providing the ability to mirror traffic for virtual ports. This would allow an administrator to granularly control port mirroring for a specific distributed port or ports. The initial offering with the VDS 5.0 was a simple configuration where you could mirror distributed ports to other distributed ports or an uplink. This is known as "Distributed Port Mirroring (Legacy)" in the VDS 5.1 and beyond, and is deprecated. Keep in mind that upgrading a vSphere environment does not automatically upgrade an existing VDS—you will have to also perform a VDS upgrade in order to enjoy the features found in later VDS versions.

Beginning with the VDS 5.1, four different port mirroring session types are available:

1. **Distributed Port Mirroring**: Mirror packets from any number of distributed ports to any number of other distributed ports on the same host. If the source and the destination are on different hosts, this session type does not function.

2. **Remote Mirroring Source**: Mirror packets from a number of distributed ports to specific uplink ports on the corresponding host.

3. **Remote Mirroring Destination**: Mirror packets from a number of VLANs to distributed ports.

4. **Encapsulated Remote Mirroring (L3) Source**: Mirror packets from a number of distributed ports to remote agent's IP addresses. The VMs' traffic is mirrored to a remote physical destination through an IP tunnel. This is similar to ERSPAN (Encapsulated Remote Switched Port Analyzer).

These options are shown in Figure 9.6.

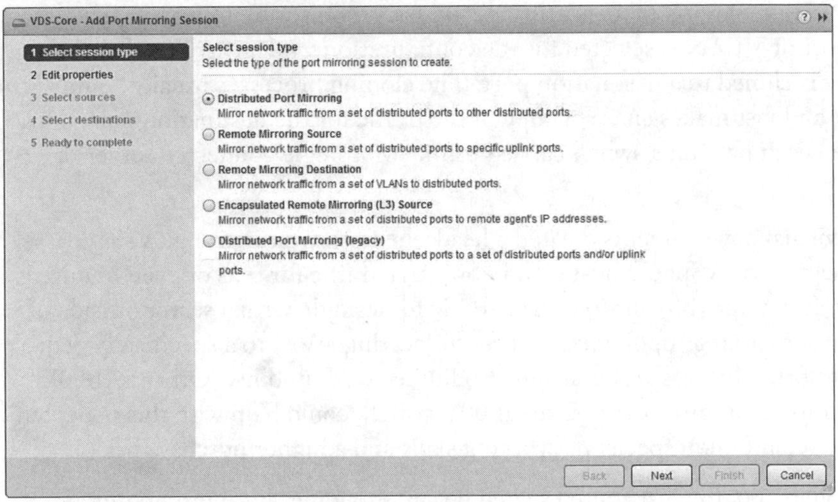

Figure 9.6   Port mirroring choices with a VDS 5.1

While the source and destination of each port mirroring choice varies, the properties are all relatively similar. In order to configure any port mirroring session, you need to define a number of standard properties for the configuration. The set of properties you need to configure will change depending on the type of port mirror chosen:

- **Name**: A name describing the port mirroring session. Try to make this as descriptive as possible without being wordy. Examples include "Mirroring ServerX to DestinationY" or "ServerX to Remote IP."

- **Status**: By default, the port mirror will be disabled. You can leave it disabled while you create the mirror and then enable later, or enable it during configuration.

- **Session Type**: This selects the type of port mirroring session. Choose one of the four described in the previous list.

- **Encapsulation VLAN ID**: The VLAN specified here will be used to encapsulate the frames that are being mirrored. This will allow you to ship frames across an uplink that might use a different VLAN ID. If you want the port mirror to remember the original VLAN ID that the traffic was using, make sure to check the "Preserve Original VLAN" option. Otherwise, the encapsulation VLAN will take its place.

There are also a few advanced properties that can be tweaked. Not all of them will be available for each port mirror type, but we cover all of them in this section:

- **Normal I/O on destination ports**: The description on this is a bit vague. It is asking you to decide if you want the destination port to act simply as a port mirror port, or if it should accept incoming traffic. By default it is set to "Disallowed" which prevents the destination port from accepting traffic into the port and effectively dedicates the port to the port mirror. For most monitoring applications that simply wish to interrogate traffic, leaving the value at "Disallowed" is desired. Keep in mind that this also prevents the port from transmitting traffic.

- **Mirror packet length (Bytes)**: This is a size limitation imposed on the mirrored traffic. If you do specify a size, packets that exceed the size will be truncated to the size you specified. This can be handy if you are monitoring traffic that includes Jumbo Frames, such as storage traffic, but only wish to capture the normal sized frames or headers rather than the full payload. Typically you'll want to leave this field empty and specify any packet length limitations on the capture software.

- **Sampling rate**: Much like with NetFlow's sampling rate configuration, the port mirror sampling rate determines how many packets to sample. The value of 1, which is default, means to capture every packet. Any other value of N means to capture the Nth packet. For example, a sampling rate of 7 will capture every seventh packet and skip the other six.

- **Description**: A description for your port mirroring session. No clue why this is listed in the Advanced properties section, as it's a way to help convey the purpose of your session, but there you have it.

These advanced properties are shown in Figure 9.7.

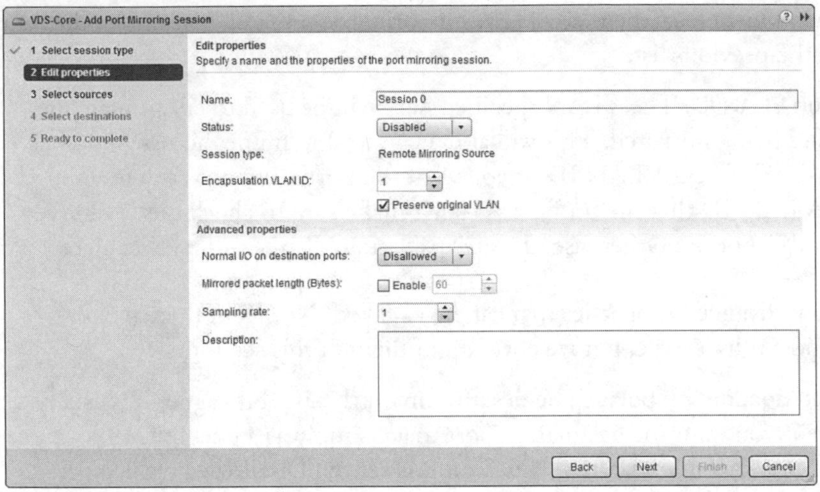

Figure 9.7   Configuration items for a port mirror session

Sources for a port mirror session can be one or many distributed ports, or even a range of ports. Ports can be used by VMs or VMkernel ports. Each port ID shows the host that is servicing the virtual port ID, the connectee of the virtual port, and the direction of the traffic that you wish to capture. Keep in mind that direction is based on perspective: An ingress enters a port, while an egress exits a port. When two people are holding a conversation, the person speaking has information egressing his mouth, while the person listening has information ingressing his ear.

Source options are shown in Figure 9.8.

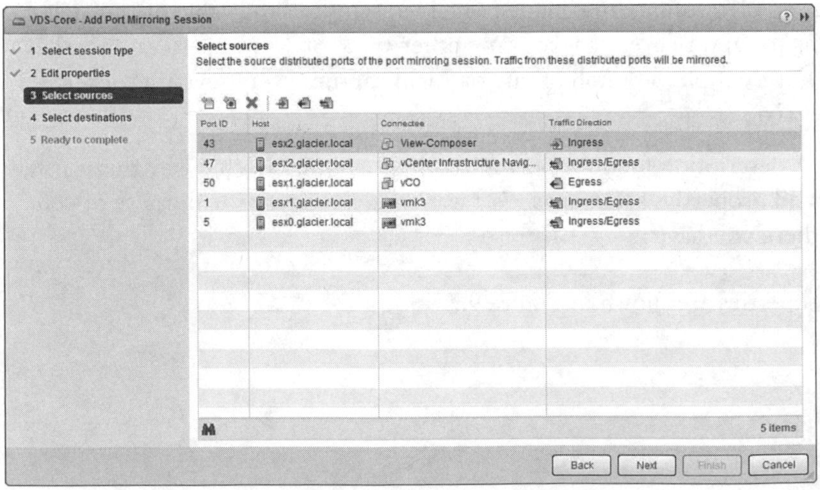

Figure 9.8   A sampling of sources for a port mirror session

The only exception to this is the Remote Mirroring Destination type, which uses one or more VLAN IDs as the source.

Choosing the destination for your port mirror has the most variety. Here is a list of destination options for each port mirror type:

- **Distributed Port Mirroring**: virtual ports

- **Remote Mirroring Source**: uplinks

- **Remote Mirroring Destination**: virtual ports

- **Encapsulated Remote Mirroring (L3) Source**: remote IP

The end result is an entry in the port mirroring section of a VDS that shows a list of all sessions. Each session shows the name, type, and status in the top panel, along with the properties, sources, and destinations in the lower panel. An active port mirroring session is shown in Figure 9.9.

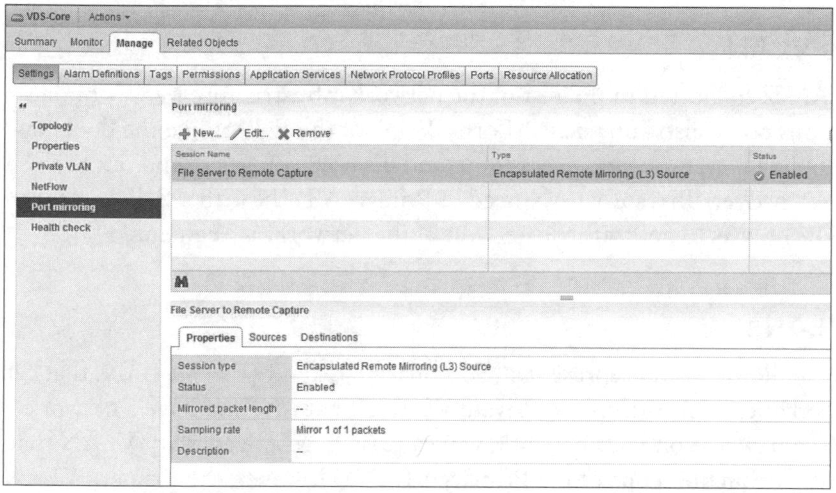

Figure 9.9 An active port mirroring session using Encapsulated Remote Mirroring (L3) Source

Private VLANs

Sometimes the use of VLANs isn't enough to satisfy a design requirement. Perhaps you wish to prevent unnecessary consumption of your 4094 VLAN IDs, or have some special tenancy requirements that mandate creating isolated environments. This is where the concept of a Private VLAN comes into play. The architectural differences are sort of like comparing a single-family home to a high-rise condo building.

In the single-family home scenario, everyone lives in the same house together but they occupy different rooms. If you have access to the house, we can trust that you belong in the house and we don't really prevent you from wandering into someone else's room—although that's typically not the polite thing to do. This is much like a regular VLAN. If you want to transfer from one person's home to another, or from one VLAN to another VLAN, you have to use a routing device—you can't just walk in between houses.

Primary VLAN

In a condo building, each condo itself is an isolated environment within the larger building. Everyone has access to the condo building's front door, but not each other's condo. This is sort of how the Private VLAN works. We use the term "Primary VLAN" to denote the common VLAN that is used to enter the private set of VLANs.

Promiscuous VLAN

The Primary VLAN is connected to the rest of the network infrastructure by way of one or more promiscuous ports, also known as P-Ports. Think of the P-Port like the doorway into the condo building—everyone has access to it, and it's how you get in and out of the private set of VLANs. Every Private VLAN needs a Primary VLAN with a P-Port, otherwise there would be no way to get traffic in and out of the networking segment.

Secondary VLANs

Each condo in the building would represent a "Secondary VLAN," or sub-VLAN, that can re-use VLAN IDs that exist outside of the Private VLAN. That is, if you have a network VLAN ID of 100 somewhere on your network, you can also have a Secondary VLAN that uses VLAN ID 100 within the scope of the Primary VLAN. However, the Primary VLAN must be unique on both networks, or else the network would become confused as to which VLAN you are intending traffic to traverse.

Secondary VLAN IDs only exist within the Private VLAN environment, and the tags are replaced with the Primary VLAN ID when traffic leaves the Private VLAN. There are three types of Secondary VLANs defined in a VMware Distributed Switch: the Promiscuous VLAN, which we already covered, as well as the Community and Isolated VLANs.

Figure 9.10 shows the process of creating a Private VLAN on a VDS.

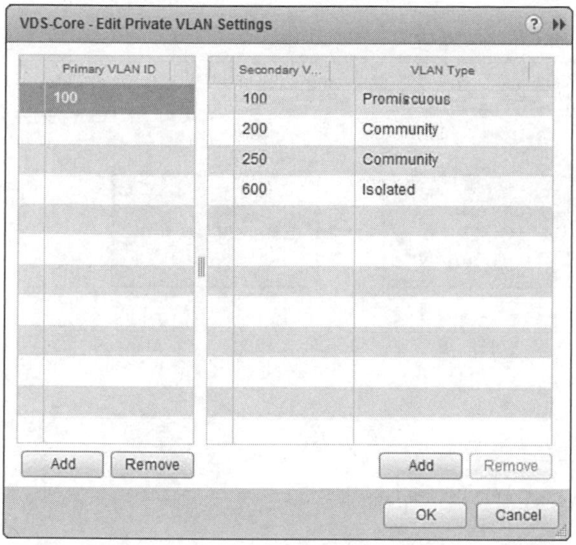

Figure 9.10   Creating a Private VLAN on a Distributed Switch

Community VLANs

A Community VLAN is one that allows members to communicate with one another and the Promiscuous VLAN. Think of it like a conference room—everyone in a conference room can communicate with one another, but cannot talk to those outside of the room without assistance. For instance, the previous diagram shows two community VLANs: 200 and 250. Any VMs placed in Community VLAN 200 would be able to talk to one another and also send traffic to the Promiscuous VLAN. They cannot, however, send traffic to the other Community VLAN 250 or the Isolated VLAN 600 without direct assistance from a routing device in either the Promiscuous VLAN or higher up the networking stack. Figure 9.11 illustrates traffic flows between secondary VLANs.

You can have as many Community VLANs as you desire, up to the VLAN ID limitation of 4094.

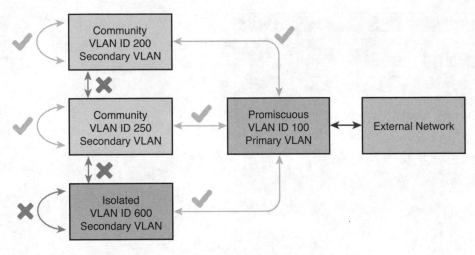

Figure 9.11   Traffic flows among Secondary VLANs in a Private VLAN

Isolated VLAN

The final Secondary VLAN type is the Isolated VLAN. In addition to the rules we covered for the Community VLAN, VMs inside the Isolated VLAN cannot even talk to one another. Any Layer 2 traffic that attempts to go from one VM to another will simply be dropped. The VMs can only communicate with the Promiscuous VLAN and beyond.

TIP

Why use an Isolated VLAN? This special type of VLAN has some fantastic uses for workloads that will be shared by guest users, such as kiosks. If you place an Internet facing gateway device in the Promiscuous VLAN, you can ensure that each kiosk is blocked from each other but can still reach the Internet. In fact, most "hoteling" situations deploy an Isolated VLAN for just this reason. Still, be careful what you do on the Internet—someone is likely monitoring your activities.

Distributed Port Groups

Because multiple hosts can use a VDS, the port groups must also be distributed. This means that no one host owns any part of a VDS, including the distributed port groups. In fact, if a VMkernel port wishes to live on a VDS, it must use a distributed port group.

This differs from a standard vSwitch configuration in that you are required to create special VMkernel network adapters directly in the vSwitch. Additionally, multiple VMkernel ports can share the same distributed port group.

> **TIP**
>
> The VDS is owned by a vCenter Datacenter container, rather than a host, and cannot span more than a single Datacenter. This means that you can create port groups on a VDS that will be consumed by hosts in any cluster that lives in the Datacenter container, or even by hosts that are not in a cluster. However, these port groups cannot be used by hosts in a different Datacenter container. This makes distributed port groups extremely powerful and highly scalable.

Every distributed port group has access to all the uplinks bound to a VDS. Additionally, configuration settings and policies, such as the security and teaming values, are applied directly to a distributed port group. This means that you can have one distributed port group that sets all the uplinks to active and uses VLAN 100, while another port group uses an active/passive mix on VLAN 200. It's common to create a modular design with a variety of port groups for different tasks, such as one for each VLAN your guest machines will use, vMotion, Management, Fault Tolerance Logging, and more. We cover a lot more on this topic in Chapter 13, "Distributed vSwitch Design."

VMkernel Ports

Because a host still needs VMkernel ports (virtual adapters) to handle tasks like management traffic and vMotion, there is still a need for VMkernel ports with a VDS. This is where things can get a little tricky. VMkernel ports are unique for each host because each host has its own vmk numbering scheme and IP configuration details. Therefore, VMkernel ports are configured on each host in vCenter, much like you would with a standard vSwitch.

The difference is that each VMkernel port exists on a distributed port group. When a host has been added to a VDS, options to place its VMkernel ports onto a distributed port group appear. A VMkernel port uses the underlying rules from the distributed port group to function. Therefore, the underlying hardware configuration is defined by the distributed port group policies, and the personality of the VMkernel port—the IP address, subnet mask, maximum transmission unit (MTU), and so on—is defined by the host itself. Figure 9.12 shows the VMkernel ports of a host on a VDS.

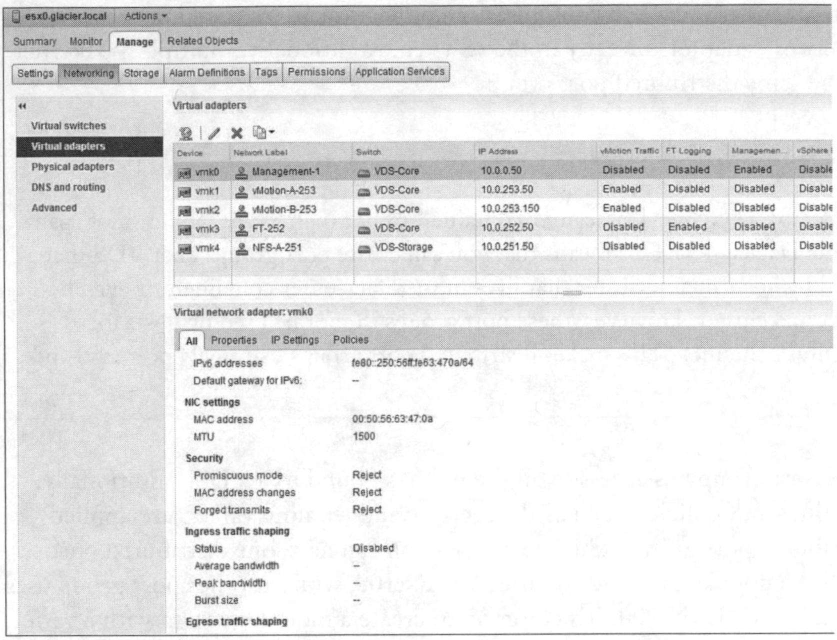

Figure 9.12   VMkernel ports on a vSphere host attached to a Distributed vSwitch

Virtual Machines

When dealing with VMs attached to a VDS, very little operational changes are required. VMs can use ports on any distributed port group, even the ones you have set aside for your VMkernel ports to use. It is often best to create specific port groups just for your VMs and use a naming scheme that best describes the network, such as the IP segment range and VLAN ID.

As an added bonus, keep in mind that because the port groups are distributed, placing a VM on a distributed port group reduces risk of a vMotion causing havoc because of a policy or VLAN ID misconfiguration at the destination host. Every host has the exact same port group settings. This makes network troubleshooting slightly easier, as you can often determine that a physical network on a host is not configured properly with little troubleshooting effort.

Traffic Shaping

We've already gone rather deep into the concept and math behind traffic shaping in Chapter 8, "vSphere Standard Switch." You should be well versed with how to define your average, peak, and burst sizes—if not, go back a chapter and read the traffic shaping section.

The reason we go into traffic shaping a second time is due to the additional feature found in the Distributed vSwitch—the ability to perform both ingress and egress traffic shaping. The standard vSwitch is limited to ingress shaping only.

Egress

Egress is the concept of controlling traffic that leaves the VDS. This could be from the VDS to a VM or a VMkernel port, or even as the traffic flows from one VM to another. The traffic shaping configuration options are the same as with ingress shaping, but are applied for traffic flowing in the other direction. Such traffic is illustrated in Figure 9.13.

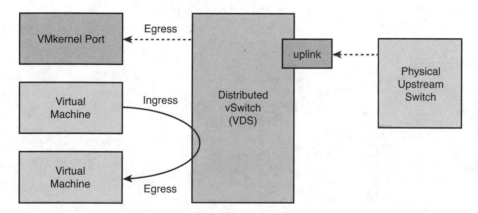

Figure 9.13   Multiple ways egress traffic can occur in a VDS

NOTE

One really great way to use egress traffic shaping is to control the amount of bandwidth that can be used for multi-NIC vMotion traffic. A corner case exists where multiple source hosts might be vMotioning VMs to a single destination host. Without egress traffic shaping, or some sort of physical traffic shaping on the upstream switch, you might end up experiencing a non-trivial amount of traffic on your host uplinks. We cover this in greater detail in Chapter 19, "Multi-NIC vMotion Architecture."

Load Balancing

Another feature that is only available in the Distributed vSwitch is a new form of load balancing named "route based on physical NIC load" which is often referred to as Load Based Teaming (LBT). This routing policy was first introduced with vSphere 4.1 and is the only true active load balancing policy available to you. All the other policies use an arbitrary factor to determine the uplink path, such as the IP address or virtual port, whereas LBT actively monitors and shifts traffic to various uplinks when certain criteria are met.

Route Based on Physical NIC Load

Let's take a closer look at how this policy works by introducing an example scenario. Imagine that you have five VMs on the same physical vSphere host that are sending and receiving Ethernet traffic on the same distributed port group. The port group has randomly assigned VM1, 2, and 3 to uplink1, while VM4 and VM5 are using uplink2. Suddenly, VM1 begins sending a massive amount of traffic that saturates all the available bandwidth on uplink1 for more than 30 seconds, as depicted in Figure 9.14.

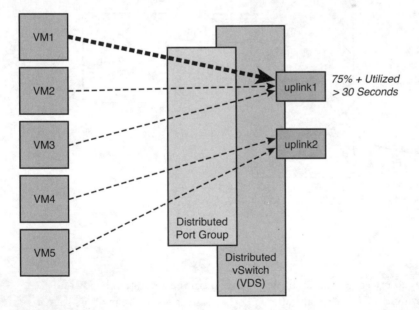

Figure 9.14   VM1 is causing uplink1 to exceed 75% of its maximum utilization for more than 30 seconds

With any other load balancing policy, the saturation on uplink1 would continue until VM1 finished sending data across the network. Meanwhile, uplink2 might be experiencing very little traffic or even be idle. What a waste!

LBT will monitor the uplinks and trigger whenever an uplink is 75% saturated or higher for at least 30 seconds. The trigger values cannot be modified. At this time, it will make the decision to move some of the VM virtual NICs to another active uplink, assuming that another uplink has enough throughput unused to accept the new VM. Keep in mind that LBT will not move traffic to a standby or unused uplink, so you don't have to worry about it violating your failover order.

In the example scenario in Figure 9.15, LBT has migrated VM2 and VM3 to uplink2, which addresses a "noisy neighbor" situation where VM1 was causing contention for networking bandwidth.

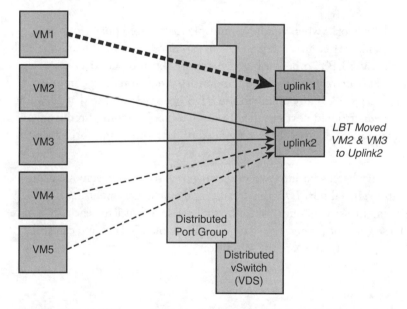

Figure 9.15   LBT has moved the virtual NICs of VM2 and VM3 to uplink2

It's important to understand a few limitations of LBT:

- The virtual NIC of a VM cannot use multiple uplinks at the same time. The policy moves the virtual NIC from one uplink to another in times of contention, but does not spread the networking traffic of a single VM across multiple uplinks.

- If you have very bursty traffic that finishes in less than 30 seconds, LBT does not trigger a migration. This 30-second threshold exists to prevent thrashing: useless, repetitive, expensive work.

> **NOTE**
>
> Although almost all documentation for LBT talks about the ability to migrate VM virtual NICs, it's important to understand that it can also move around VMkernel ports. If you are in a converged infrastructure environment with a limited number of uplinks, it might be advantageous to use LBT to move around your VMkernel port assigned to management or vMotion in times of uplink bandwidth saturation. Don't forget that LBT cannot cause traffic for a VMkernel port to use multiple uplinks simultaneously—it will only move the VMkernel port from one uplink to another.

You might wonder how LBT works when you have multiple distributed port groups all sharing the same set of uplinks. After all, each port group can have a different teaming policy applied, with some using LBT, others using virtual port ID, and perhaps a few using an explicit failover order. Fortunately, because LBT monitors saturation on the uplinks, it mixes with other policies very well. If any uplink in the VDS becomes saturated at 75% or higher for 30 seconds, any distributed port group with the LBT policy configured triggers and attempts to move around workloads. There is no need to have one giant port group with all the VMs inside.

In Figure 9.16, the VMs have been split into two different port groups: a green one using "route based on originating virtual port ID" (the default) and an orange one using LBT. When VM1 begins sending massive amounts of traffic that cause uplink1 to reach 75% or higher saturation for 30 seconds or longer, the orange LBT-enabled port group can still move VM2 and VM3 to uplink2 to alleviate the saturation.

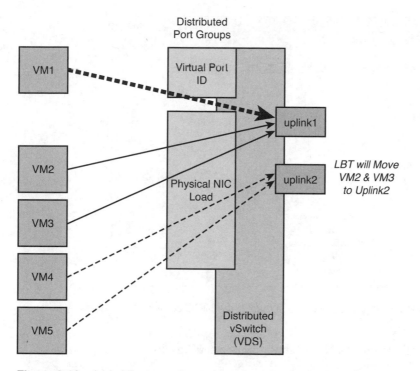

Distributed
Port Groups

VM1

Virtual Port
ID

uplink1

LBT will Move
VM2 & VM3
to Uplink2

VM2

Physical NIC
Load

uplink2

VM3

VM4

VM5

Distributed
vSwitch
(VDS)

Figure 9.16   A workload on a "route based on virtual port ID" port group can still cause LBT to move workloads elsewhere

Network I/O Control

The final feature we cover for the Distributed vSwitch is Network I/O Control, or NIOC if you're into the whole brevity thing. NIOC is a great way to further control traffic in your network. Much like the resource pools you create for your compute workloads, the idea behind NIOC is to allow you to configure limits and shares on the network for both system-generated and user-defined network resource pools. Network traffic is grouped into resource pools according to traffic type, and you can choose to apply bandwidth limitations, configure a share value, or even assign a quality of service (QoS) priority tag to each resource pool. Figure 9.17 shows where you can enable NIOC.

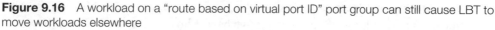

NOTE

You can find this feature in the vSphere Web Client hiding in the Resource Allocation menu. This has caused some confusion for many who were looking specifically for a "NIOC" tab.

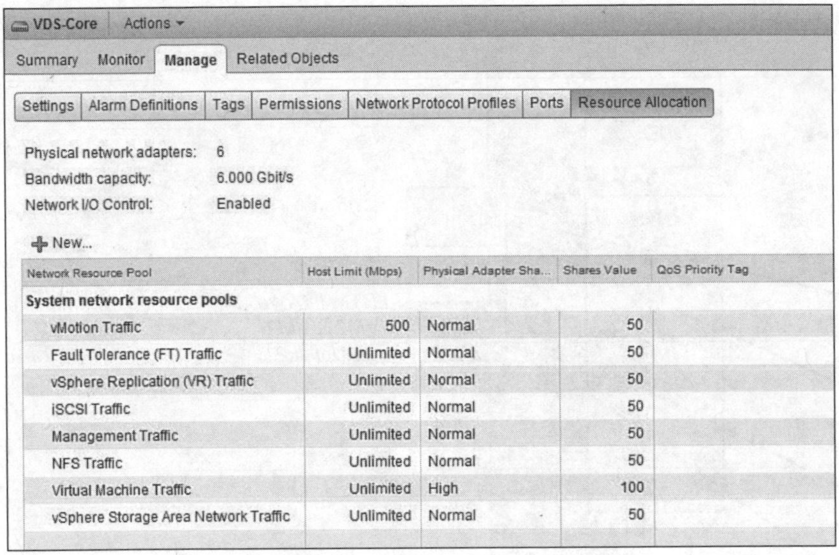

Figure 9.17   The Resource Allocation screen shows all the NIOC configuration values

Let's go over what all the various NIOC configuration settings do:

- **Physical Network Adapters**: A count of the number of uplinks each host has contributed to this particular VDS. In our case, we have 3 hosts using the VDS, each with 2 uplinks. Thus, 3 hosts x 2 uplinks = 6 physical network adapters.

- **Bandwidth capacity (Gbit/s)**: All 6 uplinks discovered from the physical network adapters run at 1 Gbit/s; therefore, my total bandwidth capacity for the entire VDS is 6 Gbit/s. Note that this is gigabits per second (little "b") not gigabytes per second (big "B").

- **Network I/O Control**: Disabled by default, or shows you Enabled if you or someone else has turned it on. When Disabled, the NIOC configuration values have no effect on traffic.

Network Resource Pools

You'll also notice a list of eight system network resource pools. Each one corresponds to a specific type of traffic and allows you to configure values that affect traffic ingress, which is from the VDS to its uplink ports. You cannot remove any of the predefined resource pools, which are as follows:

- vMotion Traffic.
- Fault Tolerance (FT) Traffic.

- vSphere Replication (VR) Traffic: Used by the VR appliance, including VMware Site Recovery Manager (SRM).

- iSCSI Traffic.

- Management Traffic.

- NFS Traffic.

- Virtual Machine Traffic: Used for all VMs, although you can create your own user-defined resource pools. We cover that later in this chapter.

- vSphere SAN Traffic: Used by the Virtual SAN technology that VMware announced at VMworld 2013 (vSphere 5.5 or higher only).

Now that you know what types of traffic we can control, let's review the configurations for each:

- **Host Limit (Mbps)**: A traffic limit, defined in megabits per second, which cannot be exceeded by the network resource pool. In vSphere 5.1, this is on a per-uplink basis, whereas prior to 5.1, it was a per-host limit. As an example with a 5.1 VDS: If you were to limit the vMotion network resource pool to 2000 Mbps, but defined multiple vMotion VMkernel ports on multiple uplinks, each uplink could send traffic upstream at a rate of 2000 Mbps. Use limits sparingly as they might artificially create network contention for no reason.

- **Physical Adapter Shares**: The configured shares for an adapter (uplink port). You can choose High (100 shares), Normal (50 shares), Low (25 shares), or Custom to define a custom quantity of shares up to 100. Shares are ultimately used to calculate what percentage each network resource pool can claim from a physical adapter (uplink). The speed of the uplink does not increase or decrease the number of shares because percentages are relative to the speed of the uplink.

- **Shares Value**: The amount of shares set on the network resource pool.

- **QoS Priority Tag**: This field gives you the ability to set the IEEE 802.1p QoS tag. Values range from 0 (lowest) to 7 (highest) priority. Many Layer 2 devices on the physical network will inspect this portion of the Ethernet frame and, based on the QoS tag value assigned, prioritize or drop traffic. Use with caution and make sure to include your network team in the discussion.

Shares

Shares cause the most confusion when it comes to resource pools. As such, let's address the share values set on the network resource pools. First off, shares are a relative value. They don't represent a specific quantity of traffic, and are not used unless the uplink becomes saturated with traffic.

When an uplink does become saturated with traffic, NIOC kicks in and begins examining two things: the share values configured and which network resource pools are being used by the uplink. In the following example in Figure 9.18, we have two uplinks configured on an NIOC-enabled VDS. One uplink is serving as the Active uplink for the Management and Fault Tolerance port groups, while the other uplink is serving as the Active uplink for VMs and vMotion port groups.

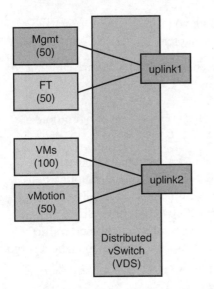

Figure 9.18   An example VDS with two uplinks and four port groups with various traffic types

If uplink1 were to become saturated with Management and Fault Tolerance, NIOC would examine the uplink and find:

- Uplink1, which is a 1 Gbps connection to the upstream switch, is the Active uplink for Mgmt (50 shares) and FT (50 shares).

- 50 shares + 50 shares = 100 shares total for this uplink

- Mgmt would get 50 out of 100 shares, which is 50%, and throttled to 50% of the full 1 Gbps link for a total of 0.5 Gbps or roughly 500 Mbps.

- FT would get 50 out of 100 shares, which is 50%, and throttled to 50% of the full 1 Gbps link for a total of 0.5 Gbps or roughly 500 Mbps.

That one was easy; let's do a harder one by looking at uplink2 and go over what would happen if it became saturated with VM and vMotion traffic:

- Uplink2, which is a 1 Gbps connection to the upstream switch, is the Active uplink for VMs (100 shares) and vMotion (50 shares).

- 100 shares + 50 shares = 150 shares total for this uplink
- VMs would get 100 out of 150 shares, which is 66.7%, and throttled to 66.7% of the full 1 Gbps link for a total of 0.667 Gbps or roughly 667 Mbps.
- vMotion would get 50 out of 150 shares, which is 33.3%, and throttled to 33.3% of the full 1 Gbps link for a total of 0.333 Gbps or roughly 333 Mbps.

Remember that shares only kick in to control active traffic. In the same scenario we just reviewed, we assume that both VMs and vMotion traffic were active and causing contention. If the entire uplink were taken up with only VM traffic, and no vMotions were occurring, no throttling would occur—there's only one type of active traffic (VM traffic). The VMs would get 100% of the uplink until a vMotion occurred.

User-Defined Network Resource Pools

Beyond the system network resource pools, which are included with vSphere and cannot be deleted, you are given the opportunity to create your own custom user-defined resource pools. These are used by VM port groups of your choosing, such as ones for production, development, mission-critical VMs, or whatever. A user-defined resource pool is shown in Figure 9.19.

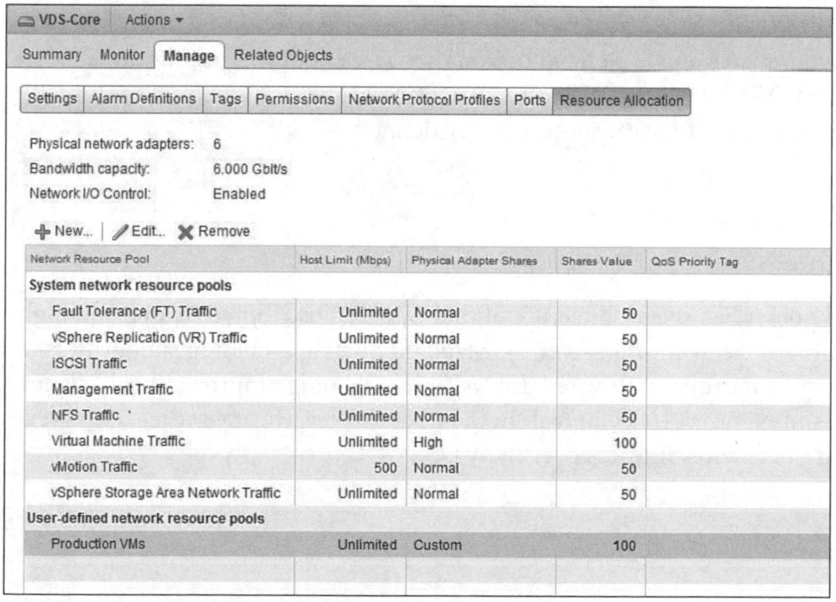
VDS-Core
Actions
Summary
Monitor
Manage
Related Objects
Settings
Alarm Definitions
Tags
Permissions
Network Protocol Profiles
Ports
Resource Allocation
Physical network adapters: 6
Bandwidth capacity: 6.000 Gbit/s
Network I/O Control: Enabled
New...
Edit...
Remove
Network Resource Pool
Host Limit (Mbps)
Physical Adapter Shares
Shares Value
QoS Priority Tag
System network resource pools
Fault Tolerance (FT) Traffic Unlimited Normal 50
vSphere Replication (VR) Traffic Unlimited Normal 50
iSCSI Traffic Unlimited Normal 50
Management Traffic Unlimited Normal 50
NFS Traffic Unlimited Normal 50
Virtual Machine Traffic Unlimited High 100
vMotion Traffic 500 Normal 50
vSphere Storage Area Network Traffic Unlimited Normal 50
User-defined network resource pools
Production VMs Unlimited Custom 100

Figure 9.19 My newly created user-defined network resource pool named "Production VMs"

You can then apply the network resource pool directly to the port group to ensure that any VM that uses the port group will be granted the NIOC configuration values. This process is illustrated in Figure 9.20.

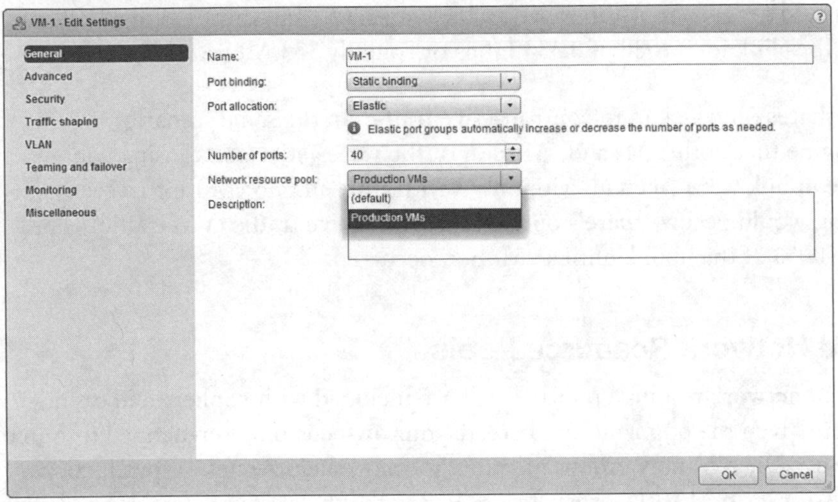

Figure 9.20   Applying my user-defined network resource pool named "Production VMs" to the VM-1 distributed port group

Any VMs that do not match a user-defined network resource pool will use the system defined pool named "Virtual Machine Traffic." You can use this as a catch-all resource pool for anything that doesn't have a specific policy defined.

Summary

In this chapter, we described the architecture of the vSphere Distributed Switch and high-lighted feature enhancements it offers over the Standard Switch, including support for LLDP, NetFlow, port mirroring, Private VLANs, egress shaping, improved load balancing mechanisms, and Network I/O Control. In the next chapter, we cover the Cisco Nexus 1000V switch and the features it offers over the VDS.

Chapter 10

Third Party Switches–1000V

Key Concepts

- Cisco Nexus 1000V
- Virtual Supervisor Module (VSM)
- Virtual Ethernet Module (VEM)
- Port Profile

Introduction

Now that we've covered the two types of built-in vSwitches, let's move into the realm of third-party virtual switches and why they came about. Historically, the VMware vSwitches have been good enough in many respects to earn a place in the datacenter but did not provide enough features or functionality to fully replace the need for intelligent physical switches. Advanced features such as ERSPAN, DHCP snooping, and Access Control are not available with either the standard or distributed vSwitch. Network administrators use these sorts of features to further enhance and control the network but were at a disadvantage in the virtual environment due to a lack of features like these.

Cisco worked to fill this gap by introducing the Cisco Nexus 1000V virtual switch at VMworld in 2008. It provided a bridge between the physical and virtual networking worlds that many Cisco Nexus and IOS professionals were familiar with using. In fact, it looks and feels much like a physical switch does, including a command line interface (CLI) and virtual modules designed to closely emulate their physical counterparts, but with improvements necessary to be relevant in a virtual environment. And while it's true that much of the feature gap between the distributed vSwitch and the Nexus 1000V has eroded, there are still many reasons that you might want to go down the path of the Nexus 1000V.

In this chapter, we dig into the Cisco Nexus 1000V from an architectural and feature set perspective.

> **NOTE**
>
> You might have also heard about another third-party switch from IBM called the Distributed Virtual Switch 5000V. We are excluding this product because neither of us, nor anyone we've worked with, has actually seen it in the wild. We've heard reports of sightings in the woods of the Pacific Northwest, and rumors of a rogue software switch attacking and drinking the blood of goats outside of San Antonio, but that's about it. It's also not called out in any of the more popular reference architectures. Just be aware that it exists, and that technically there are two choices for third-party switches with vSphere.

Integration with vSphere

The Nexus 1000V leverages the VMware vNetwork Distributed Switch Application Programming Interface (API) and, therefore, requires VMware vSphere Enterprise Plus licensing for any of the hosts that will be participating in the Nexus 1000V switch. This doesn't mean that all of your hosts in your environment must be on this license version. If you have a small collection of hosts that are running lower licensed versions, such as Standard or Enterprise, you will still be able to load the necessary modules required for operation of the Nexus 1000V on your Enterprise Plus vSphere hosts. There is also no need for physical or logical isolation—the hosts that do not use the Nexus 1000V can be managed by the same vCenter server, inside the same Datacenter container, or even reside in the same cluster together.

In order to visually represent the Nexus 1000V via the vSphere Client or vSphere Web Client, VMware constructs a special vSphere Distributed Switch (VDS) and shows which hosts are connected to it. Unlike a normal VDS, which can be edited by a vSphere administrator, the special Nexus 1000V VDS is read-only within the vSphere client. You can view some of the configuration settings from the vSphere Client but are unable to invoke any changes. This is because the configuration of the Nexus 1000V takes place on a supervisor module, just like it would in a physical environment, using the Nexus operating system (NX-OS) from Cisco. The main advantage to this method of configuration is that it is very familiar to those who operate a physical Nexus switching environment. Rather than having to train networking professionals who are already managing Nexus switches on how to use a vSphere Client interface, the Nexus 1000V provides a lightweight, but familiar, NX-OS experience. Network administrators can connect to the Nexus 1000V using tools that use SSH or Telnet, such as PuTTY or SecureCRT. They can also easily upload or download the running configuration on the Nexus 1000V, maintain the kickstart and system image versions, and make changes to the network infrastructure without any access to the virtual infrastructure. Don't worry—we cover these concepts further in the next few sections.

Architectural Differences

The Nexus 1000V is comprised of two modules: the virtual supervisor module (VSM) and the virtual Ethernet module (VEM). Each type of module has a specific set of roles to fulfill and tasks to perform to ensure the successful operation of the Nexus 1000V switch.

Figure 10.1 shows a simplified vSphere architecture that includes the Nexus 1000V.

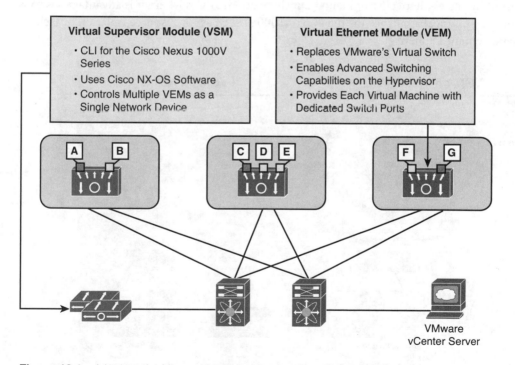

Figure 10.1 A look at the Nexus 1000V architecture in a vSphere environment

Virtual Supervisor Module

The VSM houses the control plane or "brains" of the Nexus 1000V and is deployed as a pair of VMs or on a physical appliance. The VSMs form a high availability (HA) cluster to avoid having a single point of failure. One VSM fills the active node role and the other VSM assumes the standby node role. If the active VSM were to fail for some reason, such as if the underlying vSphere host suffers a power outage, the surviving standby VSM would seamlessly take over operations and become the new active VSM node. When the failed VSM is restarted, it assumes the standby role, thus returning the VSM cluster back to an HA state.

The VSM HA cluster operates using a single IP address. This is made possible because only the active VSM manages and responds to requests for the Nexus 1000V switch. The active VSM communicates any changes to its paired standby VSM, so that the standby node can quickly assume an active role if required by a manual or automated failover.

Figure 10.2 shows the architectural differences between the VM and physical appliance deployment models. In both cases, the end result is the same—a Nexus 1000V switch is utilized by the vSphere environment—but there are use cases where it is advantageous to leverage a physical appliance for the Nexus 1000V, such as for resource isolation or lack of a management vSphere cluster.

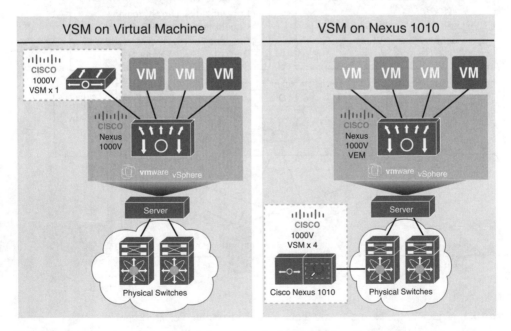

Figure 10.2   The two deployment options for the VSM: VMs or physical appliance

The VSM uses three different types of networks to control the Nexus 1000V environment: management, packet, and control. Each network has specific tasks to perform and are usually kept on different VLANs, although it is not required to do so:

- **Management Network**: This appears as the mgmt0 interface on the Nexus 1000V. It is used to perform administrative work on the Nexus 1000V, such as providing login access for configuration. It is also used to talk to the vCenter Server.

- **Packet Network**: Services such as CDP, IGMP, and LACP use this network.

- **Control Network**: The VSM uses this network to talk to one another and pass along configuration data necessary for the active-to-standby synchronization and to achieve high availability. It's also how the VSMs talk to the VEMs on the vSphere hosts.

All changes to the Nexus 1000V configuration are done via the VSMs, typically via a remote console that is connected via SSH, though you can also use the VM console session on the active node. Those changes are then communicated to vCenter by means of a Server Virtual Switch (SVS) connection, which is a special relationship created to connect the Nexus 1000V into the VMware vCenter Server. This is a requirement in order to communicate data between the two entities, as the vCenter Server will reflect the status of the Nexus 1000V configuration by way of Nexus 1000V VDS.

Here is an example SVS connection:

```
n1000V# show svs connections
connection VC:
    ip address: 10.0.0.27
    protocol: vmware-vim https
    certificate: default
    datacenter name: LabDC
    DVS uuid: ac 36 07 51 42 88 d9 ab-03 fe 4f dd d1 32 cc 5c
    config status: Enabled
    operational status: Connected
```

The connection data tells some important details:

- **ip address**: The IP address of the vCenter Server.

- **protocol**: The protocol type used to talk with the vCenter Server, either HTTP or HTTPS. In this case, the Nexus 1000V is connected to the HTTPS port, which is TCP 443, for a secure connection.

- **datacenter**: The vCenter Datacenter is LabDC. This is where vCenter will construct the distributed vSwitch.

- **DVS uuid**: The vCenter universally unique identifier (UUID) value for the distributed vSwitch that corresponds to the Nexus 1000V switch.

- **config status**: The current configuration is enabled.

- **operational status**: The Nexus 1000V is currently connected to the vCenter Server. Only one connection is allowed at a time.

At this point, you have a control plane and redundant supervisors, but no configuration. Let's move forward to the next major construct that makes the Nexus 1000V useful: port profiles.

Port Profiles

Port profiles share some similarities with port groups in VMware vSwitches. Both are used to logically define the behavior of virtual ports. The Nexus 1000V uses a variety of port profile types to control what types of virtual ports are being created, and how they map to either the virtual environment or physical uplinks:

- **Ethernet**: This type of port profile is used to define physical uplinks. There are usually two port profiles of this type: one that is used for mapping the network adapters connected to the upstream switches, and another special profile called "Unused_Or_Quarantine_Uplink" that is used by the Nexus 1000V.

- **vEthernet**: This type of port profile is used to define virtual ports. These ports are consumed by VMs and VMkernel ports on the vSphere hosts.

When you create an Ethernet port profile, the distributed vSwitch creates an empty uplink port group. The VMware administrator would then add hosts to the Nexus 1000V VDS and pick which network adapters to include, along with choosing the correct uplink port group for those adapters.

Here's an example configuration of an Ethernet port profile:

```
port-profile type ethernet SYSTEM-UPLINK
   vmware port-group
   switchport mode trunk
   switchport trunk allowed vlan 1,2,3,4,5,100-200
   channel-group auto mode on mac-pinning
   no shutdown
   system vlan 2
   description system profile for physical uplinks
   state enabled
```

Some of the configuration highlights include:

- **vmware port-group**: Specifies the type of hypervisor.

- **switchport mode trunk**: Configures the uplink as a trunk port, which allows for 802.1Q tags on multiple VLANs.

- **switchport trunk allowed vlan #**: The VLAN tags that should be passed along by the uplink.

- **channel-group auto**: This command tells the port profile how the link aggregation group (LAG) should be configured. The "mode" portion can be "mode on" for static or "mode active | passive" for LACP. The use of "mac-pinning" is useful for environments where the upstream switches do not support port channels. The MAC addresses of the VMs are pinned to the uplinks in a round-robin fashion.

- **system vlan #**: This denotes special VLANs that should be brought up immediately without waiting on communication between the VSM and VEM. It's commonly used for any management, control, or storage traffic.

> **REAL WORLD**
>
> Occasionally, there is a need to create additional Ethernet port profiles. This is a rare event, but it can be useful when you have disjointed upstream Layer 2 networks. The typical use case for this revolves around having isolated networks for DMZ traffic or PCI compliance. In this case, you would add the host uplinks (network adapters) to specific port groups that match the appropriate Ethernet port profile.

Every vEthernet port profile created on the Nexus 1000V will result in a distributed port group being created on the Nexus 1000V VDS. This allows the VMware administrator to place VMs or VMkernel ports into the port groups, while the policy remains in the hands of the network administrator that is configuring the Nexus 1000V:

```
port-profile type vethernet BobSponge
  vmware port-group
  switchport mode access
  switchport access vlan 100
  no shutdown
  state enabled
```

Note that, aside from one applying to physical uplinks and the other applying to vnics, the difference between the Ethernet and the vEthernet port profiles shown is that the vEthernet port profile is configured as an access port that only passes VLAN 100 traffic, whereas the Ethernet port profile is configured as a trunking port passing vlans 1, 2, 3, 4, 5, and 100-200.

PITFALL

Do not use the same VLAN across multiple sets of Ethernet port profiles or you will encounter some very angry users who are wondering why they can't connect to their workloads. Notice the VLANs defined in the Ethernet and vEthernet port profiles? The Nexus 1000V will determine which uplink to use based on the traffic's VLAN tag. In our previous examples, the BobSponge port group, which is on VLAN 100, would use the SYSTEM-UPLINK uplink because it is configured to pass traffic for VLAN 100. But if there were more than the Ethernet port profile carrying VLAN 100 traffic, unpredictable switching would result.

This covers the high-level functions necessary to understand some of the operational necessities of the Nexus 1000V supervisors. Let's move along toward the data plane that is provided by the VEMs.

Virtual Ethernet Module

The VEM is lightweight piece of software that must be installed on any vSphere host that wishes to participate in the Nexus 1000V switch. The VEM acts as the data plane on each host, handling all of the Layer 2 switching decisions for any traffic that is entering or leaving the Nexus 1000V. It's important to understand that the VSMs do not switch the data plane traffic, and that all traffic is still switched locally on each host by the VEM.

TIP

Installation of the VEM on a vSphere host is typically handled in one of two ways: Either embed the VEM files onto a custom vSphere installation ISO or use VMware Update Manager (VUM) to push out the VEM files. If you're using AutoDeploy, you should use a custom ISO, especially if you're operating in a stateless deployment model. For existing environments, it is often easiest to push out the software with VUM and move forward with the custom ISO for any newly created hosts. Either way, the VEM software is easy to deploy.

The VEMs must be able to communicate with the VSMs using the Control Network. This is how they are given configuration updates, licensing information, and generally operate successfully. The Nexus 1000V can use either Layer 2 mode (VLANs) or Layer 3 mode (IP) to communicate with the VEMs, as shown in Figure 10.3.

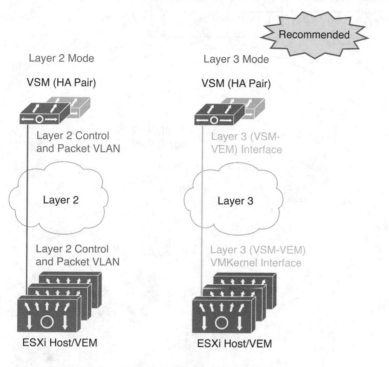

Figure 10.3   The subtle but important differences between Layer 2 and Layer 3 mode

Layer 2 Mode

In a Layer 2 mode scenario, the control and packet networks require a specific VLAN to traverse. You are given the choice to use unique VLANs or share a single VLAN, but it's advised to avoid using a VLAN with other types of traffic on it—the VLAN(s) should be dedicated to the Nexus 1000V to avoid dropping the 1-second heartbeat between the VSM and VEM. The VLAN selected must be available to the VSMs and all of the VEMs.

In a simple design where the entire datacenter has access to a single VLAN, it might seem trivial to implement Layer 2 mode. As the environment grows in complexity and scale, however, it is difficult to continue stretching Layer 2 out to all the vSphere hosts. Figure 10.4 should give you some idea as to the challenge in providing a single Layer 2 network to multiple vSphere clusters.

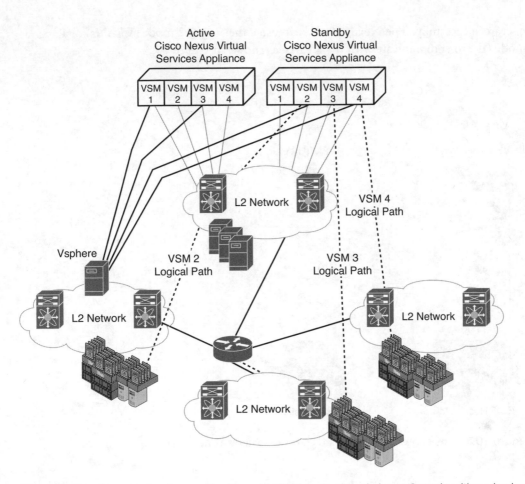

Figure 10.4   An example of a complex Nexus 1000V deployment in Layer 2 mode with a physical appliance

Nexus 1000V in Layer 3 Mode

The recommended configuration from Cisco is to use Layer 3 mode. This is a much easier configuration to support, as there is no need to ensure that the VSMs and VEMs are on the same VLAN, which can be a challenge in some datacenter configurations. Layer 3 mode can be designed in two different ways:

- Shared use of the vSphere Management VMkernel port
- Isolated VMkernel port specifically for the VSM-to-VEM traffic

The main advantage to using a shared VMkernel port is the lack of complexity with configuration of additional VMkernel ports and IPs. It does, however, require that your management VMkernel port reside on the Nexus 1000V. On the flip side, being able to put the management VMkernel port on an isolated standard vSwitch is one advantage to having an isolated VMkernel port for VEM control traffic.

An example of isolating all VSM-to-VEM traffic onto a standard vSwitch is shown in Figure 10.5.

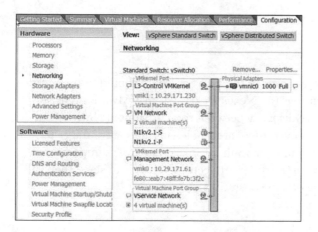

Figure 10.5   An example design showing Layer 3 control and management VMkernel ports on a standard vSwitch for isolation

---

PITFALL

It's risky to use the Nexus 1000V switch for the VSM VMs and/or the VEM's control and packet VMkernel ports. Most admins opt to use a separate standard vSwitch, and some decide to use a separate distributed vSwitch. By placing the VMkernel ports on the Nexus 1000V, you create a scenario where a network administrator could accidently sever communications between the VSMs and the VEMs with a faulty configuration, which requires a painful troubleshooting process to remedy. Be aware of the risk involved if you do decide to house the VEM's VMkernel port(s) on the Nexus 1000V, and communicate the risk to your team. A regularly updated backup of your running configuration and flagging critical VLANs as System VLANs can go a long way in mitigating the risk.

VEM Maximums

Each VEM in the environment will consume a virtual port on the Nexus 1000V Ethernet switch, which traditionally had 66 ports available: 2 for the VSMs and 64 for VEMs on the vSphere hosts. The latest code release for the Nexus 1000V allows for 130 total virtual Ethernet ports, which doubles the allowable VEMs to 128 per Nexus 1000V. Knowing that you can have 32 nodes (hosts) in a vSphere cluster, this means you could potentially have 4 fully populated vSphere clusters (32 nodes x 4 clusters = 128 nodes) managed by a single Nexus 1000V.

Advanced Features

As with most architectural decisions that occur in the network, there should be a require-ment met by selecting a technology such as the Nexus 1000V. With VMware's release of vSphere 5.5, even more of the feature disparity between the Distributed vSwitch and the Nexus 1000V has been eroded. However, there are still a handful of advantages to be gleaned from using the Nexus 1000V in your vSphere environment. It's important to review the various features provided with the different licensing models to see if they will meet design requirements or eliminate design constraints.

A Comment on Nexus OS

One of the more intangible advantages of using the Nexus 1000V is the ability to har-ness a familiar OS for network management: Nexus OS (NX-OS). Environments that already lean heavily on Nexus will find a familiar configuration environment to their other physical switches. This can offload the need for a server or virtualization administrator to handle the more nitty-gritty networking configuration and design decisions, allowing them to focus simply on consuming port groups for VM and VMkernel needs.

Licensed Modes of Operation

As of version 2.1, the Cisco Nexus 1000V offers two modes of licensing: Essential Edi-tion and Advanced Edition. For those who have vSphere Enterprise Plus licensing, you can enjoy the Nexus 1000V Essential Edition for free, or purchase the Advanced Edition if there are features you want to take advantage of beyond the free version. Licensing is purchased based on the number of physical CPU sockets in the vSphere host. A host with 2 physical CPU sockets, for example, would require 2 Nexus 1000V licenses.

Essential Edition

The Essential Edition comes with the following features:

- **VLAN, ACL, QoS**: The ability to use 802.1Q for VLAN tagging; Access Control Lists (ACL) for permitting and denying traffic; and Quality of Service (QoS) to police traffic to and from the VMs and VMkernel ports.

- **VXLAN**: Virtual Extensible LAN (VXLAN) is a Layer 2 network isolation technology that leverages encapsulation to create a large quantity of virtual LANs. It is also a popular way to do networking with VMware's vCloud Director product.

- **vPath**: Provides a forwarding-plane abstraction and a programmable framework for inserting network services such as firewalls, load balancers, and wide area network (WAN) optimization at the virtual access layer.

- **LACP**: Link Aggregation Control Protocol (802.3ad) for the creation and maintenance of multi-link LAGs.

- **NetFlow**: See the "NetFlow" section in Chapter 9, "vSphere Distributed Switch."

- **ERSPAN**: See the "Port Mirroring" section in Chapter 9.

- **vTracker**: Provides information about the virtual network environment. Based on the data sourced from the vCenter, the CDP, and other related systems connected with the Nexus 1000V virtual switch.

- **vCenter Plug-in**: Provides the server administrators a view of the virtual network and a visibility into the networking aspects of the Cisco Nexus 1000V virtual switch by way of the vSphere Web Client.

Advanced Edition

The Advanced Edition includes all of the features of the Essentials Edition, with the following additions:

- **Cisco TrustSec Support**: Enables you to build secure networks by establishing clouds of trusted network devices. Each device in the cloud is authenticated by its neighbors. Communication on the links between devices in the cloud is secured with a combination of encryption, message integrity checks, and data-path replay protection mechanisms.

- **DHCP Snooping**: This feature validates the DHCP messages received from an untrusted source, filtering out invalid response messages from DHCP servers. By default, all vEthernet ports are untrusted, and all Ethernet ports are trusted.

- **IP Source Guard**: A per-interface traffic filter that permits IP traffic only when the IP address and MAC address of each packet matches the IP and MAC address bindings of dynamic or static IP source entries in the DHCP Snooping binding table.

- **ARP Inspection**: Prevents man-in-the-middle (MITM) attacks by validating that MAC addressing being advertised by a network host is not being forged.

- **Virtual Security Gateway (VSG)**: A virtual firewall appliance that provides trusted access to virtual datacenter and cloud environments.

Summary

In this chapter, we described the operation of the Cisco Nexus 1000V and highlighted the advantages it offers over the distributed virtual switch. While enhancements to the distributed virtual switch have reduced some of the use cases for the Nexus 1000V, it remains a popular alternative for environments with a more hands-on network team. This ends our high-level overview of the types of virtual switches and their features. In the next few chapters, we show you how to actually accomplish things with them as we work through design exercises.

Chapter 11

Lab Scenario

Key Concepts

- Network Design
- Host Design
- Data Traffic Design

Introduction

Now that you are properly armed and dangerous with a bevy of networking knowledge covering the physical and virtual ecosystem, it's time to roll up your sleeves and get to building and configuring your own virtual network. As with most things in technology, try not to shoot from the hip—it's always better to start with a design, including understanding various architectural decisions. This chapter sets you up for success for a real world deployment, providing a number of design considerations that are relevant for a wide range of virtual networking deployments.

Building a Virtual Network

As you might imagine from reading the various switching chapters, there are many different paths along the journey to a viable and healthy virtual network. Where some folks will only need a standard virtual switch with a modest number of VMkernel ports, others will need multiple sets of distributed virtual switches with a large quantity of port groups and VMkernel ports. Is either of these right or wrong?

The answer to that question can be found by examining the use cases for these virtual networks and the effects they have on the overall design. Consideration must be given to factors such as redundancy, load balancing, an appropriate MTU value, and so on to create a healthy virtual network.

Before moving on to Chapter 12, "Standard vSwitch Design," let's review some of the common architectural decisions you'll need to tackle prior to building your shiny new virtual network.

Architectural Decisions

Most of the questions we go through here sound obvious when they are said aloud. We definitely will not argue that point with you. However, it is our experience that, although obvious, the questions rarely get asked. Later, when the dust clears and the trouble tickets flow, what would have been thoughtful questions to ponder become groans of pain and fixes. Even if you plan to move on after building a virtual network, it's never nice to leave a ticking time bomb for the next person who fills your seat.

The major points of thought for a virtual network revolve around the network design, host design, and your expected data traffic. It's often difficult to pin down specifics on data traffic for a new environment, so you might have to resort to a best guess and tweak as your organization grows.

Network Design

The network design portion of your architecture focuses on the logical entities necessary to create a successful virtual network. We're not so much concerned with network adapter speeds in this section, but rather want to lock down what is necessary to make the network operational.

Start by looking at the various VMkernel services offered by a vSwitch and notate which ones you will require (or think you will require later on down the road):

- **Management traffic**: Because this is used to manage the hosts and provide vSphere HA heartbeats, you will always need a VMkernel port for management. This is a no-brainer.

- **vMotion traffic**: Except for in somewhat rare cases where the network will be used by nonclustered, standalone hosts, anticipate needing a VMkernel port for vMotion. Yes, you could share this role with the management port, but using a modular design for your network is almost always preferred for ease of management and troubleshooting.

- **Fault Tolerance (FT) logging:** It's rare to see Fault Tolerance used in the wild due to the large number of associated caveats and 1 vCPU limitation. Unless your team, a business unit, or your management requests it, it's okay to skip creating this VMkernel port until a later date. Just remember that using FT, which allows you to create a "shadow" virtual machine (VM) on another vSphere host, requires a fair bit of compatibility between your vSphere hosts and sufficient bandwidth to keep the VMs synchronized between hosts.

- **vSphere Replication traffic:** Unless you plan to utilize vSphere Replication (VR), it's perfectly fine to hold off creating this VMkernel port. If you do plan to use the product later, it is a good time to evaluate your network configuration in multiple points (the wide area network [WAN] bandwidth, the quantity of workloads to replicate, and so on) and also design your VR ports.

- **iSCSI traffic:** Required if you plan to connect iSCSI storage to your vSphere hosts. If not, hold off making a VMkernel port for iSCSI until required. This is covered in Chapter 14, "iSCSI General Use Cases," and Chapter 15, "iSCSI Design and Configuration."

- **NFS traffic:** Required if you plan to connect NFS storage to your vSphere hosts. If not, hold off making a VMkernel port for NFS until required. This will be covered in Chapter 16, "NFS General Use Cases," and Chapter 17, "NFS Design and Configuration."

> **NOTE**
>
> The Management VMkernel port is already created during the ESXi installation process. That doesn't mean that you won't want to document how it is configured and have an understanding of the traffic flows to get to and from that VMkernel port.

Host Design

This portion of the architecture looks at how the network adapters are configured and consumed by the virtual network. This has become less of an exercise with the introduction of 10 Gb network adapters, which are typically fewer in number on a host, than it was during the days of using many 1 Gb network adapters (or network cards that had as many as four 1 Gb interfaces).

When looking at the network adapters and physical host design, there are a few critical decisions to make:

- **Redundancy**: Whenever possible, you'll want to make sure your virtual networks span redundant physical network adapters. This avoids a single point of failure scenario in which one single network adapter failure could interrupt the flow of an entire traffic type. It's not enough to use multiple physical ports on the same network adapter because the network adapter then becomes the single point of failure. Why do we say "whenever possible" and not "always?" Many blade server configurations can only accommodate a single network adapter. We don't want to stop you from considering these platforms, but want to highlight that you're trading a single point of failure for the ease of management and density advantages.

- **Supported Features**: Not all network adapters are created equal. Some support advanced features, such as TCP Segmentation Offload (often just called TSO) or various MTU values. Others do not. If you have a traffic type that requires specific functionality, make sure your underlying physical network adapter can support it.

- **Speeds**: Oftentimes a physical server comes with a network adapter built in. This is called the LAN On Motherboard (LOM). The LOMs are often only capable of providing 1 Gb speeds. If you are also installing cards capable of providing 10 Gb speeds, you won't want to mix the two speeds for a single traffic type. You could, however, use one speed for a specific traffic—such as Management—and the other speed for other traffic—such as VM traffic or vMotion.

REAL WORLD

Just about all 10-Gb network adapter manufacturers offer a model with a two-port configuration. We suggest you pick up at least two of these cards for redundancy, even if you only plan to use one port on each card—just make sure they are on the official VMware Hardware Compatibility List (HCL). Remember that your virtual network can only use the physical uplinks to get traffic in and out of the host. Don't skimp on such an important component unless you enjoy being called at night with an outage. Also, remember that vSphere HA might trigger a VM restart if it feels that the host has been isolated from the cluster, depending on your HA settings.

Data Traffic Design for Virtual Machines

The final component to consider is the VM networks, the real data traffic to and from VMs. This, you'll recall, is the important bit—it's why you're building the network in the first place. Think hard on how you want to configure and label your VM networks. These are the day-to-day networks that you or your team will be working with, and we've seen a lot of environments that use a very poor or confusing naming standard.

Some points to consider:

- **VLAN tagging**: In the vast majority of use cases, you will want to specifically define a VLAN ID for each VM port group. This is referred to as Virtual Switch Tagging (VST). It also gives you the operational freedom of using trunk ports on your upstream physical switch and clearly shows anyone looking at the vSphere Client what VLAN the VMs are communicating on.

- **MTU**: The default value of 1500 bytes works fine for most folks. It's rare to change this for VM traffic, but a bit more common to increase the value if you plan to use an overlay protocol such as virtual extensible LAN (VXLAN) or configure IP storage such as iSCSI or NFS. You'll recall from Chapter 4, "Advanced Layer 2," that frames larger than 1500 bytes are called Jumbo Frames. If you aren't sure if you need Jumbo Frames, leave this setting alone. Every piece of physical networking gear which passes your nonstandard-sized frames would also have to be set to the same nonstandard MTU size setting.

- **Naming**: One of the most overlooked, but probably one of the most important configuration items, is the naming scheme. Calling a VM network "virtual machine network 1" works when you have a tiny environment, but will become incredibly confusing down the road. The name should convey meaning in a compact format. Great names often have the subnet value in them, a designation of the workload type, and perhaps even the VLAN ID. For example, the name "SQL_192.168.50.X_V170" could communicate that the VM network uses the subnet 192.168.50.0/24 on VLAN 170 for SQL workloads.

> **REAL WORLD**
>
> Try to avoid using names that include spaces. Instead, use underscores or dashes, as spaces often make it more difficult when scripting with PowerShell or other scripting languages.

Lab Scenario

Rather than just talk about setting up standard and distributed vSwitches, along with the use of iSCSI and NFS storage VMkernel ports, we use our company's engineering demonstration lab to walk you through virtual switch implementation. The equipment we use is as follows:

- Cisco UCS 6120XP Fabric Interconnects running UCS Manager 2.1(2a)
- Cisco UCS 5108 Chassis with 2104 IO modules
- Cisco UCS B-series B200 M2 blades with the M81KR network adapter
- Cisco Nexus 7010 Switch

Figure 11.1 shows the architecture of our demonstration lab.

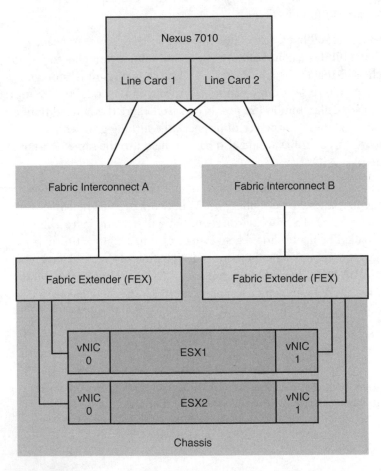

Figure 11.1 Lab scenario architecture

NOTE

Our demo lab is really something, and we love bragging about it. You can see all the toys we get to play with at www.thinkahead.com/ahead-aviation/.

That said, you don't need any of the equipment we've listed here to be successful with learning virtual switches, or even to try out creating a virtual network on your own. Much of what we cover will be done in a vendor-agnostic manner focusing on generic network adapters. You could easily substitute in hardware from HP, Dell, IBM, SuperMicro, or even use VMware Workstation at home to review much of what we cover here. Additionally, if you do not have blade servers or 10 Gb Ethernet adapters, we cover rack mount servers with both 10 Gb and 1 Gb Ethernet in Chapter 18, "Additional vSwitch Design Scenarios," and Chapter 19, "Multi-NIC vMotion Architecture."

It is, however, important to emphasize that the equipment we're using is something you might find out in a real world datacenter, so we figured you might want to know what we were using in the screenshots to follow.

We've also selected the following networks for each type of traffic:

- **Management traffic**: 10.20.0.0 /16, routable, with a gateway of 10.20.0.1, on VLAN 20

- **vMotion traffic**: 192.168.205.0 /24, non-routable, on VLAN 205

- **FT logging**: 192.168.210.0 /24, non-routable, on VLAN 210

- **VR traffic**: Not used

- **iSCSI traffic**: 192.168.215.0 /24, non-routable, on VLAN 215

- **NFS traffic**: 192.168.220.0 /24, non-routable, on VLAN 220

NOTE

The items listed are similar to a list you might see while working on a design. See the term "non-routable" used after many of the networks? This indicates that there will be no gateway for the traffic to use to crossover from one network to another. It also means that we've avoided creating a VLAN interface for inter-VLAN routing.

It is important that all the VLANs exist on the upstream physical network, as otherwise the vSphere host will not be able to communicate using the selected VLANs. In our case, the VLANs must be defined within the Cisco UCS domain itself and in the upstream Nexus 7010. Figure 11.2 shows the VLANs defined in Cisco UCS Manager.

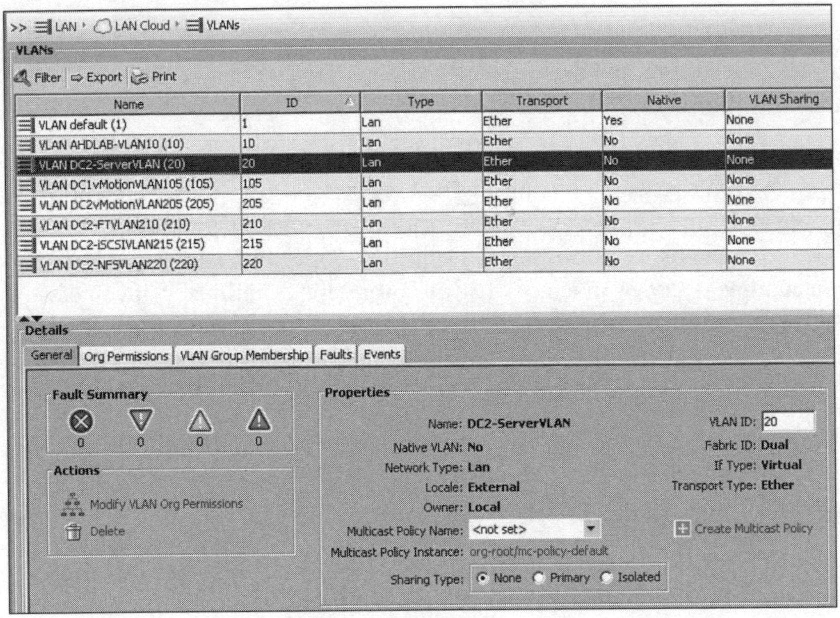

Figure 11.2   The VLANs configured on the upstream Cisco UCS domain

To tie things together, Figure 11.3 shows a basic view of the lab from the perspective of the vSphere Web Client.

The vCenter Server, named Initech Corp, contains a single datacenter in Chicago. This datacenter contains a cluster named Production, which is our focus for the remaining chapters in this section. Two blades have been added to the cluster, named esx1 and esx2, which are identical for our intents and purposes. A single VM exists named vCSA55 which runs the vCenter Server Appliance version 5.5. Nothing else has been configured—we're running off the stock default settings for the initial standard vSwitch that the hypervisor automatically creates. Welcome to our greenfield deployment, where a near infinite number of possibilities await.

You might also notice that the value for "NICs" is shown as 2. That's right, we move through the creation of distributed and virtual switching with just a pair of 10 Gb Ethernet network adapters, and discuss many of the caveats around this tactic, in Chapter 12 and Chapter 13, "Distributed vSwitch Design," on standard and distributed vSwitches.

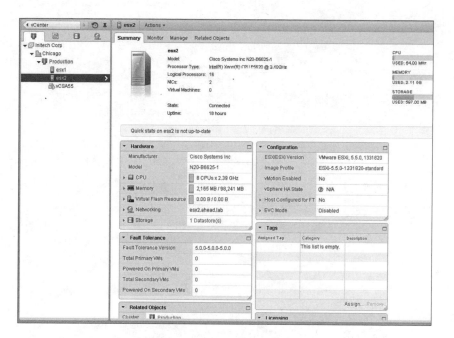

Figure 11.3   High-level perspective from the vSphere Web Client

Summary

Behind every great implementation is a great design. In this chapter, we looked over some of the decisions you will face when creating your virtual network design. We also locked down many of the variables that are used in the upcoming chapters on standard and distributed vSwitches in our engineering lab.

Chapter 12

Standard vSwitch Design

Key Concepts

- Defining a Use Case
- Naming Conventions
- Adapter Failover Order
- VMkernel Ports

Introduction

Fasten your seatbelts and please keep your arms and legs inside the car—we're ready to begin building out a network for your virtual infrastructure. If you need a moment to run around cheering wildly, we understand.

Throughout this chapter, we focus on many of the various decision points that will arise during an actual implementation of a standard vSwitch in your virtual environment. Some of the decision points will not apply to your environment, and you are welcome to skip past portions that do not apply. An example would be the creation of Fault Tolerance (FT) VMkernel ports if you do not need to use FT for your workloads.

For each decision, we spend some time talking about the reasons behind different decision paths. The goal is to arm you with the information necessary to make this chapter work for your specific environment, rather than just showing you the mundane steps to build a cookie-cutter switch configuration.

Standard vSwitch Design

A number of factors might influence the decision to use the standard vSwitch:

- **Licensing**: You might not have access to vSphere Enterprise Plus licensing, which is required to create a distributed vSwitch. Enterprise Plus is considerably more costly to acquire (and perhaps even to deploy due to the greater number of features to design around), and you might feel that the funds could be better spent elsewhere in your environment.

- **Simple Requirements**: If you only have a handful of vSphere hosts with very simple design requirements, it might be straightforward to use a standard vSwitch. Many of the advanced features found in a distributed vSwitch might not apply to your needs. This could also complement the licensing point made earlier.

- **Availability and Complexity**: The control plane of a standard vSwitch is bound to the vSphere host itself, not vCenter, making a standard vSwitch easier to troubleshoot and protecting it from vCenter outages. Although many advances in distributed vSwitch design have reduced the headaches associated with vCenter Server outages, there are still some advantages to having an "out of band" vSwitch for your management cluster or components that run critical back-end infrastructure workloads.

Remember that there is no universal right answer on vSwitch strategy as long as your requirements are met and the desired functionality is achieved.

Sample Use Case

In order to make this more entertaining, we provide a sample use case and walk through the configuration as the chapter progresses.

Initech Corp has a pair of vSphere hosts running ESXi 5.5 in their production data center located in Chicago. As the VMware Administrator for the corporation, you have been tasked with the creation and configuration of networking for your company's virtual infrastructure. Due to budget constraints, the company has purchased vSphere Enterprise licensing, which prevents you from building a virtual network on the distributed vSwitch or any other third party switches. You will need to use standard vSwitches. Each vSphere host has a pair of 10 Gb Ethernet network adapters connected to a redundant upstream physical network.

The virtual network should be capable of handling traffic for Management, vMotion, FT, and NFS storage traffic. It also needs to be able to pass along traffic for three different types of workloads: Web Servers on VLAN 100, Application Servers on VLAN 110, and Database Servers on VLAN 120.

Naming Conventions

After you have determined what networks you will need, your next step is to identify any relevant naming conventions currently in use in your organization, or if they are nonexistent, create your own. We'll assume that you don't already have one in place because that is more of a challenge.

We already know that the data center is located in Chicago, and that all hosts live in the Production cluster. Let's take a look at one of our vSphere host's network configuration, shown in Figure 12.1.

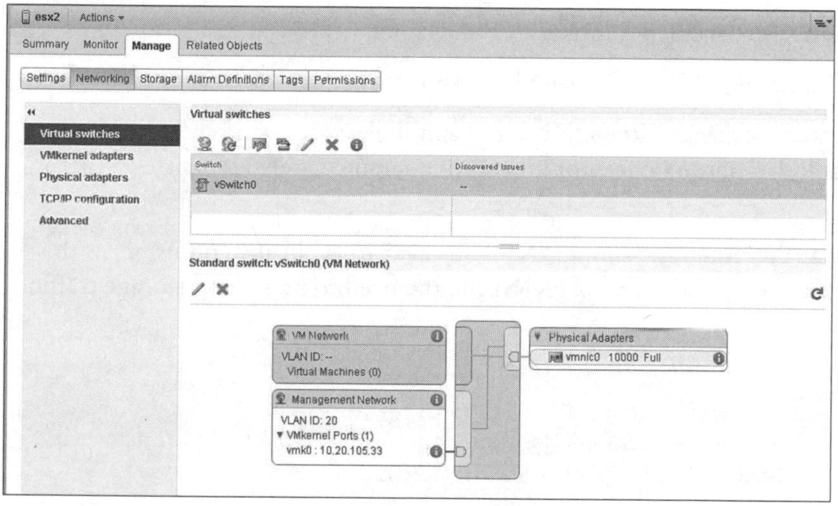

Figure 12.1   The initial vSwitch configuration of an ESXi host

Hey—someone already made a standard vSwitch. Don't worry, this is entirely normal and is part of the ESXi installation process. After all, the host needs some way to communicate with the outside world when it has been installed, right?

vSwitch0 is a special standard vSwitch that is autogenerated at the time of install. It will always contain two things:

- A Management Network with a VMkernel named vmk0 for your Management traffic

- A port group called "VM Network" for virtual machine networking traffic

You are not able to easily rename vSwitch0 to anything more descriptive unless you like digging around in the command line or through a script. But we think the default name vSwitch0 is actually a good thing—if you leave the vSwitch0 name as default, you are assured that every single host you create has a vSwitch0, which helps make a standardized environment.

> **NOTE**
>
> You're certainly welcome to change the name of vSwitch0, or even create a new vSwitch with a descriptive name and migrate the VMkernel port over, but that seems like a fair bit of extra work for no real gain.

Let's come up with some names for all of our VMkernel ports:

- **Management**: "Management Network" sounds fine.

- **vMotion**: The name "vMotion" is simple and effective.

- **Fault Tolerance Logging**: Either "FT" or "Fault Tolerance" work well, but I lean toward "Fault Tolerance" since not everyone can immediately recognize the acronym "FT."

- **NFS Storage**: You could use simply "NFS Storage" to avoid any confusion, as this easily proclaims both the protocol (NFS) and the need to pass along storage traffic.

> **NOTE**
>
> You could also add networking and VLAN information to your VMkernel port names, if desired, an example being "vMotion_192.168.205.x_V205."

Let's also come up with names for the VM traffic port groups. Great names include some sort of detail on the type of workload, the network for that workload, and the VLAN ID. Unfortunately, right now we only know the type of workload (Web, Application, and Database servers) and the VLAN ID—we don't know the networks.

After a quick chat with our network engineer friend, we find out that the VLAN networks are as follows:

- **VLAN 100**: 192.168.100.0 /24

- **VLAN 110**: 192.168.110.0 /24

- **VLAN 120**: 192.168.120.0 /24

> **REAL WORLD**
>
> As with the VMkernel VLANs, you need to ensure that the VM VLANs exist on the upstream network device. Otherwise, the VMs will be unable to communicate outside of the vSphere host. Most of the issues we've seen with VM communication tend to relate to a VLAN configuration missing somewhere in the upstream physical network.

Now we have all three pieces of the puzzle, so let's come up with some descriptive names:

- **Web Servers on VLAN 100**: Web_192.168.100.x_V100

- **Application Servers on VLAN 110**: App_192.168.110.x_V110

- **Database Servers on VLAN 120**: DB_192.168.120.x_V120

See how easily you can read those port group names and know exactly what they do? It makes life simple and efficient for any human operator, like you, that has to deal with the virtual network. As mentioned earlier, we have avoided spaces in the port group names to simplify scripting.

If you have more workloads in your environment, keep going through the exercise and identifying all the names you'll need before moving on. For example, you might need to use iSCSI traffic, vSphere Replication, or have ten different types of Database Servers to support, each with their own VLAN.

> **REAL WORLD**
>
> Why not just create a bunch of port groups called Port Group 1, Port Group 2, and so on? These names make it annoying and difficult to figure out what these port groups are used for. We've seen many environments with no understandable naming convention, requiring tribal knowledge to decipher the names. Tribal knowledge is any knowledge that only certain people know and is not documented anywhere. When someone that had tribal knowledge leaves your company, the team suffers as they try to piece together the missing information. Squash tribal knowledge by using highly descriptive names for your network objects. And document them for good measure.

Ensuring Quality of Service

The standard vSwitch has few methods of ensuring quality of service for the traffic that is being passed along. You're mainly limited to traffic shaping of ingress traffic, which is mainly traffic generated by VMs or VMkernel ports on the host to external entities—this is sometimes referred to as "outbound" traffic shaping.

You miss out on a fair number of really handy tools, such as Network IO Control (NIOC), egress traffic shaping, and the "route based on physical NIC load" policy (often referred to as load-based teaming).

There are, however, a few ways to overcome these limitations:

- **Additional network adapters**: One of the oldest methods of ensuring QoS for traffic is to increase your uplink count by way of multiple network adapters. For example, you could designate a pair of ports specifically for your IP Storage traffic. Some Converged Network Adapters (CNAs) also support the ability to logically carve up a physical network card into multiple virtual network cards, making it appear as if the vSphere host has many different network adapters. In this case, you are placing the responsibility of enforcing traffic fairness on the CNA.

- **Quality of Service (QoS) and Class of Service (CoS)**: Although the standard vSwitch does not allow you to set the 802.1p priority tag, some upstream physical network devices will interrogate and tag traffic for you. You would need to configure the upstream network device to correctly understand and prioritize your traffic when it receives traffic from the vSphere host.

- **Combination approach**: Some hardware systems allow you to both logically split up your physical network adapter and enforce QoS or CoS tagging on the various virtual network adapters. This would allow you to squeeze a fair bit of value out of your investment, as these types of solutions typically kick in only when congestion is present. If your upstream device supports this configuration, you are often allowed to weigh each traffic type against others to determine which one holds more priority, or even set hard limits as to how much traffic can be sent during a peak time.

NOTE

The increased availability of 10 Gb Ethernet has placed much of the need for QoS on hold—for now. We rarely see a 10 Gb link reach saturation on a vSphere host for any significant amount of time outside of an intentionally busy period—such as that of a vMotion event. However, as systems continue to crave more and more bandwidth, relying on 10 Gb to soak up any traffic congestion without any thought into QoS will eventually stop working effectively.

Network Adapters

At this point, you are ready to begin configuring the network. Notice how much emphasis was put on proper naming and really thinking about all the required port groups? It's essential to put in the planning time prior to implementation, otherwise you have either a sloppy environment that will require re-work to fix, or a suboptimal implementation that will haunt you further down the road.

Let's focus first on the vSphere host named esx2. To begin with, we need to take a good, hard look at our vSwitch0 to see if it has all the appropriate network adapters added to it. These will act as uplinks for the vSphere host. We'll select vSwitch0 from host esx2 and choose the "Manage the physical network adapters" option. Figure 12.2 shows the results.

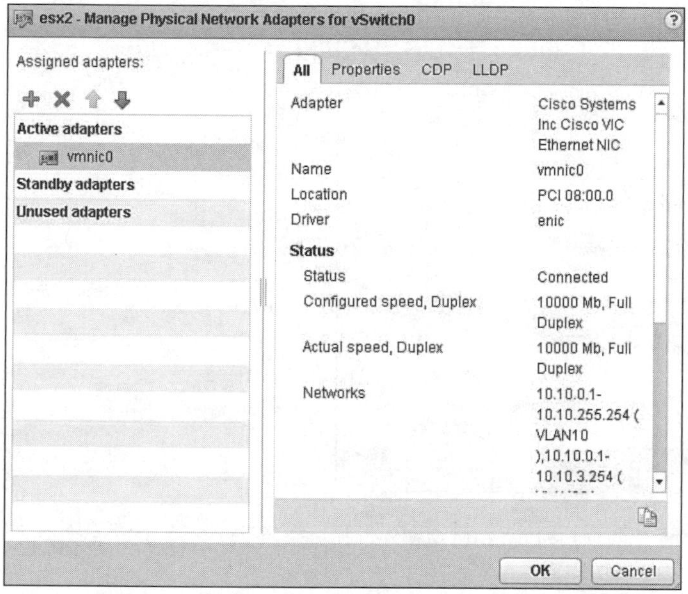

Figure 12.2 Network adapters used by vSwitch0

Whoops, it looks like only a single uplink, vmnic0, was added. This is the standard behavior for a fresh installation—vSwitch0 grabs the first network adapter, vmnic0, by default. If you recall from earlier, each host has two network adapters available, and we need to make sure that both of them are added to vSwitch0 to ensure the switch is redundant.

REAL WORLD

With very, very few exceptions, every vSwitch you build should have *at least* two physical adapters to act as uplinks. Any time you use a single adapter, you are creating a single point of failure, creating havoc if that network adapter were to fail.

We'll go ahead and click the green plus sign button to add the other network adapter into vSwitch0, as indicated in Figure 12.3.

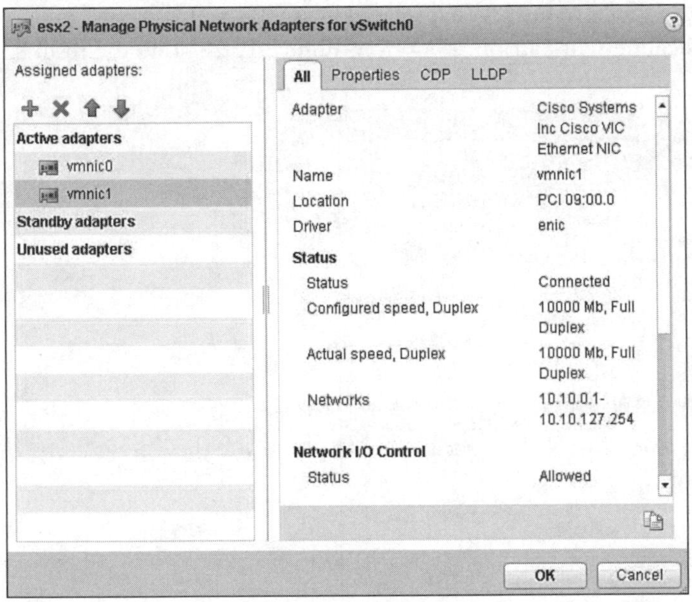

Figure 12.3   The second network adapter is now part of vSwitch0

NOTE

If your environment has more than two network adapters, it might be worth taking a glance at Chapter 18, "Additional vSwitch Design Scenarios," where we talk about systems that have four or more network adapters. We ultimately can't offer a complete walkthrough for every environment, but you should be able to roll with the punches and adapt this guide to your specific needs.

Virtual Machine Traffic

Now we have a fully redundant vSwitch0 that can use either vmnic0 or vmnic1. Let's build some port groups for our VM traffic.

Virtual Machine Port Groups

Our use case requires networking for three unique VM workloads: one for Web Servers, another for Application Servers, and a third for the Database Servers. Because each one of these workloads uses a different VLAN ID, we need three unique port groups. You might wonder, however, why the port groups must be unique?

Each port group will carry one single VLAN ID because our guest workloads, the servers themselves, are not configured to handle VLAN tags. We need to configure the vSwitch to handle this on the workload's behalf, which goes back to the Virtual Switch Tagging (VST) methodology outlined in Chapter 7, "How Virtual Switching Differs from Physical Switching." If our workloads could handle VLAN tags, another option would be to use a single port group that carried all three VLAN IDs as a trunk, which would be the Virtual Guest Tagging (VGT) configuration.

Let's begin by creating the port group for the Web Servers. To start, navigate to the Host and Clusters view in the vSphere Web Client, select host esx2, click on the Manage tab, Networking sub-tab, and then select the virtual switch named vSwitch0. Click the "Add Host Networking" link on vSwitch0, which looks like a little globe with a plus sign on it. The results are shown in Figure 12.4.

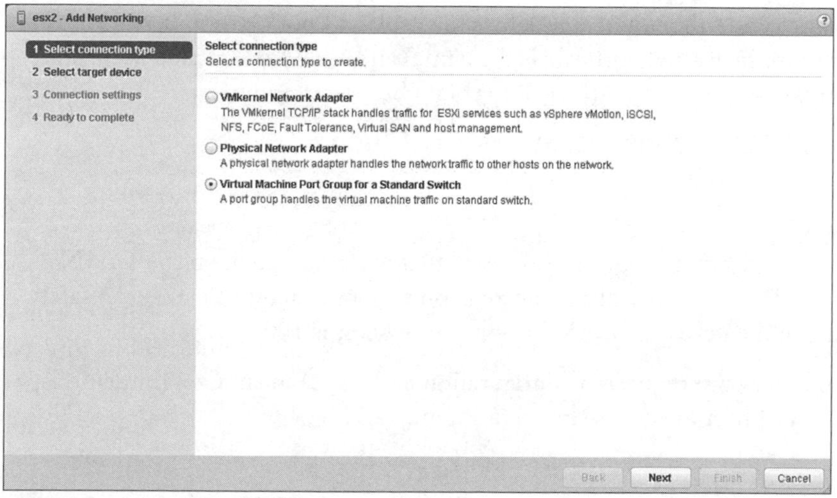

Figure 12.4   Adding a new network to vSwitch0

Because we want to make a new port group for VMs, we want to select the "Virtual Machine Port Group for a Standard Switch" radio button.

The next prompt asks what the target device is. You can leave the default selection of "Select an existing standard switch" highlighted with vSwitch0, as shown in Figure 12.5. If you chose to rename vSwitch0, or created a new vSwitch, you would want to select that vSwitch instead of vSwitch0.

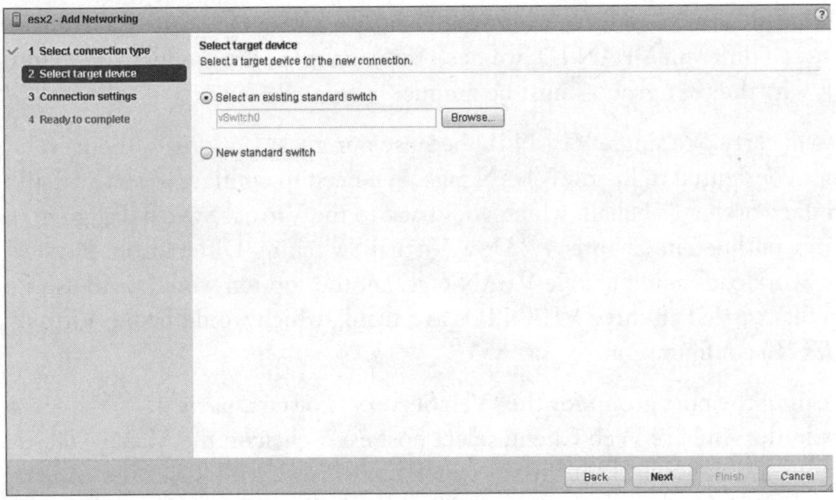

Figure 12.5   Selecting vSwitch0 as the target device

You are now ready to enter the important details for your VM port group. It really boils down to nothing more than a network label (the name) and VLAN ID. Since we're starting with the Web Server port group, the values would be:

- **Network label**: Web_192.168.100.x_V100

- **VLAN ID**: 100

I've entered the values shown in Figure 12.6. Note that when you click on the VLAN ID box, a few premade selections will appear for None (0) and All (4095). You can safely ignore these values and enter your own value—in this case, it is 100.

The last step is to review the requested configuration and click Finish. Congratulations, you have created a VM port group, as shown in Figure 12.7!

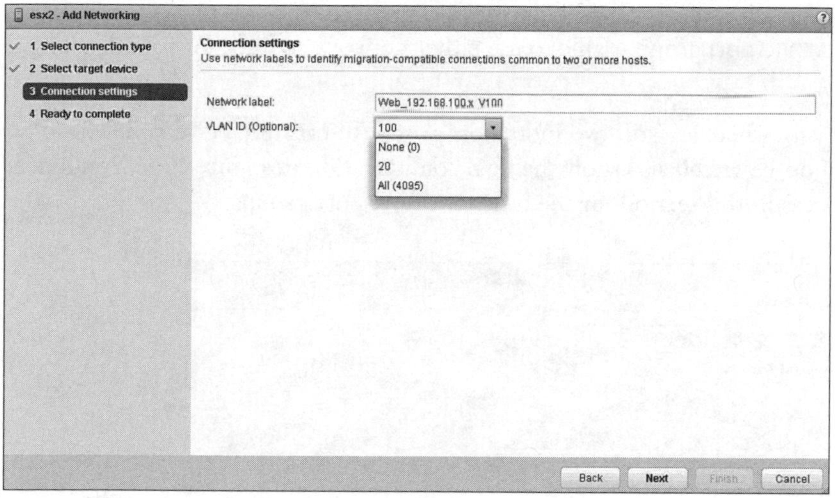

Figure 12.6   Entering the network label and VLAN ID for the Web Server port group

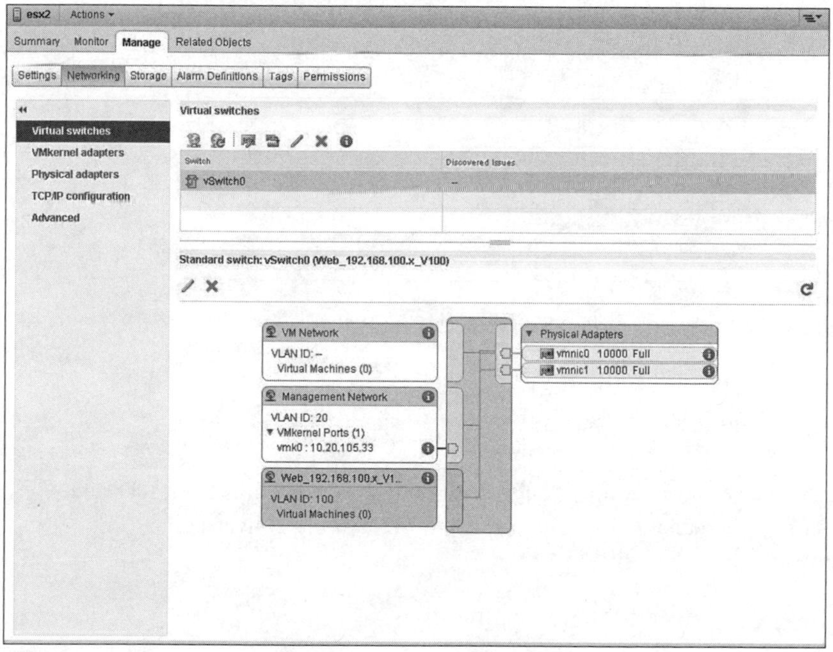

Figure 12.7   The Web Server port group is now part of vSwitch0

Note the gold line leading from the Web Server port group to the two physical adapters. This indicates that the port group is able to use either network adapter for passing along traffic.

You're not done yet—there are still two more port groups to create. We've gone ahead and created them on vSwitch0 and show the final configuration in Figure 12.8. You'll need to repeat the process in this section for the other two VM port groups.

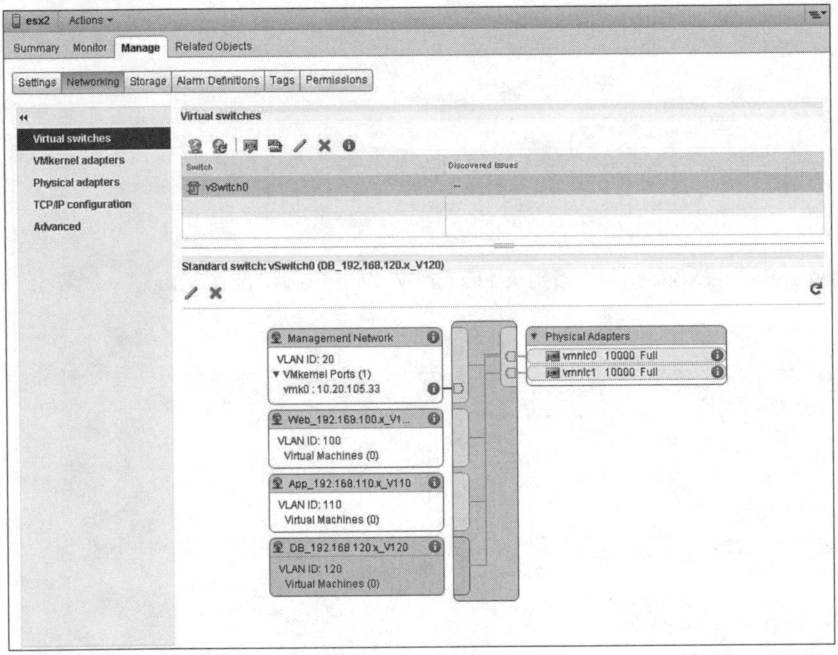

Figure 12.8   All the VM port groups have been created on vSwitch0

NOTE

Delete the "VM Network" port group if you're not going to rename and use it for something else. No sense having a name that doesn't match the naming convention.

Failover Order

By default, any new port group created will use the policies inherited by the vSwitch itself. For vSwitch0, the policy is to actively use all of the network adapters. We're going to leave this setting as-is for the VM port groups and let the VMs use either of the two available network adapters. In fact, Figure 12.9 provides a view of the default teaming and failover policies for vSwitch0. As you can see, both vmnic0 and vmnic1 are listed as Active adapters for vSwitch0, meaning they will both be used.

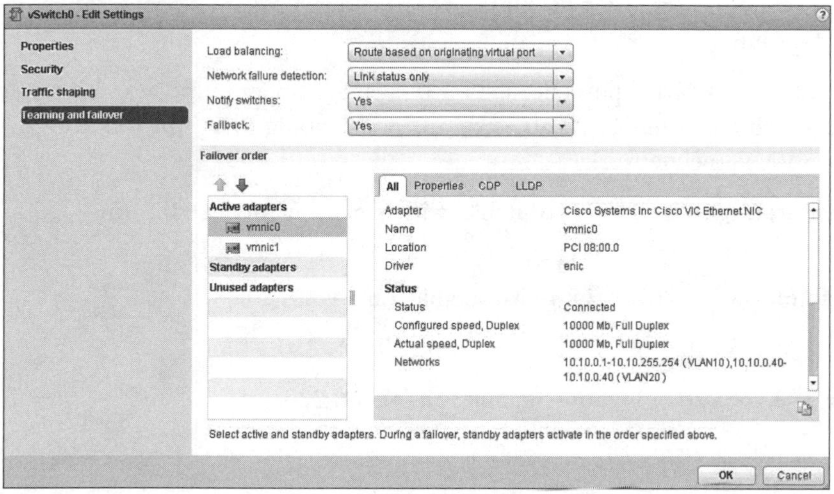

Figure 12.9   Default teaming and failover policies for vSwitch0

Why? With few exceptions, VMs are some of the least bandwidth hogging entities on a network. And, since there is no way to easily load balance them across the two network adapters, having two active uplinks with the default "route based on originating virtual port" gives them a solid chance at being spread out evenly across the uplinks.

REAL WORLD

There are some situations where you really should define specific network adapters as Active and others as Standby for VM traffic. If you have a specific use case, such as a workload that needs to use an uplink that goes to a specific network (such as a DMZ uplink), make sure to define a failover policy for that port group. It's just that we rarely find this the case specifically for VM throughput—they often consume a very small percentage (<10%) of the total bandwidth available to them.

We'll come back to this in greater detail for the VMkernel ports, since they will be using specific failover orders to help alleviate specific traffic congestion scenarios.

VMkernel Ports

Now comes the slightly trickier part of creating a standard vSwitch for the Initech Corp environment: configuring VMkernel ports. With a standard vSwitch, creating a new VMkernel port automatically generates a new port group for the VMkernel port to live inside. VMs cannot use this port group. You can only have one VMkernel port residing inside of each port group.

We'll tackle each of the VMkernel ports needed for this environment in the next few sections. As a reminder from Chapter 11, "Lab Scenario," we're going to use the following VLAN IDs for the VMkernel networks:

- **Management traffic**: 10.20.0.0 /16, routable, with a gateway of 10.20.0.1, on VLAN 20
- **vMotion traffic**: 192.168.205.0 /24, non-routable, on VLAN 205
- **FT logging**: 192.168.210.0 /24, non-routable, on VLAN 210
- **NFS traffic**: 192.168.220.0/24, non-routable, on VLAN 220

Management

The Management VMkernel port is commonly used as the means to manage a host. If you were to ping a host by its Fully Qualified Domain Name (FQDN), the IP address you received in response should be the one mapped to the Management VMkernel port. It's also what we commonly use when performing work via Secure Shell (SSH).

> **NOTE**
>
> Enabling "Management traffic" on a VMkernel port, such as what is shown in Figures 12.10 and 12.14, tell vSphere High Availability (HA) which VMkernel port to use for heartbeats. It's not actually required for managing the host. Still, it's often best to leave it on for whichever VMkernel port you wish to use to manage the host, which is vmk0 by default.

If you look carefully at vSwitch0, you'll notice that the Management Network port group is in fact just a container that houses a single VMkernel port called vmk0 (see Figure 12.10). This is used for your host management and is responsible for being the default gateway for any unknown VMkernel traffic that doesn't match a network mapped to any other VMkernel port. Don't let that confuse you—the default gateway is not used for VM traffic in any way. VMs will have a default gateway configured within their operating system. The VMkernel default gateway is there only for other VMkernel ports.

Figure 12.10   vmk0 is the default VMkernel port used for host management

You cannot put VMs inside of this port group because it is made specifically for a VMkernel port. This helps avoid any confusion when an administrator, for example, you, is looking for a network to place a VM on.

> **NOTE**
>
> vmk0 is a special VMkernel port generated by the hypervisor at the time of installation. Unlike other VMkernel ports, vmk0 uses the first network adapter's hardware MAC address—also known as the burned-in address (BIA)—as its own MAC address. We find that it's often best to leave vmk0 as the Management VMkernel port and not try to fiddle with it to become more than that, as bad things can (and do) happen.

It seems like most of your work is done for the Management VMkernel port, right? Obviously this port is operational, because otherwise the host would not be able to connect to the vCenter Server. However, it's important to review the failover order for every VMkernel port. If you edit the settings of the Management Network port group (which contains vmk0), you'll see a screen like that shown in Figure 12.11.

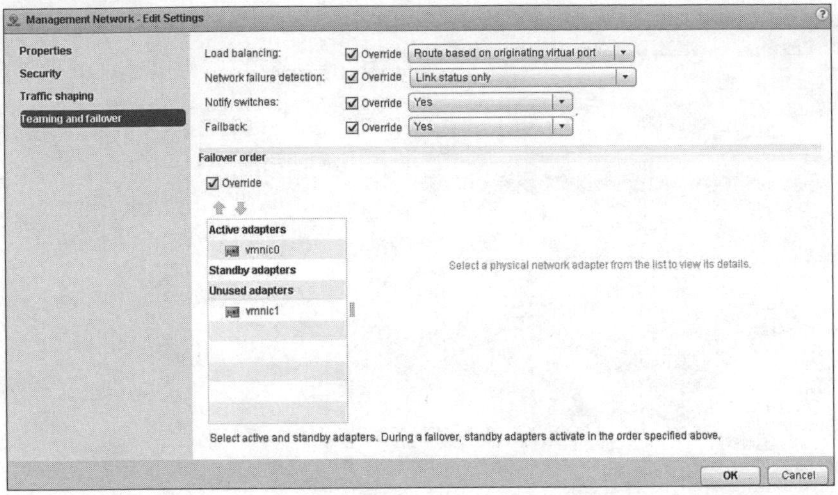

Figure 12.11   The failover policy settings for the Management Network

Hopefully, you'll see the same issue here that we see—vmnic0 is set to Active, and vmnic1 is set to Unused. This means that a failure of vmnic0 will bring down the vmk0 port, even if vmnic1 is still operational. We definitely don't want that; so let's fix it by modifying the failover order for the port group.

In order to balance out the VMkernel ports over a variety of different network adapters, we're going to purposely mark specific network adapters as Active and others as Standby. This is to help minimize traffic on any one specific network adapter. It might not make total sense now, but we will review the failover settings with each VMkernel port on a one-by-one basis here, and then go over the entire logical configuration in the final segment of this chapter. When you see all of their failover settings together, it should make more sense.

For the Management VMkernel port, vmk0, we're going to set vmnic0 as Active and vmnic1 as Standby. Select vmnic1 and click the blue up arrow to change vmnic1 from Unused to Standby, as shown in Figure 12.12.

That's much better. Now, if vmnic0 fails for some reason, vmk0 on the Management Network will be moved over to vmnic1 and the host will remain accessible on the network. When vmnic0 is repaired, vmk0 will move back over to vmnic0 due to the fact that the Failback option is set to Yes. We have introduced redundancy to this network, which is always a good thing to help avoid frantic calls in the middle of the night.

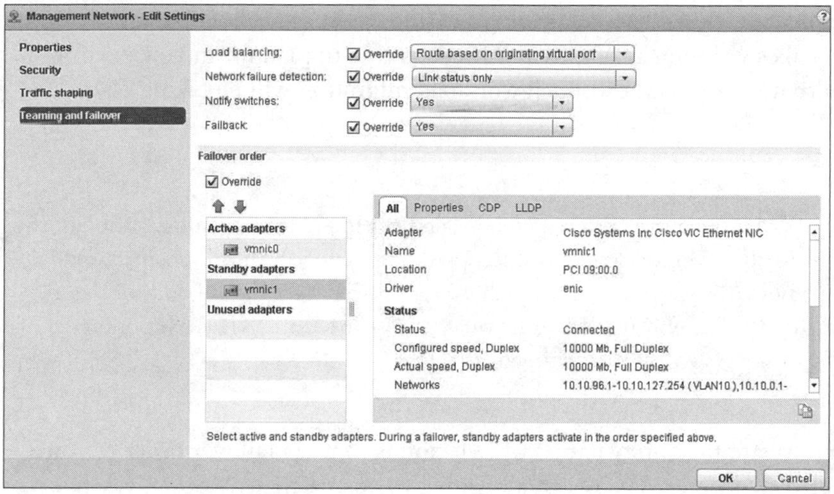

Figure 12.12   Marking vmnic1 as a Standby adapter for the Management Network

---

REAL WORLD

You might also choose to set failback to "No" for the Management VMkernel port to reduce the risk of a "Lights On" switching event during physical network maintenance. This occurs when the upstream switch is restarted, and then begins initiating the startup process and powers on the physical network port. vSphere might incorrectly believe that the port is up and available while the upstream switch is still going through the boot process and try to erroneously use the port for Management traffic.

Note that we're not talking about a blocked port via Spanning Tree Protocol (STP). Per the Portfast recommended practice mentioned in Chapter 4, "Advanced Layer 2," you should have already configured all your upstream switch ports connected to the vSphere hosts to immediately transition to a forwarding state.

---

vMotion

Whenever a VM is whisked away from one vSphere host to another, one or more VMkernel ports with the vMotion service tag will be used to transmit the VM's running state between them. As you might imagine, the amount of traffic traversing the vMotion VMkernel port is somewhat bursty. When no vMotions are occurring, the traffic being sent and received is zero. When vMotions are occurring, there is a whole bunch of traffic being sent. This makes vMotion a somewhat difficult traffic to plan for in new environments where you're not sure just how much workload migration will be taking place.

> **NOTE**
>
> Traditionally, one VMkernel port was created on each host for vMotion traffic, although the concept of multiple-NIC vMotion was introduced with vSphere 5.0. In this chapter, Initech Corp only has two network adapters, and as such, we don't want to saturate both of them with vMotion traffic simultaneously. However, we do cover multiple-NIC vMotion in detail in Chapter 19, "Multi-NIC vMotion Architecture."

One way to help mitigate the bursty nature of vMotion is to use a failover order to place it on a specific network adapter. We're actually going to ensure that vMotion is Active on vmnic1 and Standby on vmnic0, which is the opposite order we used with the Management traffic in the previous section. This keeps the two from fighting on a standard vSwitch unless we're in a scenario where one of the two network adapters has failed.

To begin with, let's create the VMkernel port for vMotion by selecting the Add Networking function on vSwitch0—the same function we used to add a VM port group earlier. This time, however, choose the "VMkernel Network Adapter" as your connection type as shown in Figure 12.13.

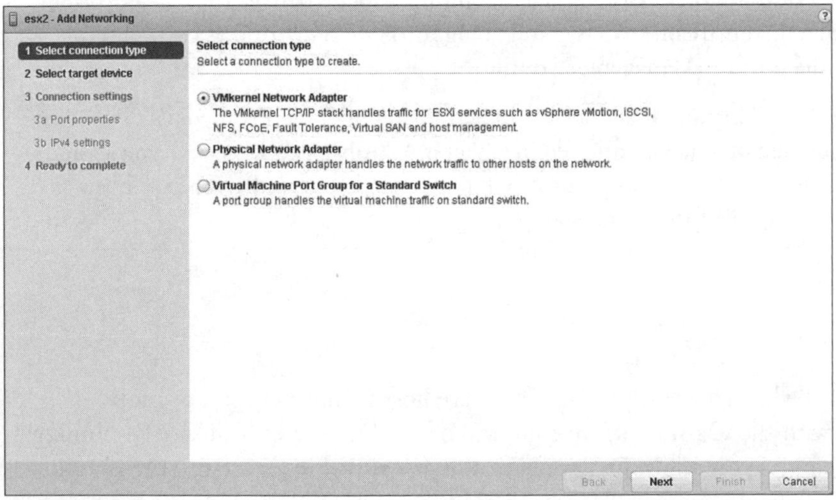

Figure 12.13   Adding a new VMkernel port to vSwitch0 for vMotion traffic

Ensure that the target device is vSwitch0 and continue forward. You'll be greeted with a screen asking for a variety of port properties. Let's review the properties:

- **Network label**: If you look back at the "Naming Conventions" section, you'll see we decided to call this port group "vMotion."

- **VLAN ID**: We've already selected VLAN 205 for vMotion, so enter 205 here.

- **IP settings**: To keep things simple, we're going to select IPv4, although if you are feeling adventurous in your environment, you can feel free to opt for IPv6.

- **TCP/IP stack**: Use the "Default" stack, as we have no need to use any custom gateways for traffic. (Our vMotion isn't even routable on our network.)

- **Enabled services**: Select the "vMotion traffic" checkbox to allow the hypervisor to use this VMkernel port for vMotion. If you forget to check this box, the host will not be marked as a valid source to send or receive VMs within the vSphere Cluster.

You can also review the settings in Figure 12.14.

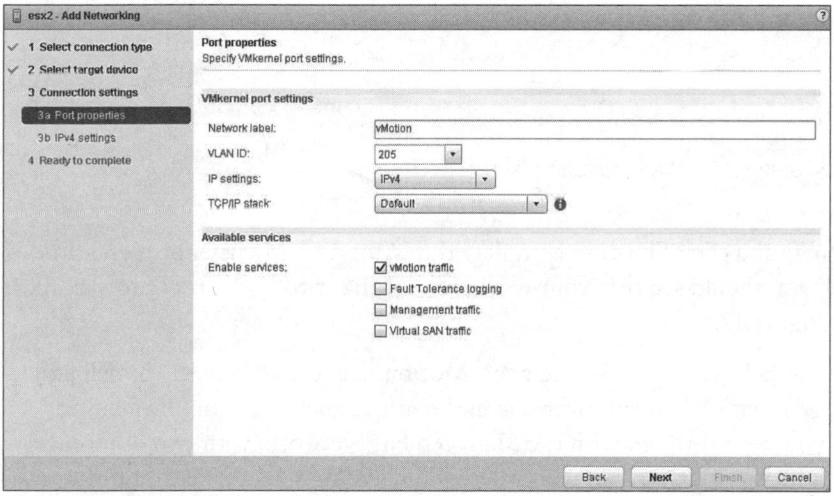

Figure 12.14   Port properties for the vMotion VMkernel port

In the next screen, we need to enter an IP address for this VMkernel port. That's different from what you might remember in the VM port group creation process. This is because a VM port group is just a housing for VMs, each of which have their own IP address, while a VMkernel port is used by the host to communicate on the network for its services.

In the case of Initech Corp, we've already been assigned a network subnet of 192.168.205.0/24 to use for vMotion traffic. To make life easier, we'll pick 192.168.205.2 since the host we're configuring is called esx2. The CIDR notation mask of /24 won't work for the vSphere Web Client—we'll have to provide a full dotted decimal mask. A /24 translates to 255.255.255.0. Thus, your screen should look something like that shown in Figure 12.15.

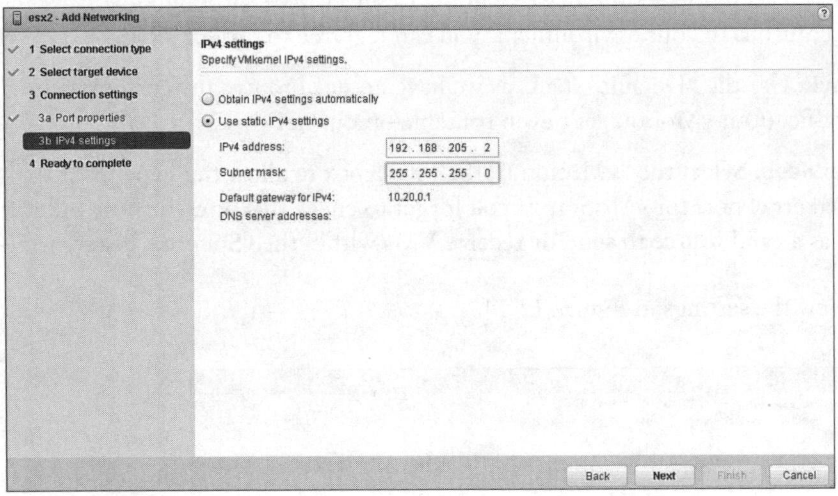

Figure 12.15   IPv4 settings for the vMotion VMkernel port

Review your settings and click Finish to complete the vMotion VMkernel port creation. If all was successful, you should see that your vSwitch0 now has two VMkernel ports similar to that shown in Figure 12.16.

However, notice the failover policy for the new vMotion network uses both vmnic0 and vmnic1 as Active adapters? We need to fix that and mark vmnic0 as a Standby adapter. Repeat the steps you went through with the Management Network, with two differences: Enable the Override checkbox for Failover order, and make sure vmnic0 is Standby and vmnic1 is Active.

Figure 12.17 shows that vmnic0 is a standby NIC for our vMotion VMkernel port.

We've now made sure that vMotion will primarily use the vmnic1 adapter, and if it fails, will switch over to the vmnic0 adapter. Again, introducing redundancy is a great thing that should be done whenever possible.

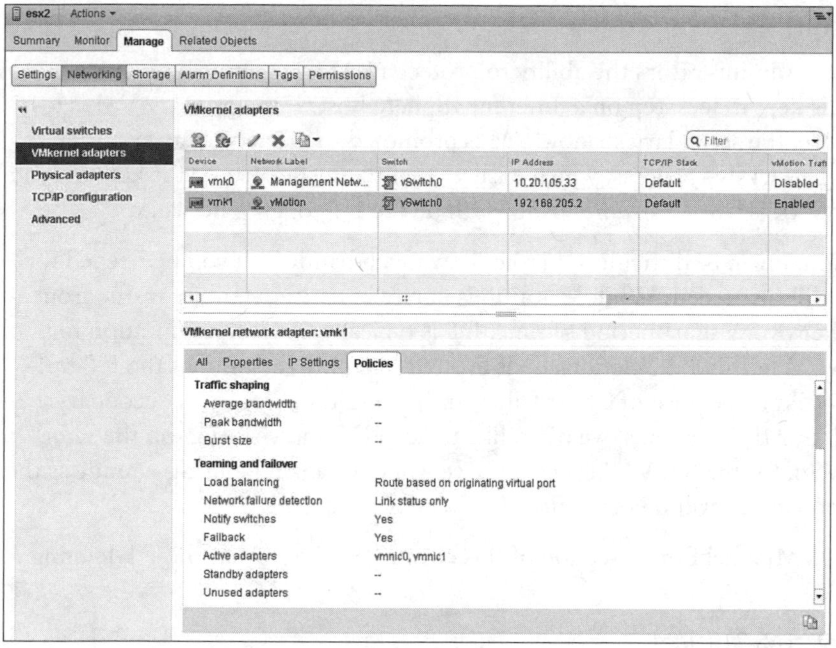

Figure 12.16   A list of VMkernel ports in use on vSwitch0

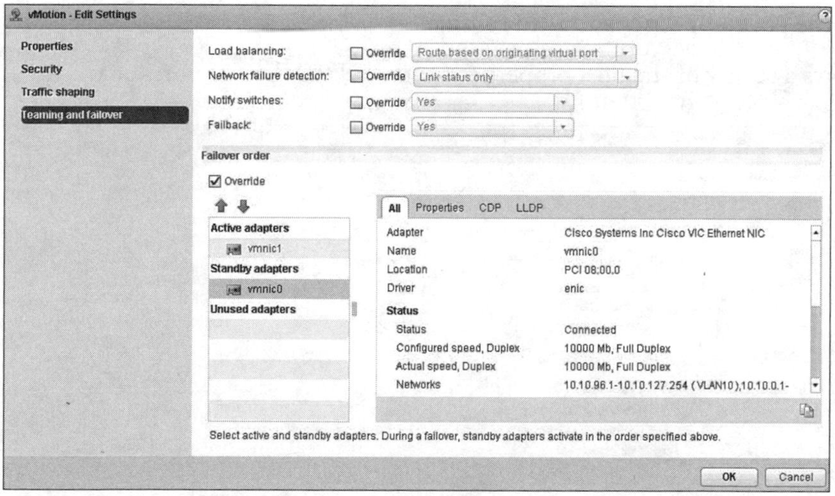

Figure 12.17   Marking vmnic0 as the Standby adapter for vMotion

Fault Tolerance

FT offers VMware Administrators the ability to protect a VM by creating a secondary shadow VM that is kept in lockstep on a different vSphere host. If the primary VM is lost due to a host failure, the secondary shadow VM is promoted to primary in a very brief period of time. The lockstep process, which ensures that the secondary VM is kept in sync with the primary VM, is what consumes bandwidth on the FT logging network.

Much like vMotion, it can be difficult to predict how much bandwidth will be needed for FT and where it will be needed. While vMotion is bursty in nature, sending traffic from one host to another over a short period of time, FT is typically of a longer duration for very specific VMs. When an FT relationship is created, the only reason that the FT traffic would cease would be because of a host failure or because the primary or secondary VM were moved. For these reasons, we often like to keep FT and vMotion on the same network adapter. So, for the FT VMkernel port, we will once again be using vmnic1 as the Active adapter and vmnic0 will be marked as the Standby adapter.

Referring to the "VMkernel Ports" section of this chapter, we know that the FT logging network is using:

- **Network**: 192.168.210.0/24

- **VLAN ID**: 210

Use this information to create a new VMkernel port on vSwitch0. There will be a few changes, such as the port properties and IPv4 settings.

Figure 12.18 shows a review of the port properties for the FT VMkernel port.

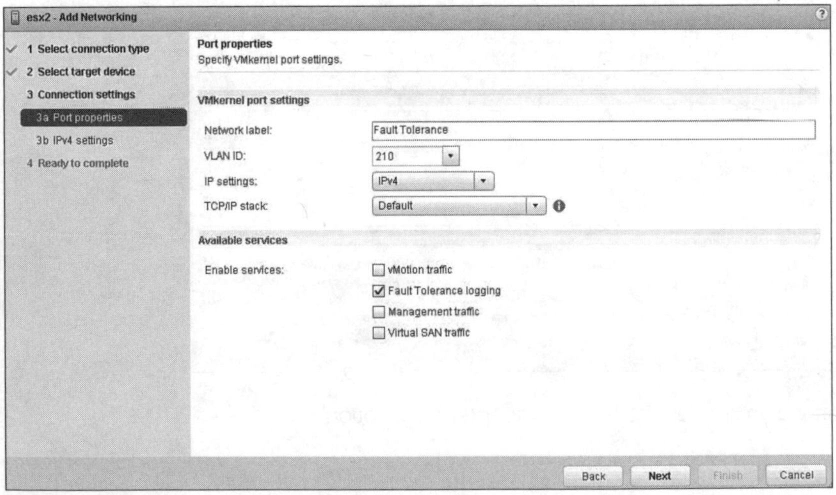

Figure 12.18   Port properties for the FT VMkernel port

The IPv4 Settings for the FT VMkernel port are shown in Figure 12.19.

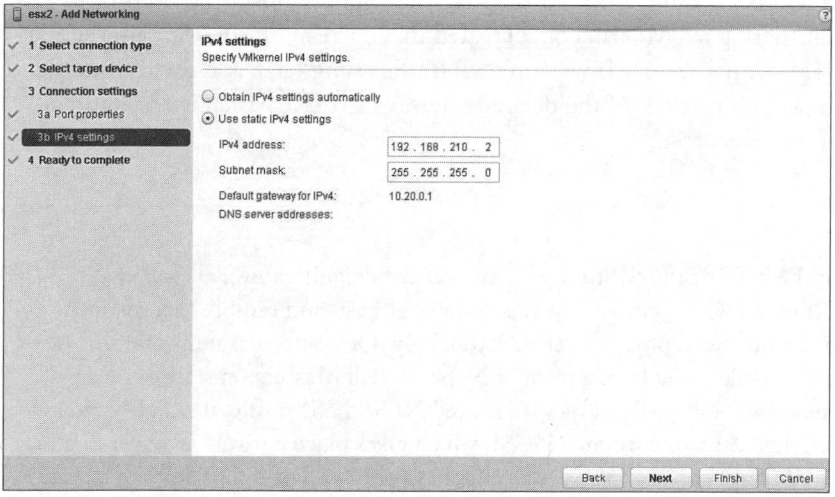

Figure 12.19 IPv4 settings for the FT VMkernel port

Don't forget to change the failover order for the FT network, making vmnic1 the Active adapter and vmnic0 a Standby adapter, by selecting vmnic0 and clicking the down arrow until it sits in the Standby adapters section. Figure 12.20 shows the end results.

You're at the home stretch—just one more VMkernel port to create to handle NFS Storage traffic.

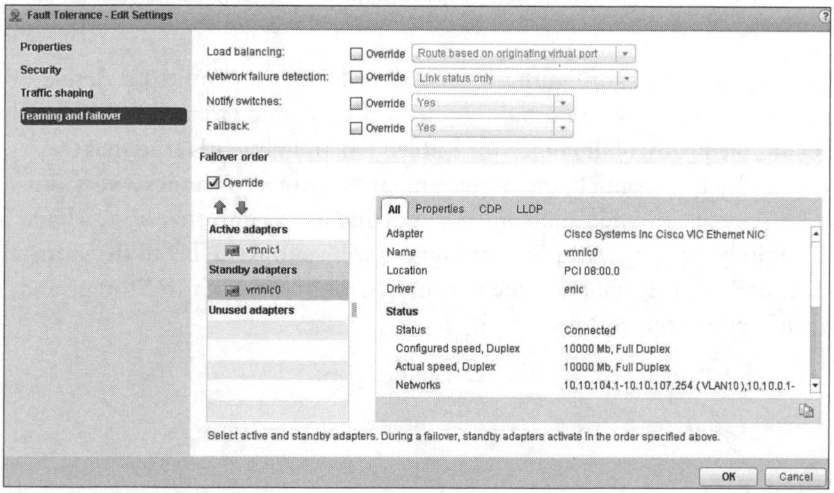

Figure 12.20 Marking vmnic0 as the Standby adapter for FT

NFS Storage

The final requirement is to connect NFS Storage to the vSphere hosts. To do this, we want to ensure that there is a VMkernel port created that corresponds to the same subnet that the NFS storage array lives on. If we don't, all traffic going back and forth from the NFS storage array will be sent out of the default gateway of vmk0, which is not optimal and typically not even supported.

> **REAL WORLD**
>
> Sending traffic to the NFS or iSCSI storage array over the default gateway is called Routed NFS or Routed iSCSI. Support for this is shaky at best, and requires a very deep understanding of the upstream physical network topology, QoS settings, and some sort of priority flow control. Unless you have a team of Network Jedi Masters on staff who can guarantee low latency and low packet loss with routed NFS/iSCSI traffic, it's highly recommended to do Switched NFS or Switched iSCSI, which takes place entirely at Layer 2. This requires having a VMkernel port on the same subnet as your NFS or iSCSI storage target. For general use cases, see Chapter 14, "iSCSI General Use Cases," or Chapter 16, "NFS General Use Cases," for more details.

It's essential to ensure a quality connection to any sort of storage array. VMs are highly sensitive to disk-related latency and tolerate loss rather poorly. This is mostly due to the fact that VMs are being tricked into thinking they are sending SCSI commands to a local device, when in fact those commands are being packaged up into packets and shot off into the network to a remote array. It is your job as the VMware Administrator to give those packets the best possible chance to reach their destination, and return, in as little time as possible.

Because of this fact, we're going to configure the failover order so that vmnic0 is Active and vmnic1 is Standby. In essence, we're somewhat dedicating vmnic0 to the IP Storage traffic, with NFS being the protocol of choice for Initech Corp. While it's true that the Management Network also uses vmnic0, the Management Network consumes a very tiny amount of bandwidth (except for when someone is importing a VM into that host, which is extremely rare). Additionally, any VM protected by FT will send write IO to the storage array and to the secondary VM. Having unique network adapters for both IP Storage and FT prevents the write traffic from competing with itself.

Let's review the network settings for the NFS Storage network:

- **Network**: 192.168.220.0/24
- **VLAN ID**: 220

Creating the VMkernel port is nearly an identical process to the vMotion and FT process you followed previously, except there is no service to enable for NFS.

Figure 12.21 shows a review of the port properties for the NFS Storage VMkernel port.

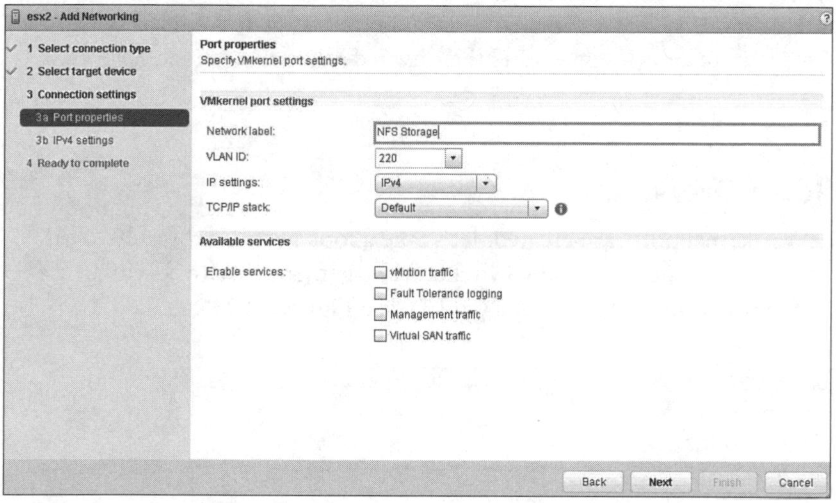

Figure 12.21 Port properties for the FT VMkernel port

The IPv4 Settings for the NFS Storage VMkernel port are shown in Figure 12.22.

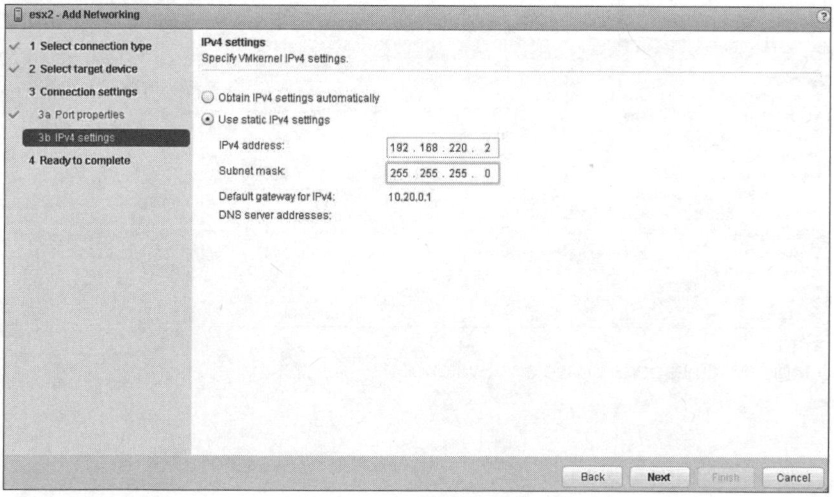

Figure 12.22 IPv4 settings for the FT VMkernel port

NOTE

Does it seem weird that there is no service checkbox for NFS Storage? It might, but rest assured, just having a VMkernel port on the same subnet as your NFS storage array will ensure that the hypervisor uses this NFS Storage VMkernel port to communicate. But don't take my word for it—SSH to your vSphere host and run "esxcfg-route -l" to view the routing table and see a list of known subnets and their related VMkernel ports.

VMkernel Failover Overview

Now that all of the VMkernel ports are created, let's take a look at the end results. You should see a list of four VMkernel ports on vSwitch0: Management Network (vmk0), vMotion (vmk1), FT (vmk2), and NFS Storage (vmk3) (see Figure 12.23).

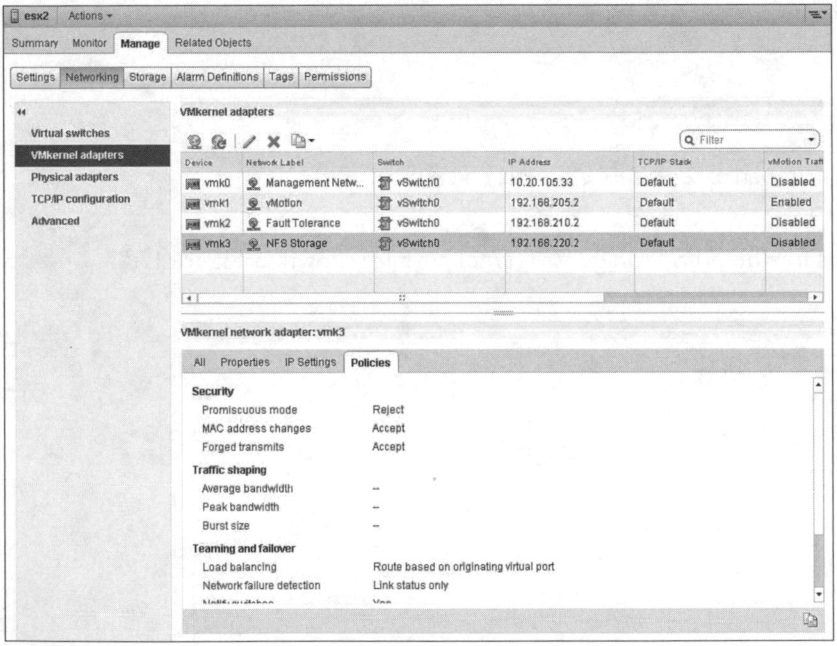

Figure 12.23   The four VMkernel ports in use on vSwitch0

Looking at the failover order for the various VMkernel ports, a pattern emerges. If you look carefully at the active and standby use of each network adapter, you'll find the following to be true:

- **Active use of vmnic0**: Management Network and NFS Storage

- **Active use of vmnic1**: FT and vMotion

- **Standby use of vmnic0**: FT and vMotion

- **Standby use of vmnic1**: Management Network and NFS Storage

- **Active use of both vmnic0 and vmnic1**: VM port groups (Web, Application, and Database Servers)

We've basically divided up the two network adapters to handle the two types of traffic that are very sensitive to latency or consume a lot of bandwidth: NFS Storage is sensitive to latency, and vMotion consumes a lot of bandwidth. They will not use the same network adapter as an uplink unless one of the uplinks fails.

The remaining traffic types—Management, FT, and VM traffic—tend to consume a little amount of bandwidth or are designed to handle a little bit more latency. VMware HA heartbeats on the Management network, for example, can miss a few heartbeats without declaring a failure. The vast majority of VMs are already well aware of how flaky a TCP/IP connection can be and will use the protocol's resiliency to handle any missed or late packets, with the exception being some legacy applications or business critical applications (BCAs) that need a large quantity of bandwidth or low latency. Also, FT is very rarely used due to the vast number of caveats and limitations.

Therefore, if we were to draw the network paths out as a solid black line for Active and a dotted grey line for Standby, it would look something like Figure 12.24.

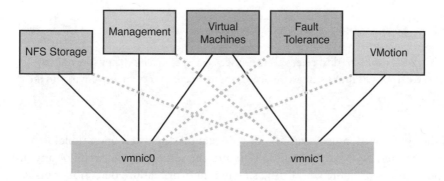

Figure 12.24　Network adapter paths for vSwitch0 traffic

Final Tuning

One last thing we want to edit is the security settings on vSwitch0. By default, a standard vSwitch allows both MAC address changes and forged transmits. This allows a VM to modify its effective MAC address for receiving frames and to transmit frames with a different MAC address than what has been configured in vSphere. While there are certain situations that warrant this, it isn't necessarily something we want enabled.

To remedy this, edit vSwitch0 and set all three security policies to Reject. Unless an administrator has manually set an override on the policies, the changes will automatically trickle down to the port groups. This configuration is shown in Figure 12.25.

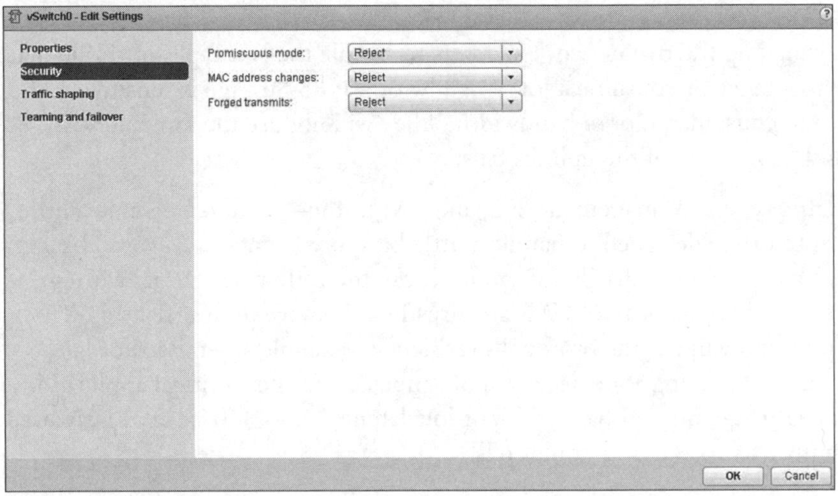

Figure 12.25   Network adapter paths for vSwitch0 traffic

> **NOTE**
>
> A distributed vSwitch is configured to reject all three security settings by default. A standard vSwitch does not. Keep this in mind when you are trying to secure your virtual environment using a standard vSwitch.

This concludes the configuration necessary to get your standard vSwitch operational in a sleek and efficient manner. Notice that we didn't go into the settings of vSwitch0 or any of the underlying port groups to fiddle with traffic shaping, network failure detection, notify switches, or failback? That's because changes to these settings are often the exception to the rule and should only be changed when the use case specifically calls out a need. The default values work great for the majority of environments that exist today.

Configuring Additional vSphere Hosts

The changes made to vSwitch0 have so far only been done on the vSphere host named esx2. We still need to execute the entire set of changes to the other vSphere host named esx1. Because each vSphere host acts as the control plane for a standard vSwitch, you must configure every single vSphere host individually, either by hand or by way of a script.

Make sure that the changes you perform on esx1 are identical to the changes you made on esx2, with the exception being IP addresses—each host needs a unique set of IP addresses. Here is a list of IP addresses you can use with vSphere host esx1:

- **Management traffic:** 10.20.105.32 /16 on VLAN 20

- **vMotion traffic:** 192.168.205.1 /24 on VLAN 205

- **FT logging:** 192.168.210.1 on VLAN 210

- **NFS traffic:** 192.168.220.1 /24 on VLAN 220

REAL WORLD

If you think configuring two vSphere hosts by hand is a challenge, try dozens of them! While ultimately out of scope for this book, we strongly recommend finding a script written in your favorite language, such as VMware PowerCLI, to perform the standard vSwitch configuration on your vSphere hosts. This is both much quicker to execute for many vSwitches and less error-prone than typing it all by hand. We're going to assume that you don't have access to Host Profiles since you're using a standard vSwitch.

Summary

You should now have a clear concept of the steps necessary to go through the entire process of creating a standard vSwitch—from the planning and design to the configuration itself. You might also now start to see some of the hassle involved with using a standard vSwitch, especially in a larger environment, along with how limited the standard vSwitch is from a feature perspective. In the next chapter on the distributed vSwitch, you'll see a much greater set of tools and features available to make life a bit easier and handling traffic more efficient.

Chapter 13

Distributed vSwitch Design

Key Concepts

- Distributed vSwitch Design
- Ensuring Quality of Service (QoS)
- Distributed Port Groups
- Health Check
- Fully Automated Design
- Hybrid Automation Design

Introduction

In the previous chapter, we took a pair of servers with a freshly installed copy of ESXi 5.5 and configured a standard vSwitch to support the Initech Corp use case. We're going to take many common components from that use case and apply them again with a few twists. By the end of this chapter, you should have a well-designed and implemented distributed vSwitch used by our two vSphere hosts and a solid understanding of the many choices that are presented with the powerful and feature-rich distributed vSwitch.

Distributed vSwitch Design

In the previous chapter, we highlighted three reasons that you might decide to forgo the distributed vSwitch: licensing cost, a small environment size, and control plane availability. Now, let's look at two good reasons why you would want to embrace the distributed vSwitch in your environment:

- **Feature Requirements**: The distributed vSwitch offers a vast number of features above and beyond the standard vSwitch. We won't enumerate them all here, but for a full list, refer to Chapter 9, "vSphere Distributed Switch." As an example—if you require the use of enhanced quality of service control that is not available with your upstream hardware, you'll need to use a distributed vSwitch. You might also need a feature that is specifically bundled with vSphere Enterprise Plus, such as Storage Distributed Resource Scheduler (SDRS), vFlash Read Cache, or Auto Deploy. You might also want to take advantage of the distributed vSwitch because it is available at that license level.

- **Larger Environment Size**: Larger environments tend to focus on supported "out of the box" features to ensure scalability. While it's true that you can script the creation of a standard vSwitch across an environment, not everyone out there wants to go through the trouble. For those with double or triple digit quantities of vSphere hosts, the ability to easily scale out a distributed vSwitch to the environment is attractive. It is worth noting that there is no "correct" environment size necessary to go with a distributed vSwitch.

This isn't the end-all-be-all list of reasons, but two of the most common that we encounter out in the field.

Use Case

Initech Corp has a pair of vSphere hosts running ESXi 5.5 in their production data center located in Chicago. As the VMware Administrator for the corporation, you've been tasked with the creation and configuration of a virtual network. Due to a requirement for providing quality of service assurances for network traffic and a need for Storage IO Control (SIOC), the company has purchased vSphere Enterprise Plus licensing, which allows you to build a virtual network on the distributed vSwitch. Each vSphere host has a pair of 10 Gb Ethernet network adapters connected to a redundant upstream physical network.

The virtual network should be capable of handling traffic for Management, vMotion, Fault Tolerance (FT), and iSCSI storage. It also needs to be able to pass along traffic for three different types of workloads: Web Servers on VLAN 100, Application Servers on VLAN 110, and Database Servers on VLAN 120.

NOTE

Yes, we're throwing you a little curve ball with the iSCSI Storage requirement. We hope this will showcase any differences between creating a VMkernel port for NFS versus iSCSI. Both NFS and iSCSI are covered in greater detail later in Chapter 14, "iSCSI General Use Cases," and Chapter 16, "NFS General Use Cases."

Naming Conventions

To start with, let's come up with names for our various VMkernel ports:

- **Management**: Let's go with simply "Management" this time around.

- **vMotion**: The name "vMotion" is simple and effective.

- **Fault Tolerance Logging**: Either "FT" or "Fault Tolerance" work well, but let's go for "Fault Tolerance" to make it as clear as possible for future administrators.

- **iSCSI Storage**: We'll use "iSCSI Storage" to avoid any confusion, as this easily proclaims both the protocol (iSCSI) and the need to pass along storage traffic.

NOTE

You could also add networking and VLAN information to your VMkernel distributed port group names, if desired. An example being "vMotion_192.168.205.x_V205"—just be careful not to make the names too similar to your virtual machine distributed port group names. A hurried administrator might add a VM's network to a VMkernel distributed port group by accident.

Just like last time, we did our homework on the various VLAN IDs and subnets used for the various VM networks. We'll keep the names the same, as there is no real need to change up the naming convention just because it's a different type of switch. A name is a just a name. Those names, again, are:

- **Web Servers on VLAN 100**: Web_192.168.100.x_V100

- **Application Servers on VLAN 110**: App_192.168.110.x_V110

- **Database Servers on VLAN 120**: DB_192.168.120.x_V120

> **NOTE**
>
> As a reminder—you need to ensure that the VMkernel and VM VLANs exist on the upstream network device to avoid any issues with upstream communications.

And finally, we need to come up with a name for the distributed vSwitch itself. You'll find that the creation wizard tends to call everything "DSwitch #" by default. We don't really see a reason to put the word "DSwitch" into your distributed vSwitch—that seems redundant. It seems fair to just call it something fitting, like "Production_LAN."

The next part of the design should focus on how we plan to provide quality of service for the network traffic types.

Ensuring Quality of Service

There are a couple of different methods available for providing some sort of quality of service in a virtual network plumbed with a distributed vSwitch. These options are Network IO Control (NIOC) and priority tagging with IEEE standard 802.1p. We covered both of these technologies in earlier chapters, but let's review at a high level how each works and how we can use them to our advantage.

Network IO Control

NIOC is a VMware technology used to weigh and limit outbound traffic types within vSphere hosts participating in a distributed vSwitch. It uses share values assigned to Network Resource Pools to provide a priority scheme for balancing traffic types. This is similar to the use of shares with CPU and memory, just with network traffic. Shares only become relevant in times of congestion and are dormant at any other time.

There are also limits available to put a hard cap on how much bandwidth can be consumed by a specific Network Resource Pool. Limits are always active, no matter the level of congestion, and therefore should be configured only when you have a complete understanding and acceptance that you might be leaving perfectly good bandwidth unused. Also, note that these limits apply only to traffic coming *from* VMs but have no affect traffic going *to* VMs.

By combining the concepts of shares and limits, we can help the virtual network understand which traffic should be granted more or less networking bandwidth. This ensures that quality of service can be provided to our guest VMs.

VMware comes with a set of NIOC default configuration values out of the box. Let's review the default pools and their default values for shares and limits:

- **Management**: Normal shares (50), Unlimited bandwidth
- **vMotion**: Normal shares (50), Unlimited bandwidth
- **Fault Tolerance**: Normal shares (50), Unlimited bandwidth
- **iSCSI**: Normal shares (50), Unlimited bandwidth
- **NFS**: Normal shares (50), Unlimited bandwidth
- **Virtual Machines**: High shares (100), Unlimited bandwidth

Figure 13.1 shows how the NIOC values look in the vSphere Web Client. Note that they are listed under the Resource Allocation section of a distributed vSwitch.

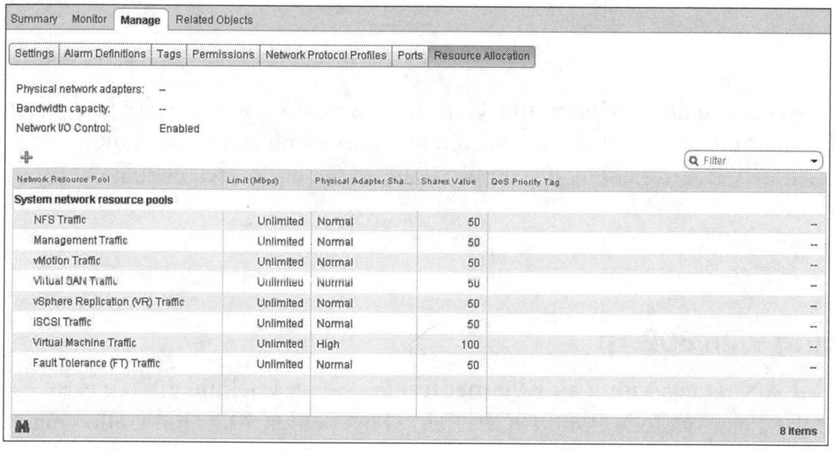

Network Resource Pool	Limit (Mbps)	Physical Adapter Sha...	Shares Value	QoS Priority Tag
System network resource pools				
NFS Traffic	Unlimited	Normal	50	--
Management Traffic	Unlimited	Normal	50	--
vMotion Traffic	Unlimited	Normal	50	--
Virtual SAN Traffic	Unlimited	Normal	50	--
vSphere Replication (VR) Traffic	Unlimited	Normal	50	--
iSCSI Traffic	Unlimited	Normal	50	--
Virtual Machine Traffic	Unlimited	High	100	--
Fault Tolerance (FT) Traffic	Unlimited	Normal	50	--

Figure 13.1 Default NIOC values for a distributed vSwitch

Did you find the idea of giving VMs a high priority and leaving everything else at a normal priority surprising? Or how about the idea of giving every type of traffic an unlimited amount of bandwidth? Let's look at it this way—there's no need to enforce limits or special share values unless your use case calls for it. By giving nearly all traffic types a Normal share value, we're saying that everyone gets an even slice of the bandwidth pie. The only exception is VMs, which can have a slice of pie that is roughly twice the size of anyone else (100 shares for VMs versus 50 shares for anyone else).

Share values only affect traffic flows during times of contention, and only for active traffic types. Adding all of the above share sizes, we have 450 shares (50 + 50 + 50 + 50 +50 + 50 + 100 + 50 = 450). And 50/450 is approximately 11%. So with the previously mentioned limits, if every single traffic type were active and causing contention, the VMs have to compete with each other over 22% of the bandwidth and the other traffic types each get 11%. It's more likely that only a few types of traffic are active at the same time—meaning only those active traffic types are used in calculating the bandwidth allocation. If you need a refresher on NIOC, refer to the "Network I/O Control" section in Chapter 9.

There's little need to change the default values for most environments. However, let's imagine that you are a bit squeamish about letting vMotion eat up your entire 10 Gb network adapter. So for our environment, we'll set a vMotion Traffic limit to 80% of an uplink by capping it at 8 Gbps, or 8192 Mbps (8 Gbps x 1024 Mbps per Gigabit). This will guarantee that vMotion will not hog all of an uplink. We'll revisit this later after the distributed vSwitch has been created and we have access to NIOC.

REAL WORLD

As a rule, you do not need to limit vMotion to 8 Gbps in your environment. We're just showing that it's something you can do if your requirements or comfort level warrant it. vMotion loves to eat up the entire uplink if it thinks it can, which has caused us some headaches in the past.

Priority Tagging with 802.1p

Much like with a VLAN ID tag within an Ethernet frame, the idea behind 802.1p is to insert a value into the Priority Code Point (PCP) field. This field is 3 bits long, allowing for 8 possibilities (2 values per bit ^ 3 bits = 8 combinations). Priority ranges from 0 (the lowest) to 7 (the highest). Within NIOC is the ability to set the priority tag for each type of traffic, which is called the "QoS Priority Tag" within vSphere.

By default, NIOC does not set any values for the PCP field. You can edit any of the various traffic types and add your own. Keep in mind that 802.1p tags apply to Ethernet frames, not IP packets, and thus have some limitations on usefulness when they leave a particular network segment.

REAL WORLD

There is no real IEEE standard behind 802.1p. The upstream physical network can ignore the tags or process them however they desire. However, it is typical to treat Ethernet frames tagged with high value PCP tags with higher priority. What we often find is that physical switches use Weighted Round Robin Scheduling (WRRS) with a buffer for each priority level. High priority buffers get picked more often. Make sure to chat with your network team and find out if they use 802.1p, agree on a value, and then move forward—don't just pick one all willy-nilly.

However, these tags can be useful when you wish to assign various levels of priority to traffic within your Ethernet environment. You could, for example, give a higher weight to your iSCSI storage traffic to help avoid congestion in the upstream physical networks.

We won't be using 802.1p in our example here, but it's important to know that it exists and can be configured on each Network Resource Pool within NIOC. Additionally, one neat feature with vSphere 5.5 is the ability to set the tag on a distributed port group with a traffic filter. In this format, the tag is called the Class of Service (CoS) value. We go into that a bit deeper in the next segment.

Differentiated Service Code Point

Another method of providing quality of service is by way of the Differentiated Service Code Point (DSCP), a new feature available with vSphere 5.5. DSCP supports 64 different tags (0 through 63) and is inserted into the IP packet rather than the Ethernet frame. This allows the DSCP tag to provide a more end-to-end level of functionality throughout the data center.

The DSCP tag is set within a traffic rule on a port group, as shown in Figure 13.2.

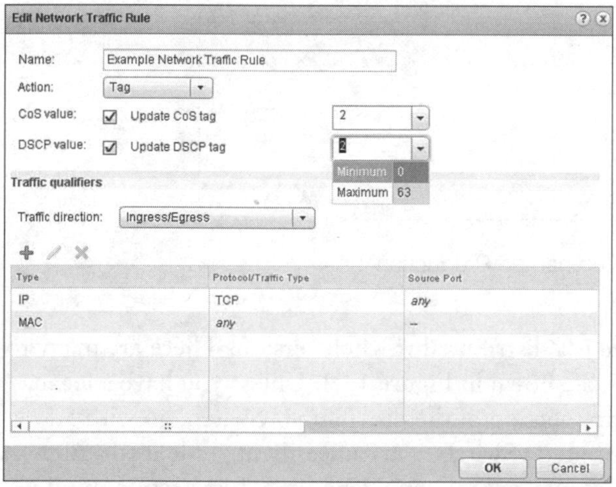

Figure 13.2   Defining a traffic rule with CoS and DSCP values

The use of DSCP is pretty far out of scope for our particular use case, but again—you should know it exists should you encounter a workload that can benefit from it.

Both CoS and DSCP are great examples of how the physical and virtual networks can work together under a common set of rules. Both technologies help ensure that your critical workloads get the network priority required to meet business demand.

Creating the Distributed vSwitch

Unlike a standard vSwitch's vSwitch0, there is no default distributed vSwitch created for you at installation. You have to roll up your sleeves and make one yourself.

To begin, navigate to the network section of the vSphere Web Client and find the Chicago data center. You can then create a distributed vSwitch by way of a right click on the data center or a trip to the Actions menu when the data center object is selected. The first requirement is a name, as shown in Figure 13.3: Production_LAN.

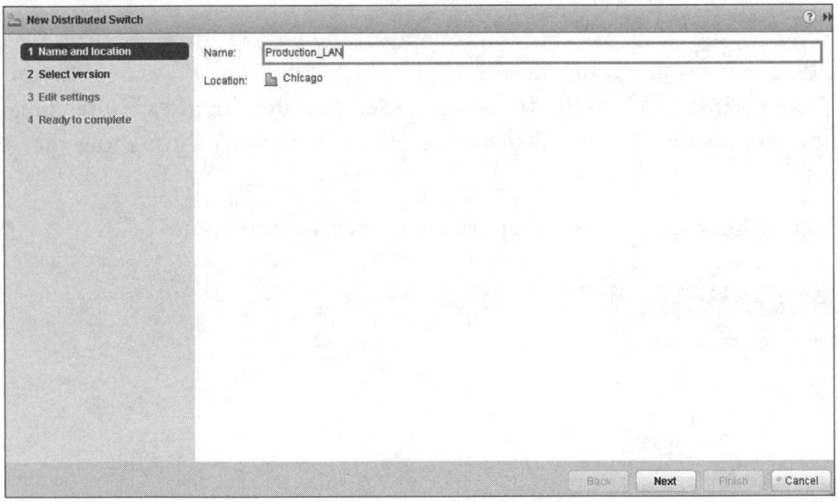

Figure 13.3 Creating a distributed vSwitch named Production_LAN

Simple enough, right? Our next choice is a distributed vSwitch version. There are many to choose from: 4.0, 4.1, 5.0, 5.1, and 5.5, as shown in Figure 13.4. Unless you have a legacy environment that requires using a legacy version of the distributed vSwitch, go with 5.5. And if you have an older existing distributed vSwitch, you can easily upgrade it to a higher version, so long as it meets the requirements, without any downtime. Just keep in mind that there is no downgrade to an older version, and that upgrades to a newer version do not happen automatically. Each version also shows off a few of the new features that were included with that release.

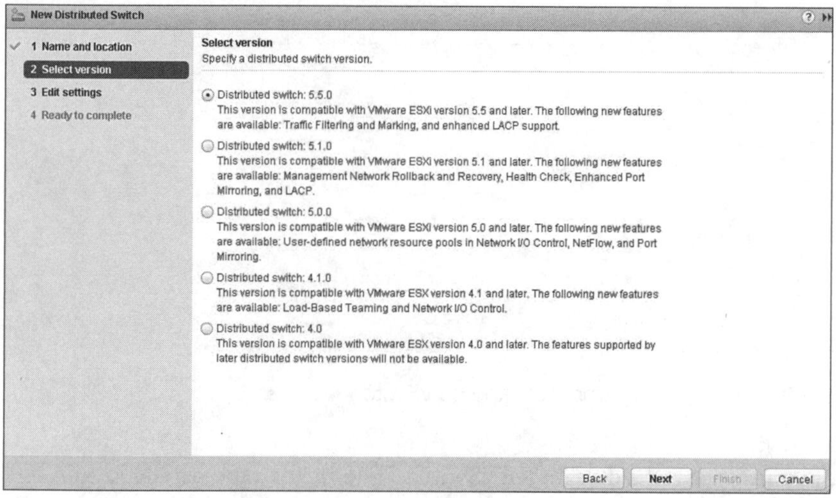

Figure 13.4   Selecting Distributed Switch version 5.5

Now we're prompted on a few specific quantities and features. Let's review them:

- **Number of uplinks**: This value determines the maximum number of NIC ports that any of this switch's hosts can connect to this switch. And because our hosts only have two network adapters, we'll set the number of uplinks to 2. You can always increase this value later if you need to.

- **Network IO Control (NIOC)**: This is enabled by default, which is exactly what we want. NIOC is one of the best things about a distributed vSwitch and was set to disabled by default in past versions.

- **Default port group**: Keep this box checked so that we can automatically generate a new port group.

- **Port group name**: Since the wizard is offering to make a port group for us, let's go ahead and have it create one for our Management traffic that we'll need later on in this chapter. Change the name to **Management** and put it aside for later.

As a result, your wizard should look like that shown in Figure 13.5.

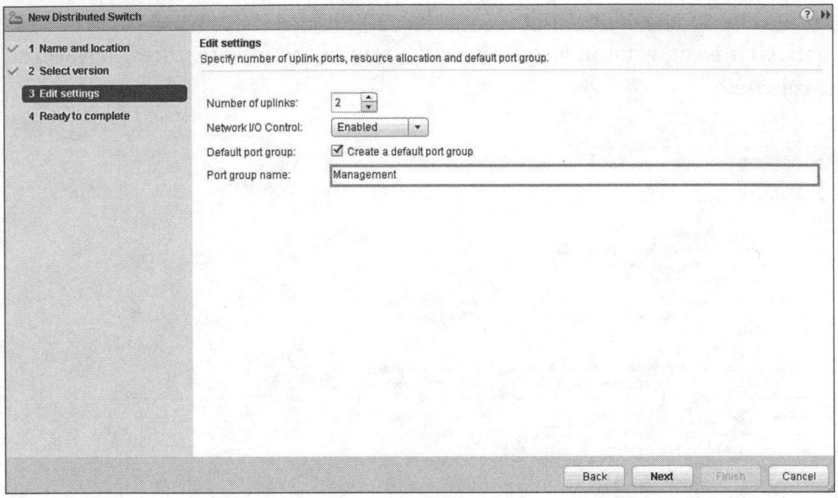

Figure 13.5   Editing the settings for our new distributed vSwitch

Congratulations, you just created a distributed vSwitch. The ticker-tape parade is on its way. If you navigate to the Network view in the vSphere Web Client, your environment should have a VM Network and a Production_LAN network. Underneath the Production_LAN network will be two entities: a port group named Management and an uplink group named Production_LAN-DVUplinks-##. Figure 13.6 shows an example of what our environment looks like to compare with.

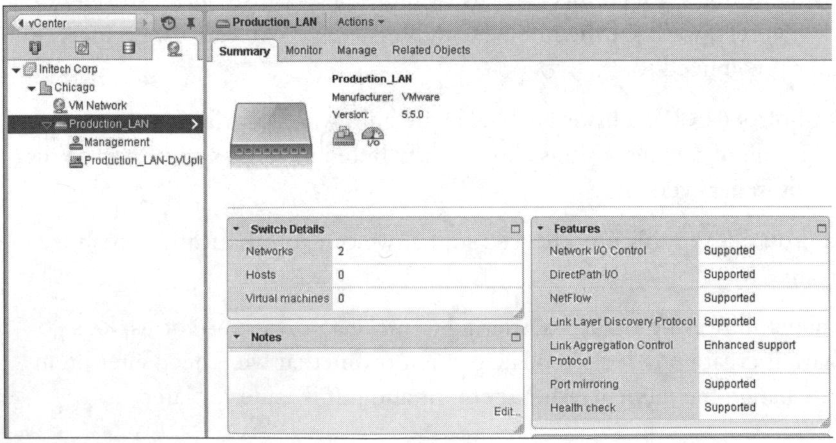

Figure 13.6   A view of the network for the Chicago data center

It should feel somewhat empty at this point. That's because the switch is effectively doing nothing right now, with only a very basic configuration. Let's change that by configuring the distributed vSwitch further and getting it ready for use.

Network Adapters

When we worked with a standard vSwitch, one of the first things you were asked to do was look at the network adapters on vSwitch0 and make sure that both were added to the switch. If you tried to do that with a distributed vSwitch, you would quickly find that it's not possible. That's because it creates a relationship between a distributed uplink and a host's physical network adapter.

If you view the topology of the distributed vSwitch, you'll see two lonely Uplinks in the DVUplinks group on the right with zero NIC Adapters listed, as shown in Figure 13.7.

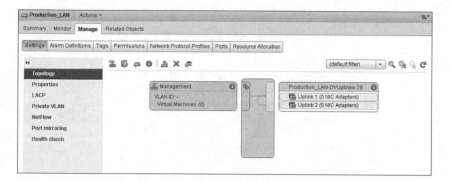

Figure 13.7   There are no uplinks added to the distributed vSwitch yet

Don't worry, this is completely intentional and normal because we haven't added any hosts to the distributed vSwitch yet—remember, the distributed vSwitch is a vCenter construct, and therefore hosts must join the switch. This is a bit different from standard vSwitches, where we create them on each host individually. As each host is added, we'll see the quantity of uplinks change. We'll also see the relationship created between a physical network adapter on a host and the logical distributed uplink assignment.

Let's move along to the port group creation sections and revisit the network adapters after we're finished adding hosts to the switch. You'll then be able to easily spot the differences.

Distributed Port Groups for Virtual Machines

We need to create three port groups for our VM traffic types: Web, Application, and Database. The naming convention chosen earlier is:

- **Web Servers on VLAN 100**: Web_192.168.100.x_V100

- **Application Servers on VLAN 110**: App_192.168.110.x_V110

- **Database Servers on VLAN 120**: DB_192.168.120.x_V120

Let's begin by creating the Web Servers VM distributed port group. To begin, make sure you have the Production_LAN distributed vSwitch highlighted in the vSphere Web Client and choose **New Distributed Port Group** from the Actions menu. Enter the name of the distributed port group (see Figure 13.8) and click **Next**.

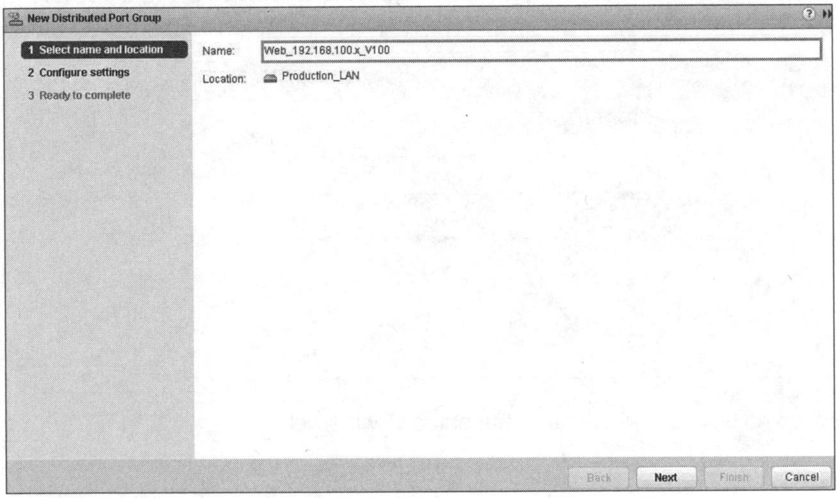

Figure 13.8   Creating the Web Server distributed port group

The next screen will require a number of settings to be filled out. We review them all here:

- **Port binding**: Although a much more important decision in prior versions, port binding has now become a trivial choice in almost all use cases. In particular, as long as vCenter is running and the maximum number of switch ports hasn't been reached, static binding, the default choice, and the choice we recommend, ensures that every VM on the port group is given a port on the switch regardless of its (the VM's) power state. Dynamic binding has been deprecated by VMware and plans to terminate their support for it soon. In other words, don't use it. Ephemeral binding (no binding) offloads port state handling to each ESXi host. This is rather intensive on the host and is only needed in corner cases where the vCenter server is offline.

- **Port allocation**: Elastic binding, the default, is a great way to ensure your ports scale and is recommended. It was introduced with vSphere 5.1 as a way to avoid having to manually adjust port counts for a distributed port group or consume a greater quantity of memory with a very large port count.

- **Number of ports**: Because elastic is enabled, the default value of 8 is just fine. You could bump up this number if you absolutely hate the number 8 for some reason, but there's little reason to do so.

- **Network resource pool**: Leave as default during creation. When we visit the NIOC settings, you'll have the opportunity to create resource pools for individual VM distributed port groups.

- **VLAN type**: The VMs will need Virtual Switch Tagging (VST), meaning you will need to select **VLAN**. If you were using External Switch Tagging (EST), the type would be None, or if you were using Virtual Guest Tagging (VGT), the type would be VLAN Trunking.

- **VLAN ID**: The Web Servers use VLAN 100, so enter 100.

- **Advanced customization**: Leave this unchecked. Rather than set up the policies on a per-distributed port group basis, we'll show you a trick to configure all of them at once.

The end result should be a settings page similar to that shown in Figure 13.9.

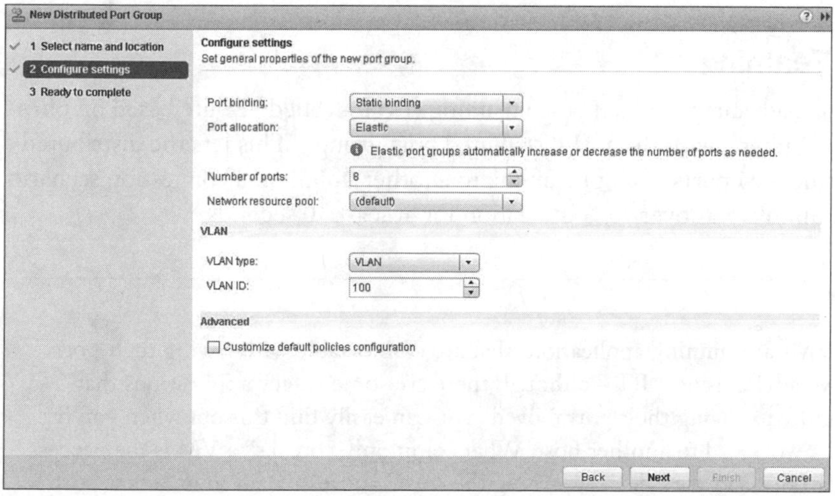

Figure 13.9   Settings used for the Web Server distributed port group

Make sure to repeat the process for the two remaining VM distributed port groups. When completed, you should have a distributed vSwitch with five total port groups—three for the VMs, one for management (that we are not using yet), and one for the DVUplinks, as shown in Figure 13.10.

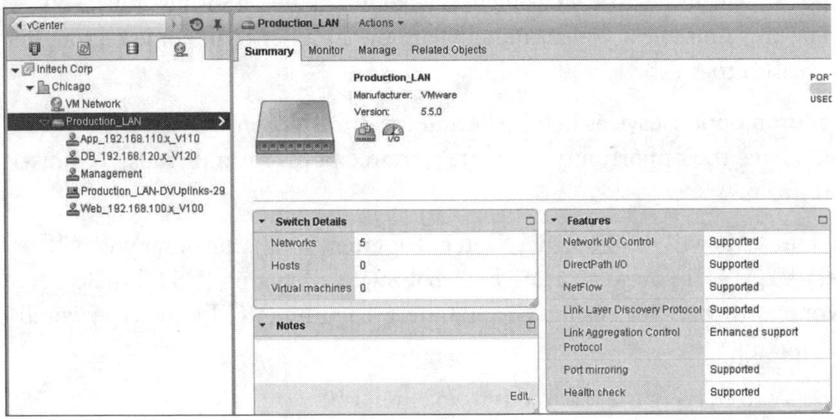

Figure 13.10   The distributed vSwitch now has all three VM distributed port groups

However, before we move on, it's important to configure the teaming policy for all of the VM port groups. Fortunately, the distributed vSwitch has some tools that make this painless. We'll walk through this process in the next section.

Load Based Teaming

We're going to take advantage of load based teaming (LBT), called "Route based on physical NIC load" in vSphere, with the VM distributed port groups. This lets the distributed vSwitch shift around VM ports from one uplink to another uplink in a congestion scenario where one of the uplinks was over 75% utilization for at least 30 seconds.

REAL WORLD

As long as your VMs are running applications that are comfortable with having their port moved around, we advise using LBT—although there are some legacy applications that don't take too kindly to having their port moved. You can easily find this out when you try to vMotion such a workload to another host. What commonly "breaks" a VM is the process of an upstream physical network device learning the MAC address location on a new port by way of a Reverse ARP (RARP). Both LBT and vMotion take advantage of a RARP to instruct the upstream network as to the new home of the VM.

To begin the process of configuring LBT, first navigate to the Production_LAN distributed vSwitch and select **Managed Distributed Port Groups** from the Actions menu. This allows you to manage multiple distributed port groups at one time. Because we only want to modify the teaming policy, select the check box next to Teaming and Failover as shown in Figure 13.11 and click **Next.**

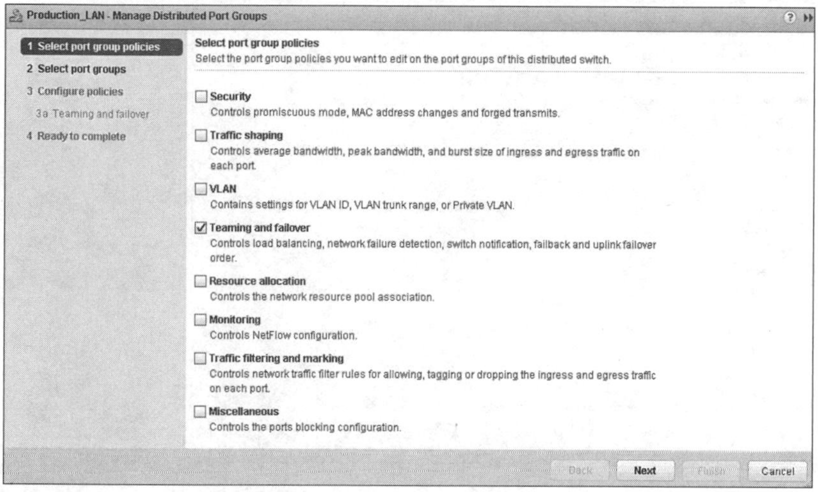

Figure 13.11   Managing distributed port groups on the Production_LAN switch

A list of port groups will appear. Hold the Control key down on your keyboard and select all three of the VM distributed port groups (see Figure 13.12). They will highlight in blue, allowing you to click **Next.**

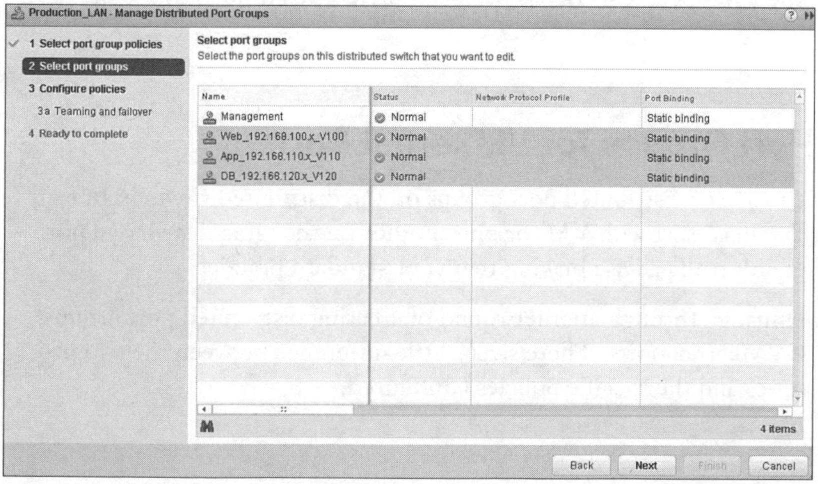

Figure 13.12   Select the 3 VM distributed port groups

The next screen will allow you to set any of the teaming and failover policies desired for those three VM distributed port groups. The only change we're looking to make is to the load balancing policy. Change it from Route ased on originating virtual port to **Route based on physical NIC load** (see Figure 13.13) and click **Next**.

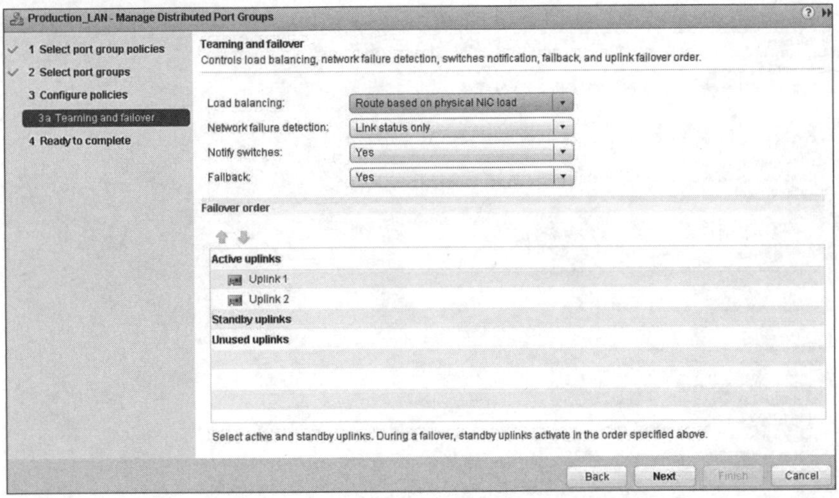

Figure 13.13   Changing the load balancing policy on the VM distributed port groups

That's all there is to it—and you've now changed the teaming policy on three VM distributed port groups at once. This is a neat trick and is one of the many time-saving features built into the distributed vSwitch.

At this point, all of the VM-specific work has been completed. It's time to tackle the VMkernel ports.

Distributed Port Groups for VMkernel Ports

VMkernel ports live inside of distributed port groups on the distributed vSwitch. In fact, VMkernel ports can even coexist with VMs or one another on the same distributed port group, although we don't really advise making that your standard practice.

This means that we must go through another round of creating distributed port groups, but this time for the VMkernel ports. There's very little difference between the two processes besides the names and the specific policies configured.

Thinking back to earlier, we know there are several distributed port groups necessary for our VMkernel ports:

- **Management**: This was done earlier when we made the default distributed port group named "Management."

- **vMotion**

- **Fault Tolerance**

- **iSCSI Storage**

We'll review each distributed port group needed for the environment and get them all created, configured, and ready for use. As a reminder, here is a list of the VLANs used by each VMkernel network that were outlined in Chapter 11, "Lab Scenario":

- **Management traffic**: 10.20.0.0 /16 on VLAN 20

- **vMotion traffic**: 192.168.205.0 /24 on VLAN 205

- **FT logging**: 192.168.210.0 /24 on VLAN 210

- **iSCSI traffic**: 192.168.215.0 /24 on VLAN 215

Management

Even though this distributed port group was created earlier, we never did get the opportunity to set a VLAN ID for it. By default, it is set to the VLAN ID of "None" which will not function for our environment. The ultimate goal is to move the vmk0 VMkernel port that sits on vSwitch0 over to this Management distributed port group, so we must make sure that the distributed port group is configured properly for Management traffic to flow. We also need to adjust the distributed port group failover settings.

First, locate the Management distributed port group in the Production_LAN distributed vSwitch and choose the **Edit Settings** function in the Actions menu. Select the **VLAN** section and make the following changes, as shown in Figure 13.14:

- Change the VLAN type from "None" to "VLAN"
- Set the VLAN ID to "20"

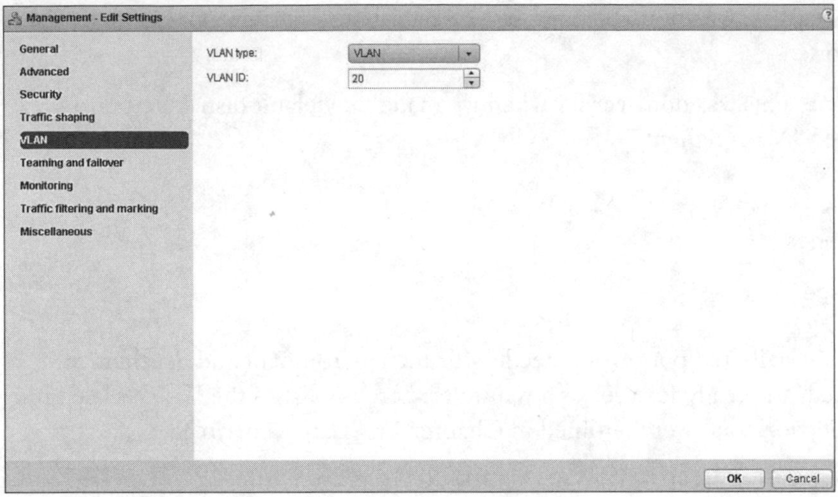

Figure 13.14   Setting the VLAN ID on the Management distributed port group

Great, now the distributed port group is on the correct VLAN needed for a management VMkernel port. Next, change over to the "Teaming and Failover" section and make the following changes (see Figure 13.15):

- Use the blue arrow button to move Uplink 2 down to the Standby uplinks section.

- Click **OK**.

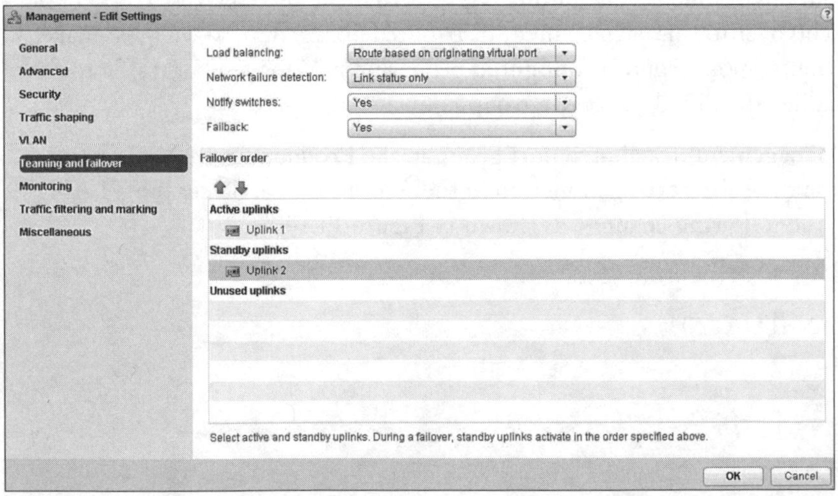

Figure 13.15   Setting the failover order on the Management distributed port group

You've now properly configured the Management distributed port group to use Uplink 1 as an Active network adapter and Uplink 2 as a Standby network adapter.

> **NOTE**
>
> Leave the load balancing policy to Route based on originating virtual port—there is no value in having it set to Route based on physical NIC load (LBT). There is only one Active uplink available and LBT will not use Standby uplinks.

vMotion

The next distributed port group we'll need is for vMotion. Select the **Production_LAN** distributed vSwitch and choose **New Distributed Port Group** from the Actions menu. Name the new distributed port group **vMotion** as shown in Figure 13.16, and click **Next**.

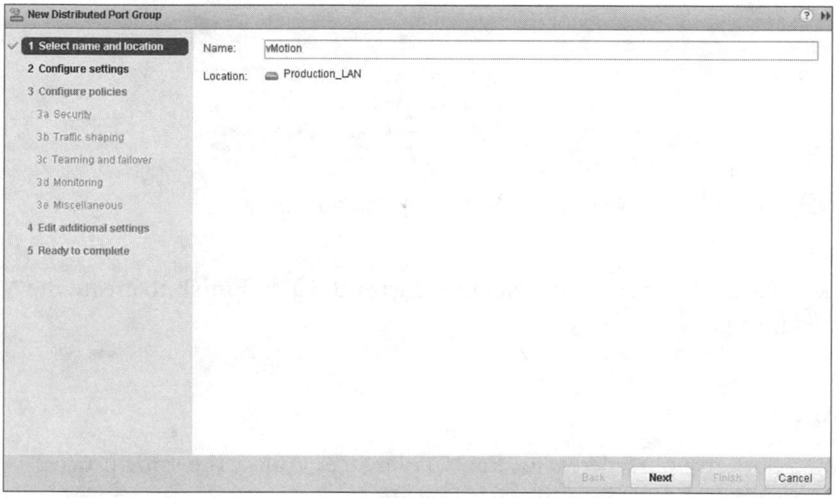

Figure 13.16   Creating the vMotion distributed port group

Next, we'll configure the settings needed for the vMotion distributed port group. Leave all the values as default, except for the following three:

- **VLAN type**: VLAN
- **VLAN ID**: 205
- **Customize default policies configuration**: Check the box.

We're checking the customize box so that you can see the alternative method for configuring the teaming policy, for when you need to make one-off distributed port groups.

Keep clicking **Next** until you reach the Teaming and Failover policy settings. Make the following change: Using the blue down arrow, drop Uplink 1 down to the Standby uplinks section as shown in Figure 13.17.

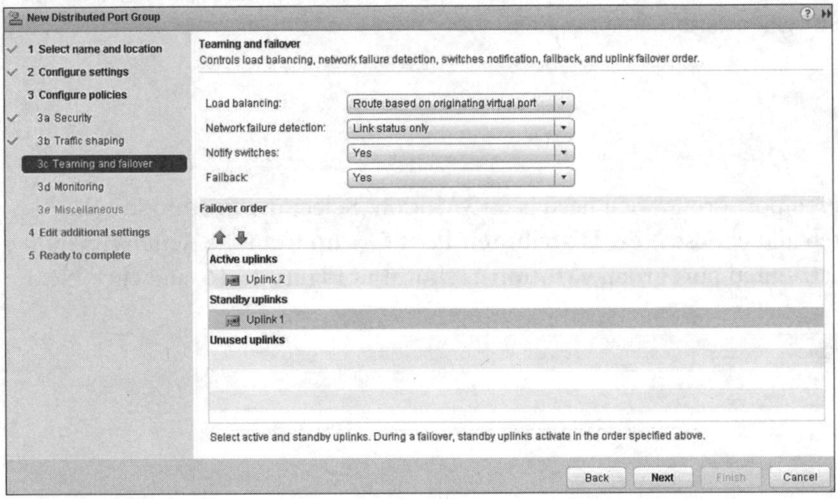

Figure 13.17   Setting the teaming policy for the vMotion distributed port group

You can now click **Next** until you reach the end of the wizard. Click **Finish** to create the vMotion distributed port group.

Fault Tolerance

The next distributed port group needed is for Fault Tolerance. Follow the same process we went through for vMotion, with the following exceptions:

- **Name**: Fault Tolerance
- **VLAN ID**: 210

The end result should look like that shown in Figure 13.18.

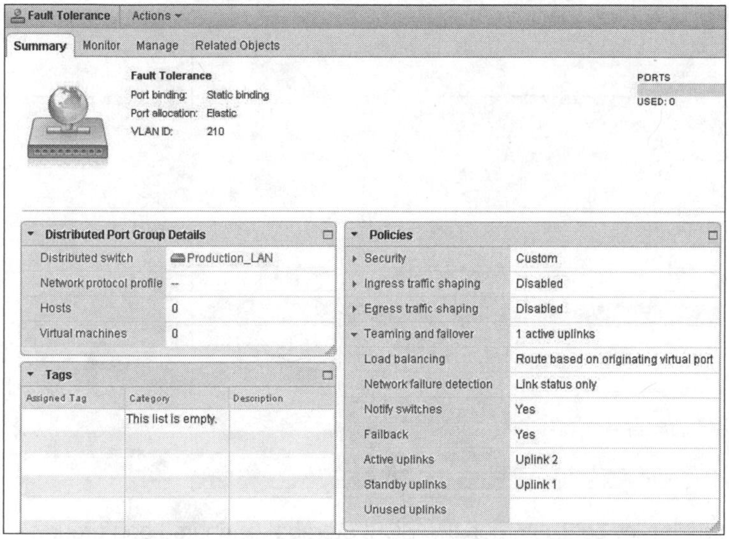

Figure 13.18   Summary of the Fault Tolerance distributed port group policies

Don't forget to set Uplink 1 as a Standby uplink for the Fault Tolerance distributed port group.

iSCSI Storage

The final distributed port group we're going to create is for iSCSI Storage network traffic. This distributed port group will be responsible for making sure that any storage arrays that use iSCSI are presented to the VM guests. Much like with our NFS Storage network used on the standard vSwitch, the iSCSI Storage network is sensitive to latency and will be Active on Uplink 1 and Standby on Uplink 2.

Start off by creating a new distributed port group named iSCSI Storage on VLAN 215. For the failover order policy, make sure that Uplink 2 is moved down to the Standby uplinks section, as shown in Figure 13.19.

This should look very similar to the failover configuration used on the Management network. Let's tie together all of the failover orders together in the next section to best understand how traffic will flow to the pair of uplinks.

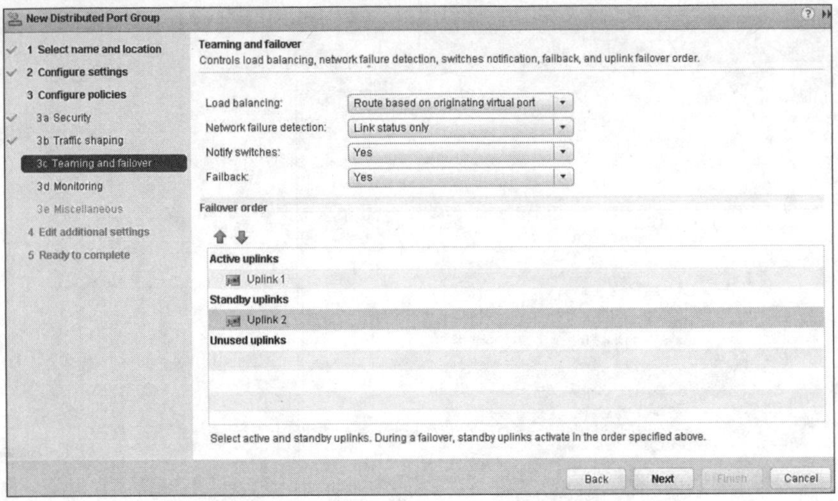

Figure 13.19   The failover order policy configured on the iSCSI Storage distributed port group

VMkernel Failover Overview

Looking at the failover order for the various VMkernel ports, a pattern emerges. If you look carefully at the active and standby use of each network adapter, you'll find the following to be true:

- **Active use of vmnic0**: Management Network and iSCSI Storage

- **Active use of vmnic1**: FT and vMotion

- **Standby use of vmnic0**: FT and vMotion

- **Standby use of vmnic1**: Management Network and iSCSI Storage

- **Active use of both vmnic0 and vmnic1**: VM port groups (Web, Application, and Database Servers)

Figure 13.20 shows a visual way of looking at the failover settings.

We've basically divided up the two network adapters to handle the two types of traffic that are very sensitive to latency or consume a lot of bandwidth: iSCSI Storage is sensitive to latency, and vMotion consumes a lot of bandwidth. They will not use the same network adapter as an uplink unless one of the uplinks fails.

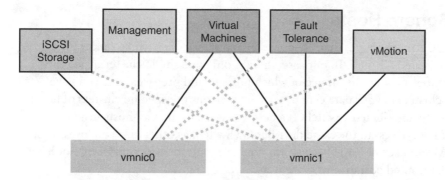

Figure 13.20   Failover order for the distributed port groups

NOTE

The iSCSI design used in this chapter supports only a single path to the iSCSI storage array. We're doing this to show isolation methods within a vSwitch, but it's typically wise to have multiple paths to your storage array. If you need multiple paths to your iSCSI storage, it's worth referring to Chapter 14 and Chapter 15, "iSCSI Design and Configuration."

We've now completed all of the preparation work necessary to fully configure the distributed vSwitch. Yours should look similar to that shown in Figure 13.21.

The vSphere hosts can now be added to the distributed vSwitch.

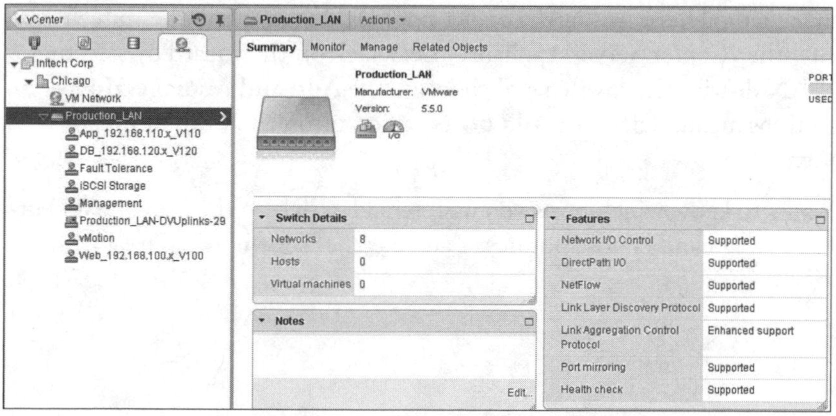

Figure 13.21   All of the distributed port groups have been created on the distributed vSwitch

Adding vSphere Hosts

If you're feeling a strange tingle, that's because the moment has arrived to add vSphere hosts to the distributed vSwitch. In our case, there is only one single cluster inside the Chicago data center, making the choice of which hosts to add pretty easy. If you have many different clusters in your data center, you can pick out the specific clusters of hosts you wish to join the distributed vSwitch. It's best to make sure that all hosts inside of a vSphere cluster have access to the same distributed vSwitch, as otherwise you lose out on the ability to vMotion across hosts because the source and destination hosts will not have the same VM distributed port groups.

There are a few different methods of adding hosts to a distributed vSwitch:

- **The kid gloves method**: This is sometimes called "walking the host" into a distributed vSwitch and is commonly used for migrating existing hosts that are running VMs without taking an outage. At a high level, this method involves stealing a single network adapter from whatever existing vSwitch the host is using and adding it to the new distributed vSwitch. We then migrate all the VMs and VMkernel ports over to the distributed vSwitch. Finally, we steal the other network adapters and remove the old vSwitch.

- **The hammer method**: This is a "move everything at once" option and is typically used for new hosts that are not yet running VMs. Because these are brand new hosts, moving them into a distributed vSwitch is somewhat trivial from a risk perspective. There are no existing workloads running on the hosts to worry about breaking. As such, we can migrate the network adapters and VMkernel ports over in one swoop.

We use the hammer method here, as there is only a single VM running in the Initech Corp environment—the vCenter Server Appliance. Let's kick off the wizard by selecting the **Production_LAN** distributed vSwitch and choosing the **Add and Manage Hosts** option from the Actions menu. Select the **Add hosts** radio button as shown in Figure 13.22 and click **Next**.

The next screen wants to know which hosts you wish to add. Click on the **New hosts** button with the green plus sign and choose both **esx1** and **esx2**, as shown in Figure 13.23. Click **Next**.

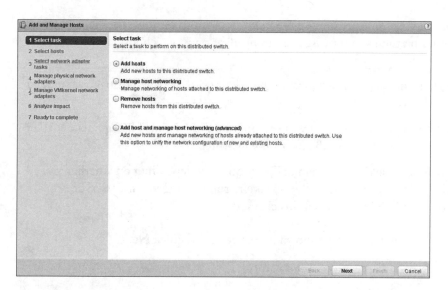

Figure 13.22   Adding the hosts to the Production_LAN distributed vSwitch

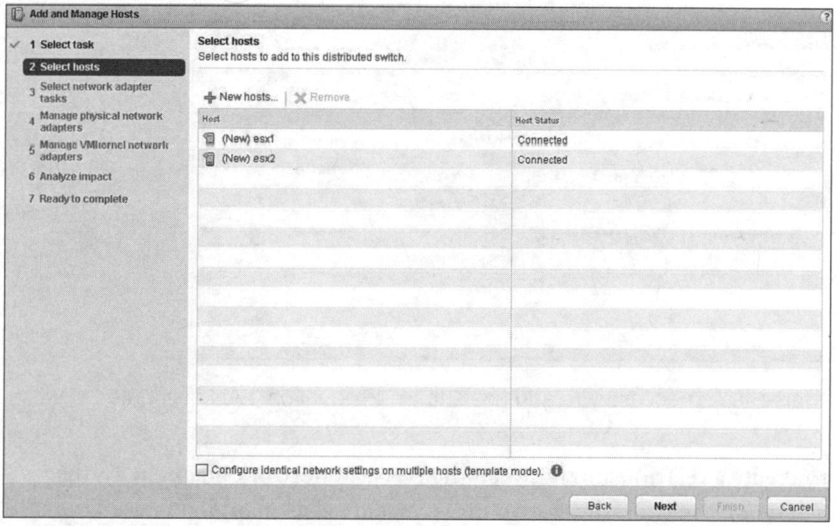

Figure 13.23   Adding the esx1 and esx2 hosts to the distributed vSwitch

The next screen requests information on the tasks you wish to perform. Because we're doing the hammer method and moving everything all at once, we choose the following check boxes:

- **Manage physical adapters**: Establishes the relationship between distributed uplinks and physical network adapters.

- **Manage VMkernel adapters**: Allows us to migrate the existing Management VMkernel port named vmk0 over to the distributed vSwitch.

- **Migrate virtual machine networking**: This is optional depending on whether you have VMs in your environment. Because we're running the vCenter Server Appliance on one of the hosts, we need this checked.

Your screen should look like the one shown in Figure 13.24. Click **Next**.

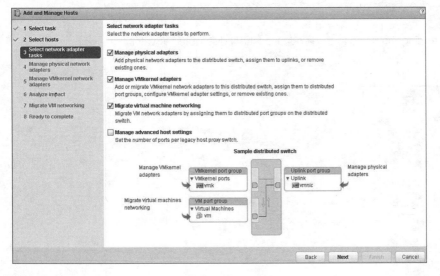

Figure 13.24   The three tasks necessary to add hosts to the Production_LAN distributed vSwitch

Your first task is to create a relationship between the physical network adapters on the hosts and the distributed uplinks on the distributed vSwitch. This mapping is used to build a relationship between physical hardware and logical uplinks.

For both hosts, make the following change:

- Select **vmnic0** and click the **Assign uplink** button. Choose **Uplink 1**.

- Select **vmnic1** and click the **Assign uplink** button. Choose **Uplink 2**.

Review your results (see Figure 13.25) and click **Next**.

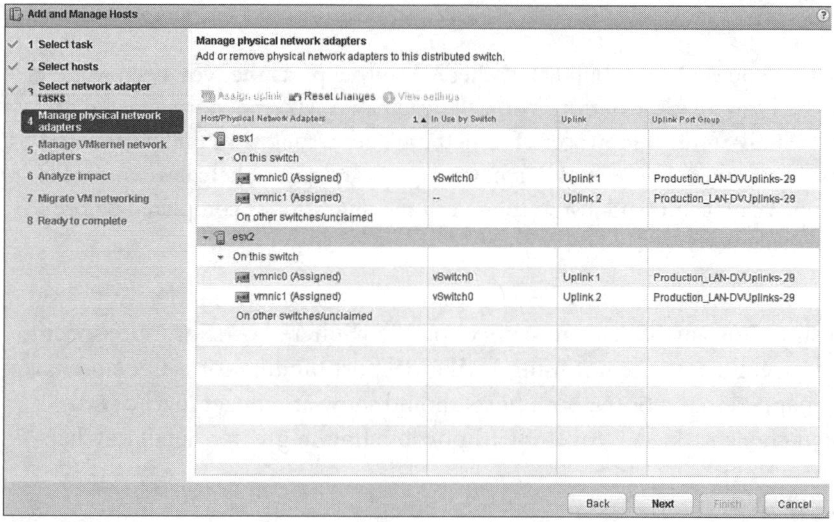

Figure 13.25 Creating a relationship between physical network adapters and the distributed uplinks

The next task is to migrate the Management Network VMkernel port, vmk0, over to the Management distributed port group. The process is very similar to the previous task: For each host, click on **vmk0**, click on the **Assign port group** button, and then choose the **Management** distributed port group (see Figure 13.26). When completed, click **Next**.

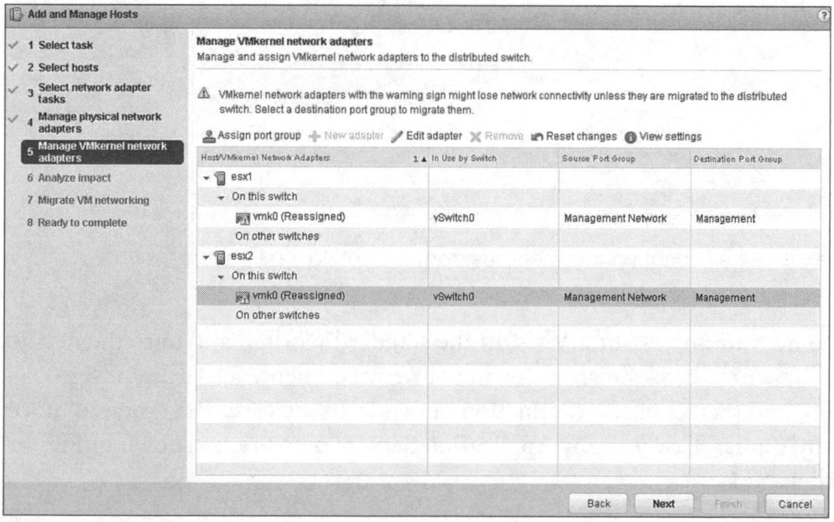

Figure 13.26 Migrating the Management Network VMkernel ports over to the Management distributed port group

---

REAL WORLD

It's worth noting that you could also build any other VMkernel ports that you need while in this screen using the **New adapter** button. You will need new VMkernel ports created for vMotion, FT, and iSCSI Storage. However, if something goes wrong with the migration, you will have wasted a fair bit of time building new adapters and most likely have to repeat the work over again. We recommend just waiting until the migration is completed before building new VMkernel ports.

Figure 13.27 will show you any impacts to services on the vSphere hosts, or more specifically, the iSCSI service. Since we're not using VMkernel port binding for iSCSI and have no iSCSI storage mapped to the hosts, both hosts should show an impact level of No impact with a green checkmark. We cover iSCSI port binding in greater detail in Chapter 14. You can click **Next**.

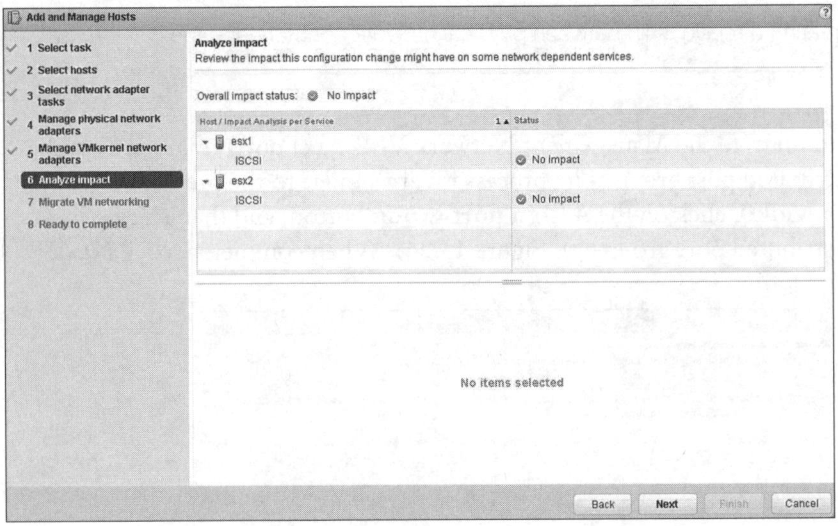

Figure 13.27   Analyzing the impact on host services from the network migration

The final task is to migrate any existing VMs off the standard vSwitch and onto the newly minted distributed vSwitch. Click on any VMs in your environment, select the **Assign port group** button, and then choose a destination network. In my case, I'm going to move the vCenter Server Appliance over to my Application Servers network, as shown in Figure 13.28, and then click **Next**.

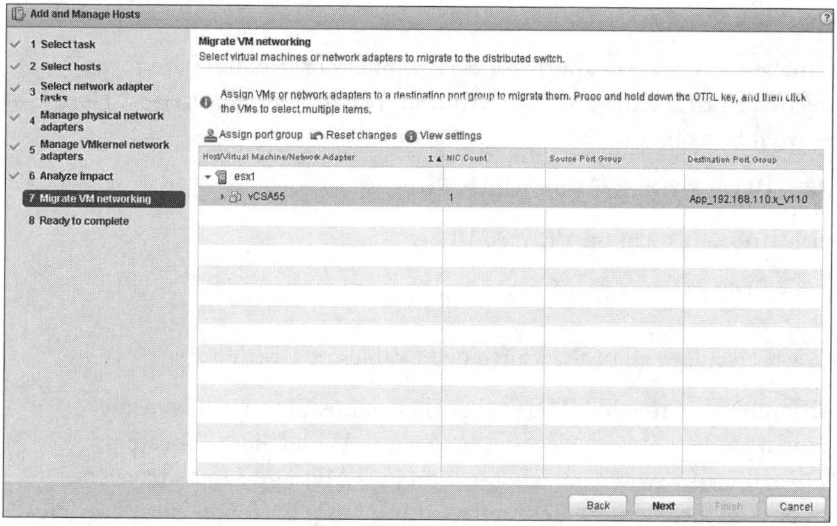

Figure 13.28   Migrating the vCSA55 VM over to the App network

---

REAL WORLD

Don't have any VMs to migrate over? Try creating a fake VM on the standard vSwitch so you can migrate it over. Or, better yet, download a small Linux VM appliance off the Internet and practice migrating it over to see what happens with performance and pings in your lab or test environment. Practice makes perfect.

Click **Finish** to begin moving over all your vSphere hosts into the distributed vSwitch. If you accidently caused an issue where your hosts are unable to talk to vCenter, the Rollback feature introduced in vSphere 5.1 should automatically revert your networking configuration back to the previous settings in about 30 seconds. At this point, the vSphere hosts are now participating in the distributed vSwitch.

REAL WORLD

Always make sure you have out-of-band access to your vSphere hosts, just in case you blow up the network to the point of needing ESXi Shell or Direct Console User Interface (DCUI) access. It happens.

Creating VMkernel Ports

It's finally time to make the VMkernel ports for each vSphere host. There are three VMkernel ports needed to satisfy the use case: vMotion, FT, and iSCSI Storage. Here is a list of IP addresses we'll be using on esx1:

- **vMotion traffic**: 192.168.205.1 /24 on VLAN 205

- **FT logging**: 192.168.210.1 /24 on VLAN 210

- **iSCSI traffic**: 192.168.215.1 /24 on VLAN 215

For the other host, esx2, replace all of the fourth octet values of 1 with a 2.

There are many different ways to add VMkernel ports to a host, but we'll be using a method that begins with the network view in the vSphere Web Client. Locate the Production_LAN distributed vSwitch and choose **Add and Manage Hosts** from the Actions menu then choose the **Manage host networking** radio button, as shown in Figure 13.29, and click **Next.**

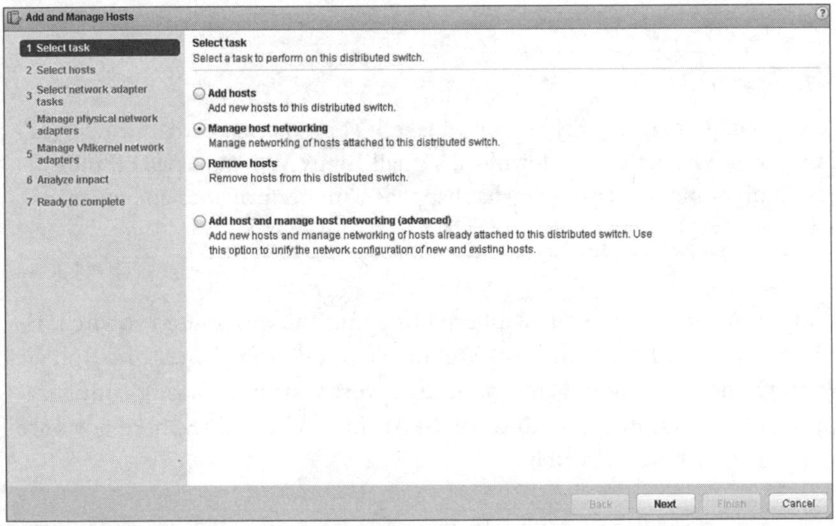

Figure 13.29   Using the Manage host networking feature to add VMkernel ports

In the host selection screen, use the **Attach hosts** button to select both of the vSphere hosts, click **Next**, then choose **Manage VMkernel adapters** in the tasks screen—uncheck all of the other check boxes, as shown in Figure 13.30.

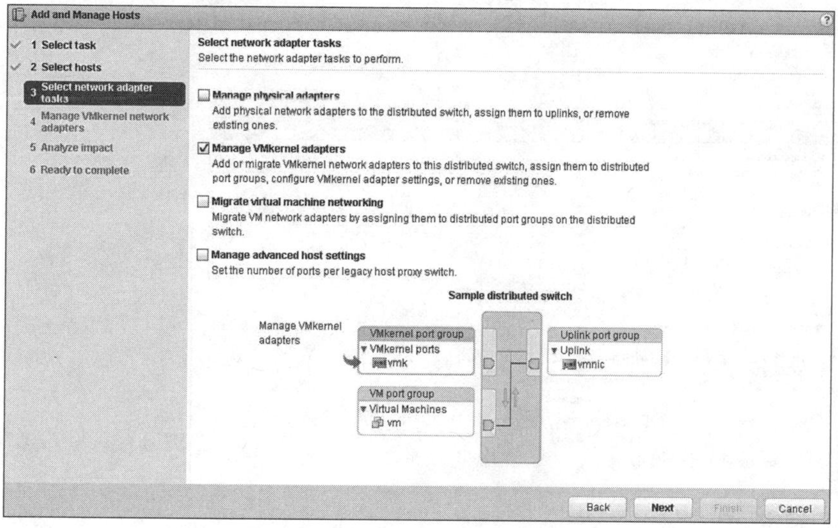

Figure 13.30   Manage VMkernel adapters to create new VMkernel ports

Select the vSphere host named **esx1** and click the **New adapter** button (not shown). Use the **Browse** button to find the vMotion distributed port group (see Figure 13.31), click **OK**, and then click **Next**.

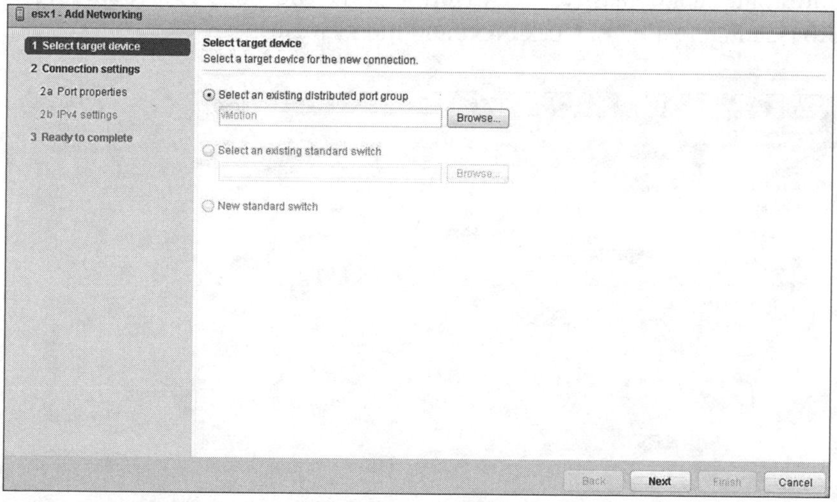

Figure 13.31   Adding a VMkernel port to the vMotion distributed port group

In the Port properties screen (see Figure 13.32), select the **vMotion traffic** service and click **Next**.

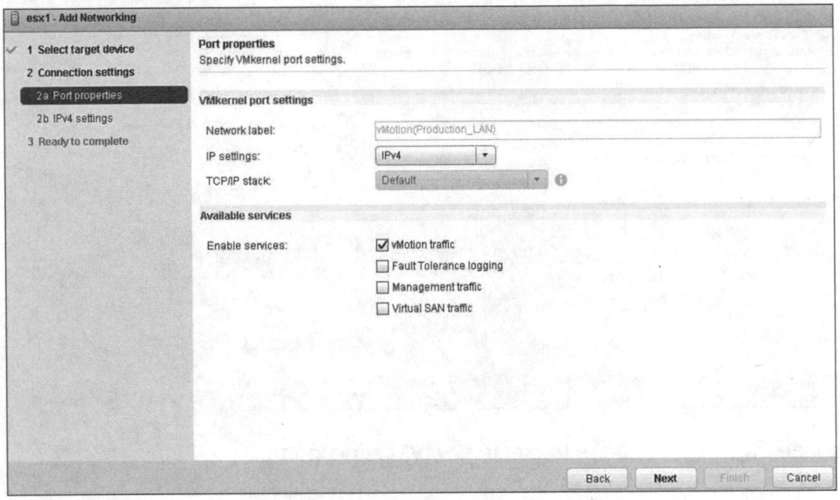

Figure 13.32 Select the **vMotion traffic** service

For the IPv4 settings page, choose the radio button for **Use static IPv4 Settings** and enter the IPv4 address and subnet mask for the vMotion VMkernel port: **192.168.205.1** and **255.255.255.0** (see Figure 13.33). Click **Next** and then **Finish**.

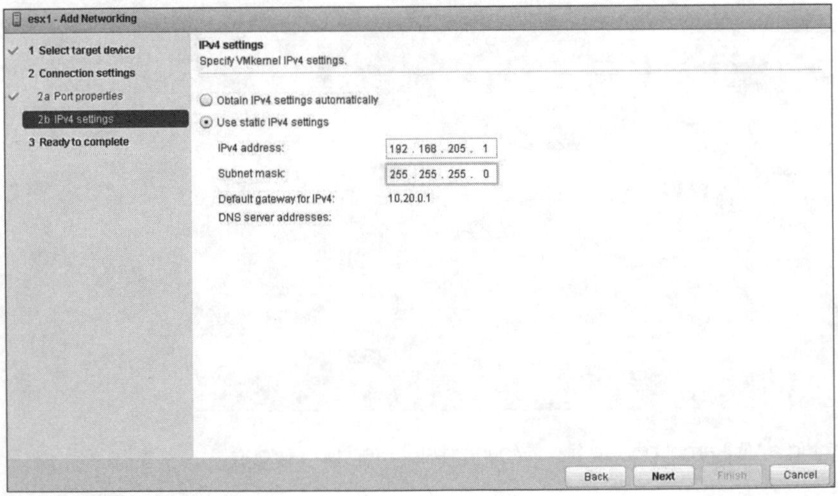

Figure 13.33 Setting the IPv4 address and mask for the vMotion VMkernel port

Repeat the process in this section for each VMkernel port required:

- **Host esx1 Fault Tolerance**: Fault Tolerance logging service, IPv4 address 192.168.210.1, subnet mask 255.255.255.0

- **Host esx1 iSCSI Storage**: No service, IPv4 address 192.168.215.1, subnet mask 255.255.255.0

- **Host esx2 Fault Tolerance**: Fault ToleranceFT logging service, IPv4 address 192.168.210.2, subnet mask 255.255.255.0

- **Host esx2 iSCSI Storage**: No service, IPv4 address 192.168.215.2, subnet mask 255.255.255.0

The end result will look like that shown in Figure 13.34.

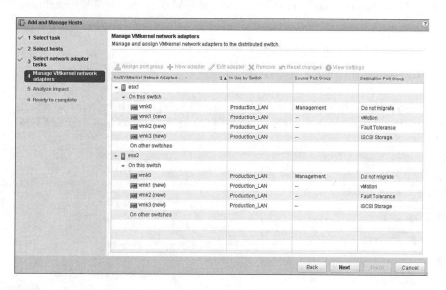

Figure 13.34   The new VMkernel ports pending creation

When you've reviewed the new VMkernel ports and verified they look correct, click through the wizard and choose **Finish**. It can take a little while to create that many VMkernel ports, so patience is required. When completed, a long list of "Add virtual NIC' tasks will show completed.

Moving the vCenter Virtual Machine

When vCenter Server is running as a VM in the environment, additional considerations must be made when attempting to migrate the underlying vSphere to a distributed vSwitch. It is highly recommended to use the more delicate method of migration to "walk" the VM over to the distributed switch in such a way that negates any network interruption. Oftentimes the hammer method ends up failing because vCenter attempts to move the vCenter Server VM and the physical network adapters at the same time, which ends up failing.

We review the steps here at a high level, and then perform a migration:

- Add the vSphere host running vCenter Server to the distributed vSwitch with a single network adapter.

- Migrate the VMkernel ports and the vCenter Server VM over to the new distributed vSwitch.

- Add any remaining network adapters to the distributed vSwitch.

- Remove the old standard vSwitch, if desired.

Let's take it step by step in the Initech Corp environment. I've placed the vCenter Server VM on esx1 and reverted it back to being on a standard vSwitch, as shown in Figure 13.35.

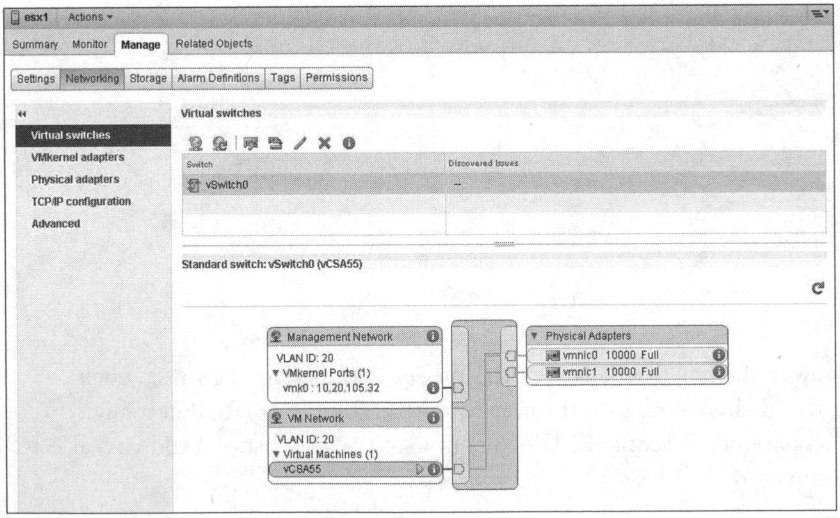

Figure 13.35 The vCenter Server VM using a standard vSwitch on host esx1

Let's begin by adding the vSphere host esx1 to the Production_LAN distributed vSwitch and taking one of the network adapters away from the standard vSwitch. Switch to the network view in the vSphere Web Client and choose **Add and Manage Hosts** from the Actions menu, then click **Next**.

Select the host named **esx1** and click **Next** again; then choose the task named **Manage physical adapters** and uncheck the boxes next to any other tasks, as shown in Figure 13.36.

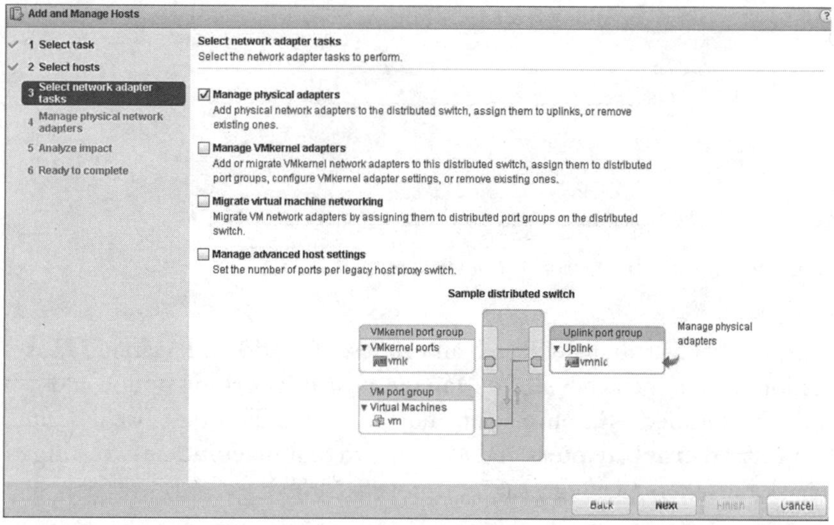

Figure 13.36   Select the **Manage Physical Adapters** task to begin with

When presented the network adapters for the vSphere host, map vmnic0 to Uplink 1 but leave vmnic1 alone (see Figure 13.37). This is the first step in "walking" the host into a distributed vSwitch.

Finish the wizard and let it complete changes to the vSphere host. The host has now joined the distributed vSwitch with a single network adapter. You can now migrate the VMkernel port and vCenter Server VM over to the distributed vSwitch.

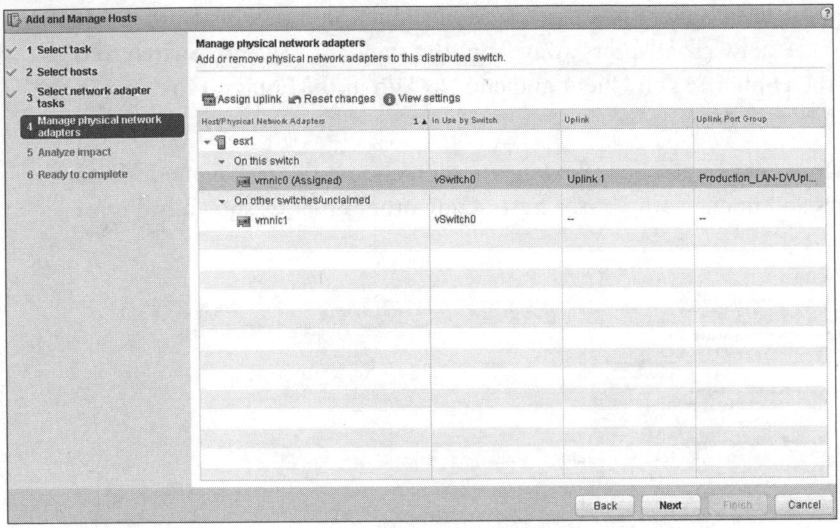

Figure 13.37   Migrate only vmnic0 into Uplink 1, but leave vmnic1 alone

Select the **Production_LAN** distributed vSwitch and choose the **Add and Manage Hosts** option from the Actions menu, then choose the **Manage host networking** option and click **Next**. Select the host named **esx1** once again and click **Next**. This time, we'll want to choose the **Manage VMkernel adapters** and **Migrate virtual machine networking** check boxes—uncheck the others (see Figure 13.38) and click **Next**.

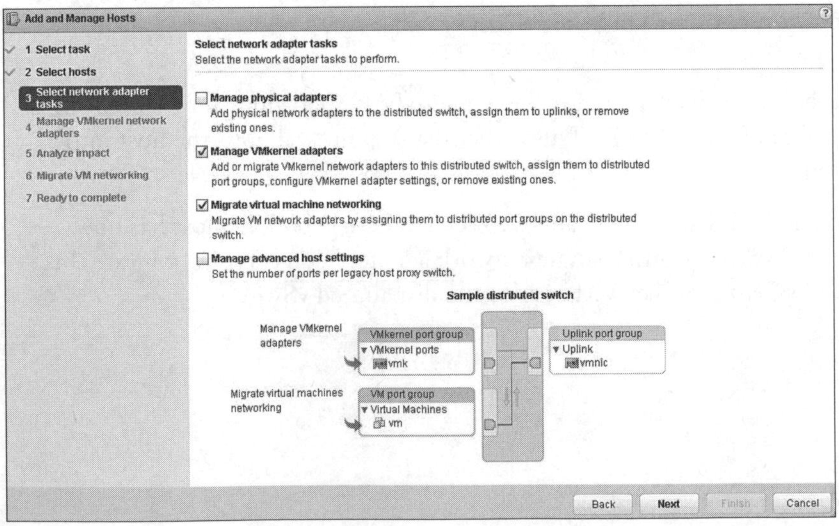

Figure 13.38   This time we migrate the VMkernel ports and VM networks

For the VMkernel network adapter task, select **vmk0**, which is on the Management Network on vSwitch0, and assign it to the Management distributed port group (see Figure 13.39). Click **Next** and skip the impact analysis screen by clicking **Next** again.

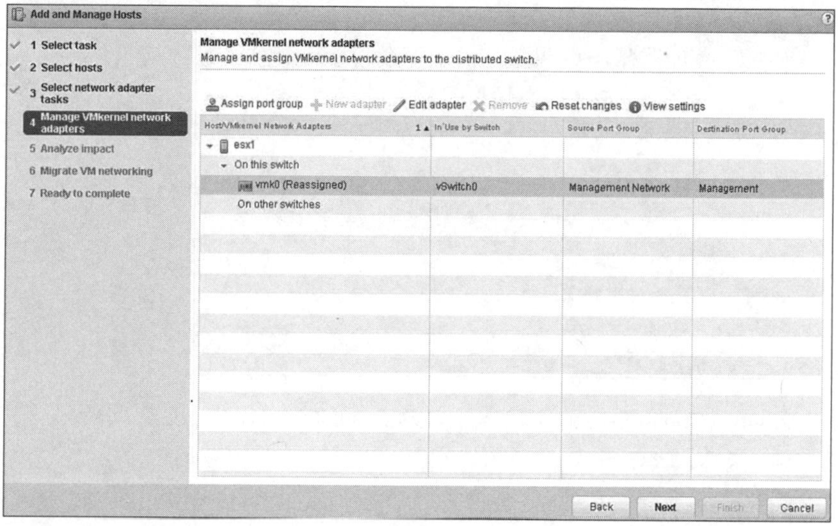

Figure 13.39   Migrating the vmk0 VMkernel port to the distributed port group named Management

The next task is to migrate VM networking. Select the vCenter Server VM and assign it to the App Servers distributed port group (see Figure 13.40). Then click **Next** and **Finish** the wizard to complete the migration.

You might lose connection to your vSphere Web Client for a moment, as the upstream switches must receive notifications that the MAC address for your vCenter Server VM has moved. The connection should restore itself after a few seconds and you'll see the tasks have completed successfully.

You can now go back through the wizard and assign the remaining network adapter, vmnic1, to Uplink 2. Make sure to also go back and delete vSwitch0 if you do not plan on using it further, satisfying your inner administrative OCD.

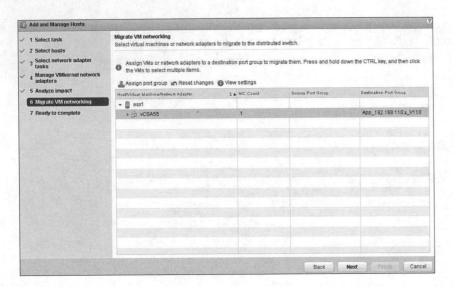

Figure 13.40   Migrating the vCenter Server to the App Server distributed port group

Final Steps

Before moving on, there are a few tuning steps that are advantageous to walk through. These provide some final tuning to your distributed vSwitch, along with some warm and fuzzies that it has been configured properly.

Health Check

One final step that is very helpful with the distributed vSwitch involves the Health Check feature. This checks the status of the configured VLANs, the MTU size, and any Teaming and Failover policies. Before the introduction of Health Check, administrators would have to resort to ping tests on each VLAN to ensure that the upstream physical network was properly configured and plumbed into the virtual network. Since the feature is free and available to use, might as well fire it up to make sure everything is configured properly.

It's an incredibly easy feature to enable. Navigate to the vSphere Web Client and find the Production_LAN distributed vSwitch. Click on the **Actions** menu, choose **All vCenter Actions** and then **Edit Health Check**, as shown in Figure 13.41.

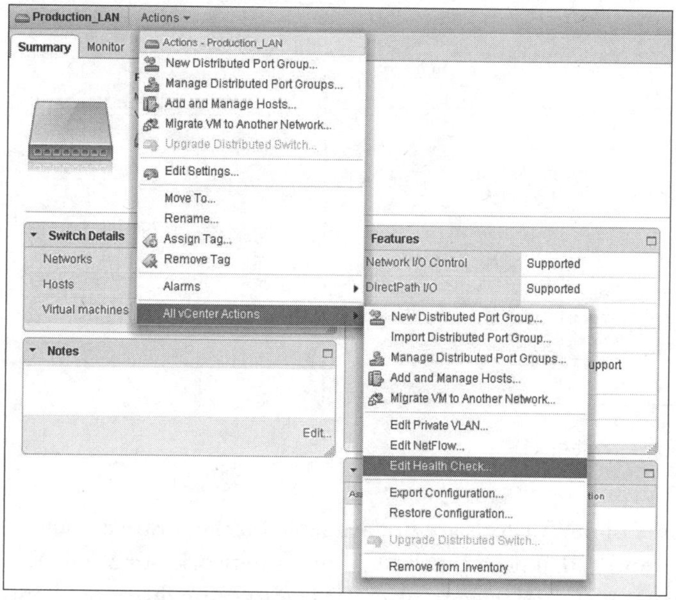

Figure 13.41   Navigating to the Health Check feature

From here, click the **Edit** button and set both the VLAN and MTU and Teaming and Failover options to **Enabled**, as shown in Figure 13.42; then click **OK**. You've now turned on the Health Check feature for your distributed switch.

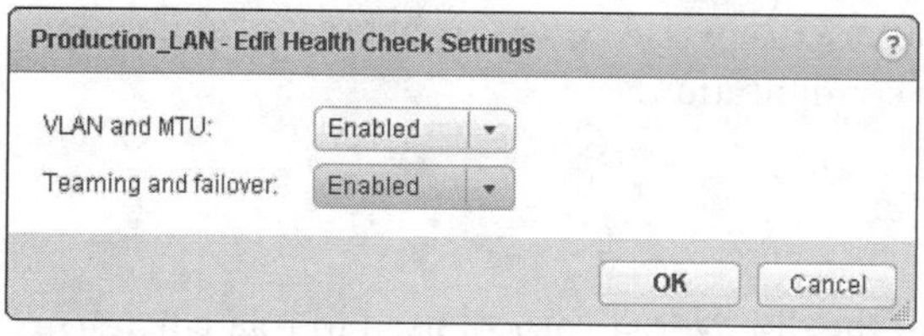

Figure 13.42   Enabling the Health Check settings

When the Health Checks are enabled, click on the **Monitor** tab and **Health** sub-tab to see the Host member health status. It might take several minutes for the checks to complete and the status entities to change from Unknown to another value like Up or Warning.

Let's look at the VLAN results first to see if any trouble exists. Choose one of the hosts in the list to view status details—in this case, we're choosing to click on **esx1** with the results shown in Figure 13.43. Can you spot the issues?

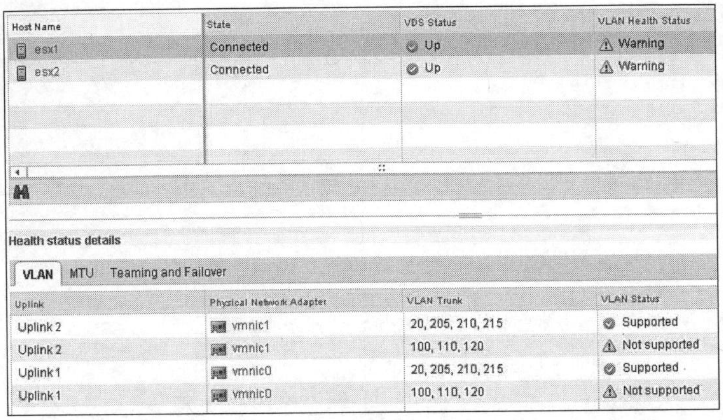

Host Name	State	VDS Status	VLAN Health Status
esx1	Connected	⊘ Up	⚠ Warning
esx2	Connected	⊘ Up	⚠ Warning

Health status details

| VLAN | MTU | Teaming and Failover |

Uplink	Physical Network Adapter	VLAN Trunk	VLAN Status
Uplink 2	vmnic1	20, 205, 210, 215	⊘ Supported
Uplink 2	vmnic1	100, 110, 120	⚠ Not supported
Uplink 1	vmnic0	20, 205, 210, 215	⊘ Supported
Uplink 1	vmnic0	100, 110, 120	⚠ Not supported

Figure 13.43 VLAN health status on host esx1

According to Health Check, three of our VLANs are not available on the upstream network device—VLANs 100, 110, and 120. Those are the VM guest networks for Web, Application, and Database Servers. If we had tried to place VMs into those distributed port groups, they would have failed to communicate with the upstream network.

In this particular case, we purposefully removed some VLANs to show you a failure scenario. Hopefully, you can see just how valuable it is to confirm that the upstream VLANs exist prior to putting workloads on the distributed port groups. You can repeat the previous process to ensure the MTU values match from a host and upstream port perspective, and if your teaming and failover policy is proper for the upstream device—this really just plays into situations where a Link Aggregation Group (LAG) has been created and will typically appear as "Normal" for any other configuration.

Network Discovery Protocol

Another option you can set revolves around the discovery protocol used to relate neighbors in the virtual world to the physical world. We previously covered the two options: Cisco Discovery Protocol (CDP) for Cisco equipment and Link Layer Discovery Protocol (LLDP) for all other equipment. By default, a distributed vSwitch is configured for CDP in Listen mode, meaning it will listen for CDP advertisements but not generate any advertisements. You can change this from Listen mode to Both mode—meaning it will both Listen and Advertise.

To make the change, click on the **Production_LAN** distributed vSwitch, open the **Actions** menu, and choose **Edit Settings**. Click on the **Advanced** menu item to reveal the discovery protocol configuration. Select the protocol that can be used in your environment and change Operation to **Both** as shown in Figure 13.44.

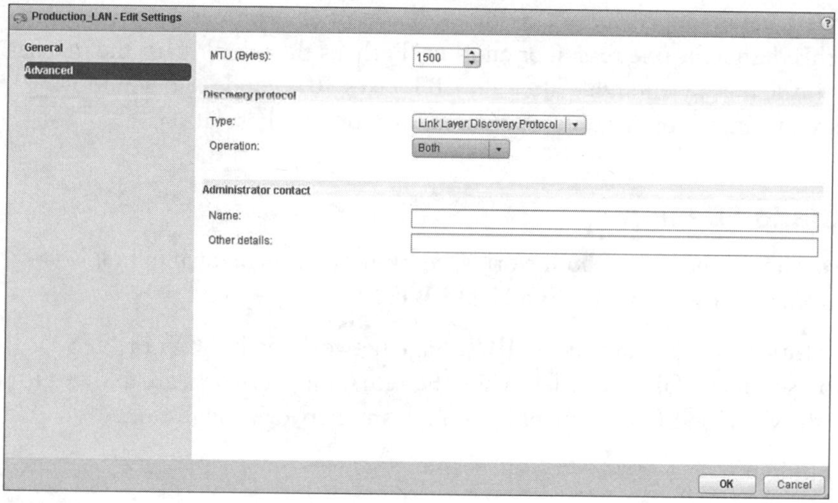

Figure 13.44   Allowing the discovery protocol to listen and advertise

The end result of this change means that the physical network can understand who their virtual neighbors are, which can be handy when either troubleshooting or making changes to the environment. There are some companies that frown upon having this enabled in some segments of the network—such as the DMZ—so ensure that you are cleared to advertise to the network prior to making this change.

Other Design Considerations

For those looking to ride along the wave of more progressive network design, there are design alternatives that we wanted to make you aware of.

Fully Automated Design

In this particular design, a combination of NIOC and LBT is used to allow the hypervisor to completely control and move around traffic. It's a bit like throwing all the network traffic types into a big pot and letting automation handle the rest.

The teaming for all port groups would be configured to LBT with all network adapters set to Active. In a congestion situation, NIOC would begin to enforce bandwidth controls based on share values, and LBT would help move traffic from one adapter to another in the case of single adapter congestion situations.

This design sounds great in theory, but we've found that most environments choose not to go forward with this design for one reason or another. Perhaps they don't trust the mechanisms to control traffic quickly enough—after all, LBT takes 30 seconds to begin moving traffic—or they are just more comfortable with some form of uplink isolation.

Hybrid Automation Design

This design approach uses the best of both worlds, combining some manual uplink isolation and some automated triggers with NIOC and LBT.

Oftentimes the vMotion network and/or the IP Storage network (be it iSCSI or NFS storage) are set to use explicit failover order, while the remaining networks are allowed to use any uplink with NIOC and LBT controlling uplink and network congestion.

The teaming would look a bit like this:

- **Active use of both vmnic0 and vmnic1 with LBT**: VM port groups (Web, Application, and Database Servers), Management Network, FT
- **Active use of vmnic0**: iSCSI Storage
- **Active use of vmnic1**: vMotion
- **Standby use of vmnic0**: vMotion
- **Standby use of vmnic1**: iSCSI Storage

Which Is Right?

Ultimately, your comfort level of the design is key. The design method we presented throughout this chapter is widely accepted and tested, giving you confidence that it will work for the majority of environments. However, it's important to both be aware of and understand that there are many different ways to cobble together your virtual networking policies, with no one design being the "right" one. If it works, and works well, be satisfied.

Summary

Having gone through a full distributed vSwitch design and implementation, you should now have a pretty good idea as to the level of effort and planning necessary to create a successful virtual network. Compared to the standard vSwitch, there's a lot more effort and configuration potential with the distributed vSwitch during the initial setup period. However, once utilized, the distributed vSwitch will provide you with a large quantity of time savings from an operational and administrative standpoint.

Many decision points require collaboration with your networking team. Even if you have a grand architecture in mind, you'll often find that having an engaged networking team, where communication flows frequently, to be a huge help. Ultimately, you cannot work in a vacuum or else projects will not work as expected.

Chapter 14

iSCSI General Use Cases

Key Concepts

- Ensuring Quality of Service (QoS)
- iSCSI Initiators, Targets, and Names
- Challenge Handshake Authentication Protocol (CHAP)
- Software iSCSI Adapter
- Hardware iSCSI Adapters
- Network Port Binding

Introduction

One really neat thing about virtualization is that it touches upon so many different disciplines. Up to this point, we've focused heavily on physical and virtual networking concepts, and applied them to example designs in a realistic data center. We're not done yet—it's time to get your hands dirty with some storage-related work. Or at least storage as it relates to virtual networking.

The goal of this chapter is to introduce you to the design choices involved when consuming storage for your vSphere hosts and virtual machines that rides on an Ethernet network. Specifically, we're going to cover the iSCSI protocol.

Understanding iSCSI

So, what exactly is iSCSI? It stands for Internet Small Computer System Interface. Fortunately, no one actually ever says that, because it sounds awkward and takes a long time to say. Let's translate the meaning to "moving SCSI commands over an Ethernet network" to make life easier, because that's what happens with iSCSI. A SCSI command, which is pronounced "scuzzy" and used to read or write data to disk, is encapsulated inside of an IP packet and fired off into an Ethernet network to travel toward a storage array and back. The network mentioned could be one specifically for iSCSI traffic or your common LAN used by servers for other types of traffic. In fact, that brings up a great point—how do we make sure that the iSCSI packets reach their destination when there are periods of congestion? After all, Ethernet loves to just drop traffic when congestion occurs, which is a very bad thing with storage traffic.

Lossless Versus Best Effort Protocols

Ethernet is a best effort protocol, meaning it doesn't guarantee delivery. That's why we let Transmission Control Protocol (TCP) handle session data—it can monitor the data traffic and request a resend of any missing or dropped packets. The idea is that traffic put into the Ethernet network is of a "best effort to get it there" quality. We try our best to make sure it reaches its destination, but ultimately it's no big deal for most traffic types to have a few lost packets that are re-sent every once in a while.

Storage IO is much less tolerant of packet loss than most other traffic types. Imagine that your server is trying to read a chunk of data on a storage array, but the network keeps losing it. The server will continue to wait for the data chunk—this is called *latency*—while most likely queuing up additional read requests. Suddenly, you have a bottleneck of read requests on the server and it locks up, waiting to get data chunks off the storage array. If the server has to wait long enough for the data chunk, the operating system may end up crashing (or worse).

It is important, although not strictly required, to provide some sort of priority mechanism for your iSCSI storage traffic. This leads us to the concept of Priority Flow Control.

Priority-Based Flow Control

We aren't the first to notice a need for prioritizing iSCSI traffic. In fact, the IEEE 802.1Qbb standard outlines a method for allowing Ethernet to do flow control with Priority-based Flow Control (PFC).

The idea is simple, and we won't go too far into the weeds on it. Imagine you have a busy network filled with frames all zooming around going from place to place trying to reach their destinations. All of a sudden, a frame holding an iSCSI packet shows up on the network. Using PFC, the iSCSI packet can be assigned a specific Class of Service (CoS) that allows it to have a higher priority on the network. When congestion occurs, a switch is able to pause other classes of traffic, such as people surfing the web for cat photos. The iSCSI frame is given priority on the network and allowed to continue along, while some of those cat photo frames are dropped.

Figure 14.1 shows an example of the default Quality of Service (QoS) configuration for Cisco UCS, in which each Priority level is also assigned a CoS.

>> ☰ LAN ▸ ○ LAN Cloud ▸ QoS System Class

General | Events | FSM

Priority	Enabled	CoS	Packet Drop	Weight		Weight (%)	MTU		Multicast Optimized
Platinum	☐	5	☐	10	▾	N/A	normal	▾	☐
Gold	☐	4	☑	9	▾	N/A	normal	▾	☐
Silver	☐	2	☑	8	▾	N/A	normal	▾	☐
Bronze	☐	1	☑	7	▾	N/A	normal	▾	☐
Best Effort	☑	Any	☑	5	▾	50	normal	▾	☐
Fibre Channel	☑	3	☐	5	▾	50	fc	▾	N/A

Figure 14.1   Default values for Cisco UCS QoS

Two priorities of traffic are enabled—best effort and fiber channel. In times of congestion, UCS gives equal bandwidth weight to both traffic types (hence, the 50% value for both traffic types). However, fiber channel does not allow packets to be dropped and has a CoS of 3, which is higher than the "Any" set by best effort. You could take a similar approach and configure iSCSI traffic with a similar priority schema as the fiber channel traffic by guaranteeing it a higher CoS and making sure packets are not dropped.

REAL WORLD

For the most part, the creation of various CoSes and their priority in the network will be the responsibility of whoever manages the physical network. It is advantageous, however, to understand these concepts. There are other methods of controlling QoS, such as creating a completely isolated iSCSI network or using rate limits, which exist on the other end of the spectrum.

No matter which method you ultimately end up choosing for prioritizing the storage traffic, it's a good idea to create some level of isolation to curtain off the iSCSI network. We dig into this concept with the use of VLANs for iSCSI.

VLAN Isolation

There are multiple advantages to using a dedicated VLAN for your iSCSI storage traffic:

- It can potentially provide a security layer for containing and protecting your storage traffic against unwanted attention through proper design and configuration.

- The VLAN can be created without a gateway, essentially making it non-routable. This avoids worrying about other traffic types entering the iSCSI network, or having the iSCSI packets somehow route into another network.

- A VLAN acts as a broadcast domain, eliminating unwanted chatter that would be reviewed and dropped from the network adapters responsible for sending and receiving storage traffic.

Since there is really no charge for creating an additional VLAN, there is little reason not to move forward with a dedicated iSCSI VLAN. Performance is king with storage, as we've tried to emphasize repeatedly, and anything you can do to enhance performance should be considered and reviewed for your design.

iSCSI with Jumbo Frames

Since we're on the topic of performance, it's definitely worth taking a look at the Maximum Transmission Unit (MTU) used for the iSCSI network. You might recall that the default MTU value is 1,500 bytes for an Ethernet frame. This is effectively how much data can be stuffed into a frame before it is considered full.

The default value of 1,500 bytes is perfectly fine and will operate without issue, but many folks often wonder if increasing the MTU value will help with performance. Whenever the MTU value is increased beyond the 1,500-byte point, the frame is considered a jumbo frame.

> **NOTE**
>
> Most people you chat with are going to assume that a "jumbo frame" has an MTU value of 9,000 bytes. Strictly speaking, anything over 1,500 bytes is considered to be a jumbo. But knowing that 9,000 is the de facto standard can help avoid confusion when talking with other networking professionals.

The logic behind increasing the MTU to something like 9,000 bytes is that fewer frames are required to send the same amount of data. For example, if you needed to send 9,000 bytes of data, it would take six regular-sized frames with an MTU of 1,500 bytes (1,500 bytes * 6 = 9,000 bytes). It would only take one jumbo frame with an MTU of 9,000 bytes.

Thus, you have used five fewer frames, which is about 83% more efficient. Additionally, the network adapter only had to create one iSCSI frame, meaning less work went into packaging and sending the data. With all these positives, you would think everyone would be turning on jumbo frames—so why don't they?

In reality, jumbo frames are hard to implement for existing infrastructures. They require ensuring that every single network device between your vSphere host and the storage array support jumbo frames: adapters, switches, the array, and so on. For some environments, this is relatively simple, while others will have to tackle a swath of red tape, change controls, and "it isn't broke" arguments. And there are some situations where you'll need to set the MTU value for your physical network switches to be higher than the VMkernel ports, such as 9,216 bytes (see Figure 14.2), due to additional overhead.

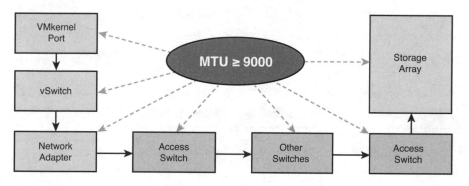

Figure 14.2 A complex network topology using jumbo frames

Unfortunately, we can't make a clear recommendation either way on this one. It depends heavily on your specific use case, network hardware, and company politics. Some folks love jumbo frames, other people hate them. Countless masses have done study after study showing minor improvements in performance with jumbo frames, while still others show minor losses in performance. If you have a new environment where making the MTU changes are relatively simple, there's nothing stopping you from giving it a shot to see if it works as advertised in your environment. In Chapter 15, "iSCSI Design and Configuration," we use jumbo frames just to give you a taste of the process.

Let's move on to the guts of what comprises iSCSI.

iSCSI Components

The high-level components of iSCSI are relatively straightforward to learn: an iSCSI *initiator*, which lives on the vSphere host, requests storage from the iSCSI *target*. The two exchange data over an iSCSI session. We go deeper into this in the next few sections.

Initiators

Initiator is a fancy term to describe the host or device that is accessing the storage array. In our case it's a vSphere host, but it could also be just about any device that is capable of speaking iSCSI. When you configure your vSphere host for iSCSI, you are configuring the iSCSI initiator with a personality (name), IP information for the network, and perhaps some security information.

iSCSI initiators are responsible for locating iSCSI targets, which creates a session for exchanging SCSI commands over the IP network. You can see a few examples of some iSCSI initiators in Figure 14.3.

Storage Adapters							
Adapter	Type	Status	Identifier	Targets	Devices	Paths	
vmhba37	Block SCSI	Unknown		0	0	0	
vmhba35	Block SCSI	Unknown		0	0	0	
vmhba34	Block SCSI	Unknown		0	0	0	
Emulex OneConnect OCe10100 10GbE, iSCSI UCNA							
vmhba1	iSCSI	Online	iqn.1990-07.com.Emulex.02-00-c9-01-15-9c	0	0	0	
vmhba2	iSCSI	Online	iqn.1990-07.com.Emulex.02-00-c9-01-15-9c	0	0	0	
No model provided - vmhba39							
vmhba39	SCSI	Unknown		1	2	2	
iSCSI Software Adapter							
vmhba38	iSCSI	Online	iqn.1998-01.com.vmware:esx2-11c1afa6	2	2	2	

Figure 14.3   A few examples of iSCSI initiators on a vSphere host

Targets

An iSCSI target is controlled by the storage device or storage array. The target is responsible for maintaining the stored data and making it available to the initiator. The target knows what data to make available because it has been associated with any number of Logical Unit Numbers (LUNs) on the storage array, usually by way of a storage group or some other vendor-specific name for a container of LUNs. The relationship between a target and the presented LUNs is called *masking*—it's how the storage administrator is able to define what is presented to each specific host. Otherwise you'd see all devices on the entire storage array, which wouldn't be all that secure, would it?

Figure 14.4 shows a quick look at an iSCSI software adapter's target list against a single iSCSI server (storage array) named "nas1.glacier.local" on port 3260. Don't worry; we go much deeper into the concept of software and hardware iSCSI adapters in the "iSCSI Adapters" section of this chapter.

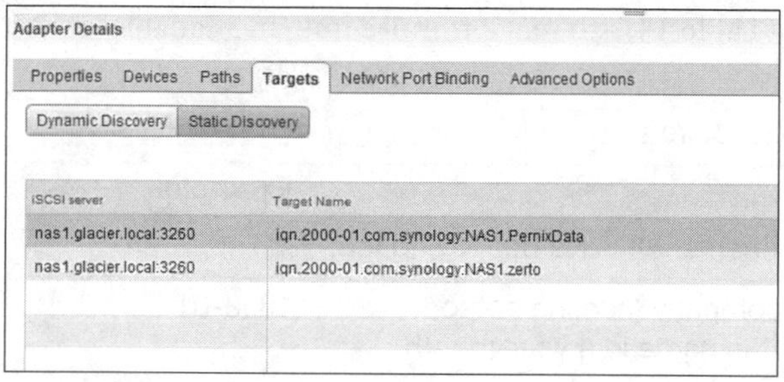

Figure 14.4 Targets discovered and in use with an iSCSI adapter

Notice how there are two buttons available—one for Dynamic Discovery and another for Static Discovery? This allows you, the administrator in control, to determine how the initiator is made aware of the targets:

- **Dynamic Discovery**, also commonly referred to as "Send Targets" in VMware documentation, is a method in which the initiator simply asks the storage array for a list of available targets. The storage array will then respond with a list of all the targets that can be reached by the initiator. If you are using a large number of targets, or just want the targets to automatically appear as they are created, dynamic discovery can be quite handy.

- **Static Discovery**, also called static targets, works very similar to how it sounds. You manually enter a list of targets that you wish to establish a session with. The list of targets never changes unless an administrator goes in and adds or removes targets from the list.

Both the initiator and target have a special naming format. There are a few different types of names and methods used when naming iSCSI devices.

Naming

Warning—here's where it gets a little confusing, so it may take you a few passes through this segment and some hands-on time with iSCSI to really get it to stick. Let's start with the basics.

Every iSCSI device, no matter if it is an initiator or a target, has a name. This name is called the IQN, which means iSCSI Qualified Name. It has a very odd format that looks like this:

```
iqn.1998-01.com.vmware:esx1-12345678
```

Weird, right? Let's break that down in Table 14.1 to make it more human-readable.

Table 14.1   iSCSI Qualified Name (IQN) Structure

Field	Purpose	Example
Type	Denotes the type of name. All IQNs begin with iqn.	iqn
Date	Denotes when the company (naming authority) took possession of the name in a year-month (YYYY-MM) format.	1998-01
Naming Authority	Naming authority in reverse, the name of the company (naming authority) that produced the initiator or target.	com.vmware
Unique String	This is the unique string field created by the naming authority. For VMware vSphere, it's the name of the vSphere Host with a dash and random characters—you can change it to something more meaningful if you'd like (such as just the hostname).	esx1-12345678

This structure is used for both sides of the equation—the initiator and the target. Let's break down a target name in a similar fashion to what we did with the initiator name previously:

```
iqn.2000-01.com.synology:NAS1.PernixData
```

- The first part of the target name starts with iqn, telling us we're dealing with an iSCSI Qualified Name.

- Next, we can see the date that the company (naming authority) registered the name, which was January 2000 in this case.

- The naming authority is com.synology, which is synology.com in reverse.

- The final portion, which is the unique string, indicates that the name of the storage array is NAS1 and the target's locally significant name is PernixData. Remember that the target can put whatever it wants in this segment, so it will change depending on the vendor and/or your specific configuration of the storage.

Knowing all the nitty-gritty about the IQN isn't all that important for day-to-day operations, but we find it is good to know how the vendor is using the unique string portion and how to read an IQN.

There are also two other another naming formats that you might encounter, although rarely:

- Extended Unique Identifier (EUI)
- T11 Network Address Authority (NAA)

Now that we know how the initiator and target talk to one another, let's move onto ways to secure the connection with authentication.

Security with CHAP

Even if the iSCSI Server (storage array) is limited to a specific VLAN, and you have made that VLAN nonroutable and isolated, there is still a chance that some unwanted entity could find a way to communicate with your server. In this case, some folks wish to secure the connection between their vSphere environment and the iSCSI storage with one additional layer of authentication.

Rather than encrypting the traffic itself, VMware vSphere only supports the use of the Challenge Handshake Authentication Protocol (CHAP) to secure iSCSI connections. Either one or both sides of the exchange require a password, called the *secret*, in order to establish an iSCSI session. And additionally, the password exchange occurs periodically throughout the duration of the iSCSI session to prevent relay attacks. Also, a hash of the password, rather than the password in clear text, is what actually gets exchanged.

There are two major methods you can employ with CHAP:

- **Unidirectional CHAP**: The target authenticates the initiator.
- **Bidirectional CHAP**: The target authenticates the initiator and the initiator authenticates the target.

The choice of CHAP implementation largely depends on what your storage array supports and what type of iSCSI network adapter you are using. Table 14.2 shows publicly published support for the various CHAP security levels with VMware vSphere 5.5.

Table 14.2 CHAP Security Levels

Security Level	Description	Support
None	No authentication.	Software iSCSI
		Dependent hardware iSCSI
		Independent hardware iSCSI

Security Level	Description	Support
Use unidirectional CHAP if required by target	The host prefers a non-CHAP connection, but can use a CHAP connection if required by the target.	Software iSCSI Dependent hardware iSCSI
Use unidirectional CHAP unless prohibited by target	The host prefers CHAP, but can use non-CHAP connections if the target does not support CHAP.	Software iSCSI Dependent hardware iSCSI Independent hardware iSCSI
Use unidirectional CHAP	The host requires successful CHAP authentication. The connection fails if CHAP negotiation fails.	Software iSCSI Dependent hardware iSCSI Independent hardware iSCSI
Use bidirectional CHAP	The host and the target support bidirectional CHAP.	Software iSCSI Dependent hardware iSCSI

Managing and editing the authentication type for an iSCSI adapter is relatively straight-forward. Select the network adapter and edit the Authentication method from the default of None to whichever method you have determined is necessary in your environment. In the example shown in Figure 14.5, **Use unidirectional CHAP** has been chosen. It's good to have a chat with your security team to find out if this is necessary since it can add an extra dimension of complexity to your host and storage configuration.

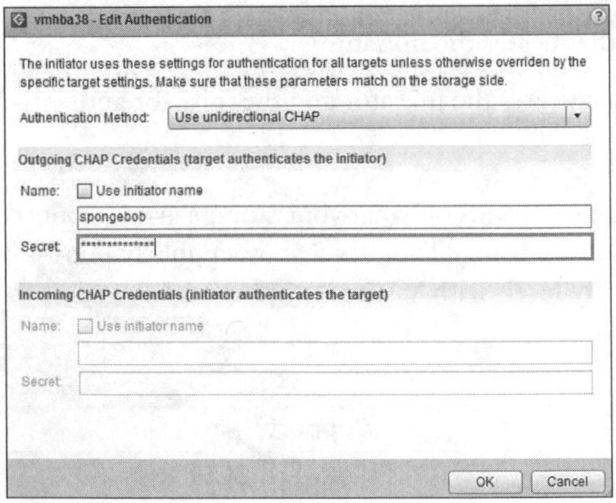

Figure 14.5 Configuring CHAP on an iSCSI network adapter

REAL WORLD

It's relatively rare to see a data center deploy CHAP authentication without a good reason. If you properly isolate your iSCSI network and use masking to limit what IP addresses can talk to the iSCSI server and targets, it's rather difficult for someone to infiltrate your storage network. We strongly suggest that you test the feature with a nonproduction target to get comfortable with how your vendor implements it before rolling out into production.

iSCSI Adapters

There have been many mentions made toward three different types of adapters over the course of this chapter:

- Software iSCSI

- Dependent hardware iSCSI, sometimes referred to as TOE (TCP Offload Engine) cards

- Independent hardware iSCSI, sometimes referred to as iSCSI HBAs (Host Bus Adapters)

Before we go into the differences, let's spend a little time talking about the iSCSI stack. In fact, Figure 14.6 shows the various OSI layers required to make iSCSI do its thing.

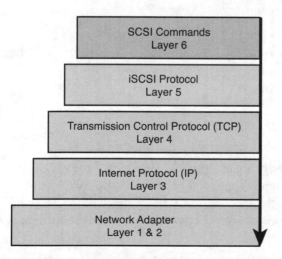

Figure 14.6 The layers hierarchy used for iSCSI

The SCSI commands and data at Layer 6 (Presentation) are encapsulated by Layer 5 (Session) into iSCSI data units. A further nesting of encapsulation occurs as we move down the OSI model: iSCSI data goes into TCP segments, which are put into IP packets and ultimately Ethernet frames.

These modular layers have to be handled by something—either software or hardware—that ultimately drives the major differences that exist between the types of network adapters available.

Software iSCSI Adapter

The software iSCSI adapter is provided by VMware to allow any vSphere host to participate in an iSCSI SAN without any special hardware. The entire IP and iSCSI stack is run in software using the host's CPU and memory along with a physical network to send and receive the packets, as shown in Figure 14.7.

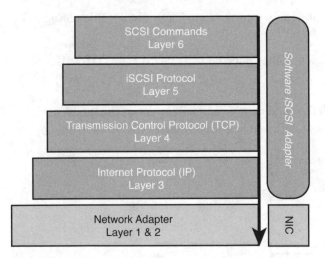

Figure 14.7   Responsibilities of the software iSCSI adapter

Creating a software iSCSI adapter is relatively simple—you just request that the vSphere host add a new software adapter, and it promptly appears. The underlying physical network adapter becomes largely irrelevant, as the vSphere host is handling all of the heavy lifting from Layers 3 through 6. The network adapter will typically just build the Ethernet frame and transmit it over the wire.

However, this does place some stress, even if it is slight, on the vSphere host because it is doing all of the work to encapsulate every single layer for all iSCSI traffic. If you plan to run your hosts aggressively with a high number of workloads, or just wish to ensure that the workloads' performance is not impacted by the overhead of processing storage traffic, another option exists: the use of hardware iSCSI adapters that are specifically designed to handle iSCSI traffic.

Dependent Hardware iSCSI Adapters

The first type of network adapter is the dependent hardware iSCSI adapter. Think of it as a hybrid solution—the network adapter isn't a fully featured iSCSI network adapter, but does have some special hardware in play that can offload the TCP portion of the work from the vSphere host. The reason we call this a "dependent" hardware adapter is that it is in fact dependent on the creation of a software iSCSI adapter to handle the creation of iSCSI data.

The division of labor looks like the example in Figure 14.8.

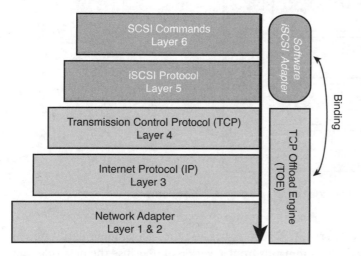

Figure 14.8   Responsibilities of the dependent hardware iSCSI adapter

Essentially, as the iSCSI protocol data is generated by the software iSCSI adapter, it is tossed over to the dependent hardware iSCSI adapter for further encapsulation and transmission into the network.

The software iSCSI adapter and the dependent hardware iSCSI adapter form a relationship with one another called a network port binding. Every dependent hardware iSCSI adapter in use requires its own software iSCSI adapter and the two are bound together in a one-to-one relationship. We go deeper into the concept of binding a little later.

Dependent hardware iSCSI adapters are often a nice middle ground between performance and cost. The host has less work to deal with, which might fit nicely with your design requirements, by using a network adapter that handles the TCP, IP, and Ethernet efforts.

But what if you want the network adapter to handle the iSCSI protocol data, too?

Independent Hardware iSCSI Adapters

If you want to offload the maximum amount of iSCSI work to a piece of hardware, you're in the market for an independent hardware iSCSI adapter. As the name indicates, this card can completely handle the entire iSCSI stack, as shown in Figure 14.9.

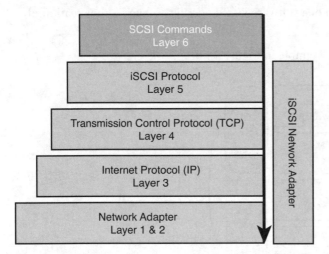

Figure 14.9   Responsibilities of the independent hardware iSCSI adapter

There is no need to create a software iSCSI adapter because the independent hardware iSCSI adapter can accept raw SCSI commands from a workload. Because the network adapter handles all of the work, it also needs to be configured with an IP address and IQN. As an example, let's look at our Emulex OCe10102-FX card (see Figure 14.10), which is an independent hardware iSCSI network adapter.

Notice how the adapter doesn't even have a tab for network port binding and also includes a field for the IP Address configuration? These are hints that you're looking at an independent hardware iSCSI network adapter. The one shown here has no IP address configuration because it's not in use, but if we wanted to set it up, it would just require using the **Edit** button and assigning a network address.

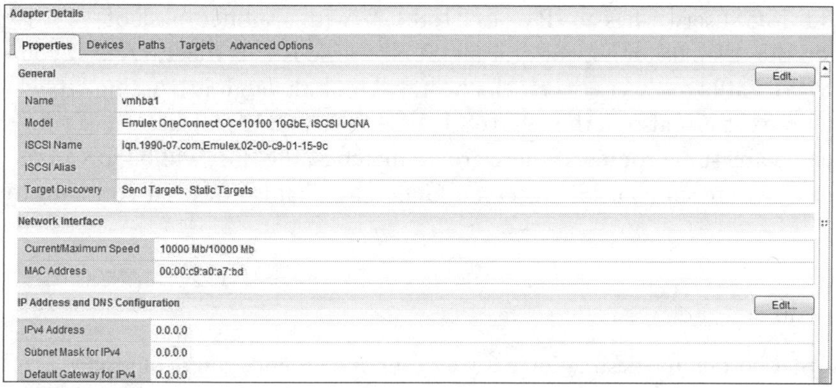

Figure 14.10 Adapter details from an independent hardware iSCSI adapter

NOTE

Many Converged Network Adapters (CNAs) or Universal CNAs (UCNAs) have the ability to perform both standard Ethernet networking and iSCSI or Fiber Channel over Ethernet (FCoE) functions—but not both iSCSI and FCoE at the same time. Just be on the lookout for TOE versus full protocol offload. This applies to network adapters in both traditional PCIe card format and blade server mezzanine card format.

iSCSI Design

Now that you are armed and dangerous with a solid understanding of iSCSI, its components, and the various adapters, let's shift into a design discussion. There are a few different methods available to you for designing the virtual network for iSCSI, and you should be aware of the benefits and drawbacks of each.

Because iSCSI uses the TCP/IP stack, it is reliant upon certain rules followed by the vSphere host. One such rule is how routing table lookups are performed. Whenever you are trying to reach a destination in a network, the vSphere host examines its routing table to determine if it has a VMkernel port on the intended network.

NOTE

If you are using an independent hardware iSCSI adapter (iSCSI HBA), the routing table on the vSphere host is no longer relevant. The iSCSI adapter handles all of the IP connectivity without involving the host.

For example, if your iSCSI server has an IP of 192.168.1.22 with a subnet mask of 255.255.255.0, then the destination network for all iSCSI traffic is 192.168.1.0 /24. If you attempt to send iSCSI traffic to this network, the host will look through its routing table to find a VMkernel port that is also in the 192.168.1.0 /24 network. It will also see if you have manually created any static routes. If there are no matches, the host will be forced to use the default gateway to reach your iSCSI server. Generally, that is not what you want to happen.

> **REAL WORLD**
>
> Any time a VMkernel port on the destination network cannot be found, you're entering the realm of routed iSCSI. This means we are using routing to reach the destination, which involves multiple networks and ultimately increased latency due to additional hops. Routed iSCSI is nearly always a corner case and should be avoided unless absolutely necessary.

Knowing this, let's discuss some design ramifications of the two methods available for relating iSCSI traffic to physical network adapters.

NIC Teaming

The first design option is to use NIC teaming, which is something you should be reasonably familiar with from other traffic types like Management and VM Traffic. NIC teaming dictates that we provide two or more network adapters and allow the teaming policy to determine where to place the workload. It works great for VMs and some types of management traffic. Unfortunately, it's not a very good way to handle iSCSI traffic.

To understand why, let's go back to the routing table discussion from earlier. Let's say there is a VMkernel port, vmk1, named "iSCSI" that is operational and on the same subnet as the iSCSI server. When iSCSI traffic wants to reach the iSCSI server, the host locates the VMkernel port because the routing table tells the host that the "iSCSI" VMkernel port is on the same subnet as our iSCSI server. However, the VMkernel port can only operate on a single physical network adapter, even if multiple adapters are available, as shown in Figure 14.11.

Therefore, all iSCSI traffic would use only vmnic0. The other network adapter, vmnic1, would sit there idle unless vmnic0 failed—at which point vmnic1 would take over as the active network adapter and vmk1 would point itself at vmnic1.

You might think that you can get around this issue by creating a second VMkernel port. So you add a second VMkernel port, vmk2, and name it "iSCSI2" with an IP address of 192.168.1.110. A diagram of this model is shown in Figure 14.12. Let's see how that would work.

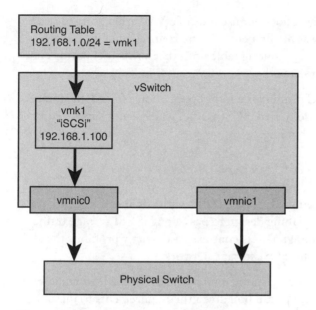

Figure 14.11   The iSCSI vmk1 is using vmnic0

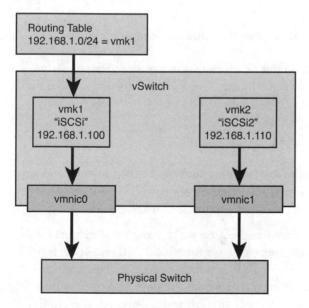

Figure 14.12   Using two VMkernel ports for iSCSI

The routing table is unchanged. The host does not use multiple VMkernel ports to reach the same network. In this case, vmk1 was the first entry in the routing table for the network 192.168.1.0 / 24. It will remain in the routing table until that VMkernel port is either removed or reconfigured to a different network.

Because of this behavior, standard NIC teaming is a rather poor choice for iSCSI storage. Its only real advantage is the ability to do routed iSCSI traffic, which is not supported by the other design method: network port binding.

Network Port Binding

The highly preferred method for doing iSCSI storage traffic with vSphere is network port binding. This allows you to use a multipathing design to pass along iSCSI storage traffic. There's really no reason to avoid this design unless your use case strictly prohibits the ability to use switching, not routing, for your iSCSI storage network.

Network port binding requires a rather stringent configuration so that the host understands exactly what you are trying to do. We can boil down the requirements to these items:

- Every network adapter that will pass along iSCSI traffic has a single, unique VMkernel port for iSCSI traffic.

- Each VMkernel port cannot be used by more than one single network adapter.

There are two different ways you can build this relationship—a multiple vSwitch design and a single vSwitch design. They are both equally effective and are ultimately driven by the quantity and layout of your network adapters.

Multiple vSwitch Design

The multiple vSwitch design uses an entire vSwitch to isolate the VMkernel ports and network adapters from one another. Each vSwitch will house a single iSCSI VMkernel port and a single network adapter. Figure 14.13 shows the multiple vSwitch design.

Notice that the routing table is no longer shown? Because we're using network port binding, the routing table is no longer the determining factor for which VMkernel port is used for iSCSI traffic. The Path Selection Policy, or PSP, is now in charge of determining which network adapter will send traffic. Using this approach, we have effectively minimized the importance of the vSphere network configuration and are instead living in the realm of storage.

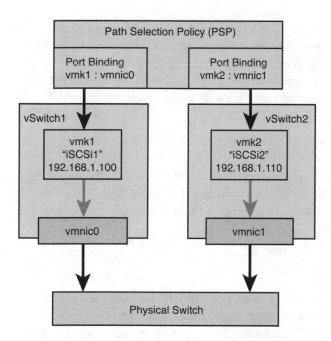

Figure 14.13   Multiple vSwitches for iSCSI VMkernel ports

There are three types of PSPs available with vSphere by default:

- **Most Recently Used (MRU)**: The host selects the path that it used most recently. At boot time, the PSP selects the first working path it discovers. When the path becomes unavailable, the host selects an alternative path. The host does not revert to the original path when that path becomes available again. There is no preferred path setting with the MRU policy. MRU is the default policy for most active–passive storage devices.

- **Fixed**: The host uses the designated preferred path, if it has been configured. Otherwise, it selects the first working path discovered at system boot time. The host automatically returns to the previously defined preferred path as soon as it becomes available again. If you want the host to use a particular preferred path, you must specify it manually. Fixed is the default policy for most active–active storage devices.

- **Round Robin (RR)**: The host uses an automatic path selection algorithm rotating through all active paths when connecting to active–passive arrays, or through all available paths when connecting to active–active arrays. RR is the default for a number of arrays and can be used with both active–active and active–passive arrays to implement load balancing across paths for different LUNs.

The multiple vSwitch design is handy when you have dedicated NICs specifically for iSCSI storage traffic. This usually means you're using a rackmount server with many 1 Gb Ethernet adapters, but it can sometimes reveal itself in a blade design, too. Just remember that this design isn't recommended if you plan to use the network adapters for other types of traffic, because you're effectively creating a vSwitch with a single point of failure—one network adapter.

Having a single network adapter on a vSwitch is okay with the network port binding design because each bound port works as part of a greater team. If one network adapter fails, all traffic is shifted off the "dead" network port binding and onto the surviving network port binding(s). This can be a bit difficult to swallow at first blush, since we've been stressing the need to have multiple network adapters on a vSwitch over and over again—but this leads us into the second design: single vSwitch design.

Single vSwitch Design

In many cases—when using just a pair of 10 Gb network adapters, for example—you'll want to use the physical uplinks for more than just iSCSI traffic. In these cases, creating additional vSwitches will not be possible. Fortunately, there is a design that addresses the use case with just one vSwitch, as shown in Figure 14.14.

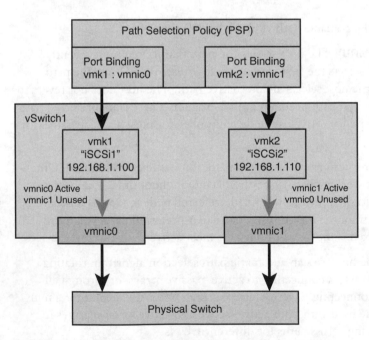

Figure 14.14   A single vSwitch for iSCSI VMkernel ports

The major difference with the single vSwitch design is that it uses failover order to isolate the VMkernel port onto a network adapter. Let's review the failover order for the two VMkernel ports:

- **vmk1**: Active on vmnic0, Unused on vmnic1

- **vmk2**: Active on vmnic1, Unused on vmnic0

> **NOTE**
>
> The design diagram assumes only two network adapters named vmnic0 and vmnic1. If you have more adapters, make sure that all but one adapter is set to Unused for each VMkernel port. It is very important to select **Unused** and not Standby for port binding; the wizard does not allow a configuration where Standby has been chosen.

By setting this failover order, we've isolated each VMkernel port to a single network adapter. If the Active network adapter fails, the VMkernel port will no longer remain functional, which is the desired result. The PSP will cease using this dead path and shift all traffic to the surviving paths. Additionally, assuming your vendor supports RR IO, you can utilize two or more network adapters simultaneously, which can lead to an improved quantity of throughput.

Boot from iSCSI

It can be somewhat annoying to have hard disks inside your vSphere server, especially at scale. One potential solution to this is to avoid using local disks inside of the server and instead boot from a LUN on your storage array. This is usually referred to as "Boot from SAN" or BFS if you're short on time. VMware has supported booting from SAN using the iSCSI protocol since ESXi 4.1. This is supported even with the software iSCSI adapter. But wait, you might ask—how do I boot from the SAN using a software iSCSI adapter when the hypervisor isn't installed yet?

The trick is to use a special type of network adapter that supports iSCSI Boot Firmware Table (iBFT). Think of this as a type of helper that knows the details necessary to find the iSCSI server, connect to a target, and mount a LUN for booting. You can find over 200 supported network adapters in the Hardware Compatibility List (HCL) on VMware's website. Just make sure to set the "What are you looking for?" field to **IO Devices**, the I/O Device Type to **Network**, and then look for the keyword iBFT, as shown in Figure 14.15.

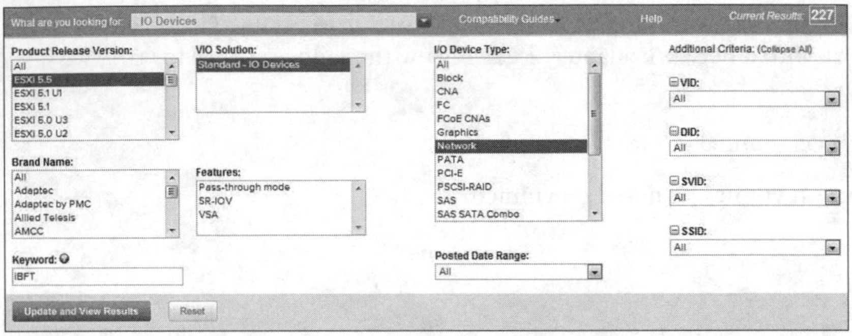

Figure 14.15   A list of network adapters that support iBFT

The high level steps necessary to install ESXi using this method are:

1. Boot up your server and press the vendor-required keystrokes to enter the configuration of your network adapter.

2. Configure the adapter with your iSCSI IP, mask, and target information.

3. Save your configuration and restart the server, but do not enable the iSCSI boot.

4. Present the VMware ESXi installation media to the server using an ISO, DVD, or whatever method you prefer.

5. While the server boots up, the network adapter will contact your storage target and connect to the boot LUN.

6. When prompted by the installation media, begin an install of ESXi to the iSCSI boot LUN.

7. Remove the ESXi installation media and restart.

8. Reconfigure your network adapter to boot to iSCSI.

Keep in mind that the detailed steps vary depending on the type of hardware you select.

REAL WORLD

When creating a unique LUN for your server to boot from, try to make sure the host-facing LUN ID (often called the Host ID) is 0. Almost all vendor hardware that has a boot configuration will assume LUN 0 is the boot LUN, although we have run into a few that look for some oddball number. Consider LUN 0 the de facto standard booting ID or read the vendor documentation carefully. Additionally, we often like to make sure that only the boot LUN is presented to a host the first time you install the hypervisor onto it. After all, you don't want to accidently install ESXi to the wrong LUN, especially if it contains valid data and is wiped by the install process!

There are many advantages to using a boot from SAN architecture:

- **Hardware Upgrades**: If you need to upgrade the ESXi server hardware, just remove the server and plug in a new one, then reconfigure the network adapter—no hypervisor reinstall necessary.

- **Hardware Mobility**: The ESXi server can change personalities by changing boot LUNs, such as a boot LUN for ESXi 5.1 production and a boot LUN for ESXi 5.5 to test the new features.

- **Reduced Capital Expenses (CapEx)**: You've already purchased that big, redundant storage array, and wish to use it for booting to save on a large quantity of hard drives inside of your servers.

Do keep in mind that booting from SAN increases your vSphere host failure domain to include your SAN and the storage array itself. If the SAN is unavailable, your hosts can no longer boot, though running hosts should chug along fine as the hypervisor is loaded into RAM. Usually, though, if the SAN is unavailable, you have bigger concerns.

> **NOTE**
>
> Let's be clear. We're not fans of booting from iSCSI—there are much better ways to do this, such as stateless Auto Deploy. This doesn't mean iSCSI boot can't or shouldn't be used, but we view it as a lot of additional complexity added for something as trivial as the hypervisor, which should be as stateless as possible anyway. Simplicity is the cornerstone of all great designs.

Summary

Whew, what an adventure through the land of iSCSI. You should now be familiar with all the components within the iSCSI stack, along with a foundational knowledge around the architecture necessary to get iSCSI humming along. We also poked into the two major design scenarios used with iSCSI networking. It's time to apply all that newly found knowledge! The next chapter focuses on the design and configuration steps needed to create a real-world, working implementation of iSCSI networking to connect to an iSCSI LUN.

Chapter 15

iSCSI Design and Configuration

Key Concepts

- iSCSI Network Address Scheme
- Network Port Binding
- iSCSI Server and Target Discovery
- CHAP Authentication
- Path Selection Policies

Introduction

It's time for the fun part: getting your hands dirty with some iSCSI design and configuration. This chapter focuses heavily on a real-world scenario involving the use of iSCSI to map and present storage for your virtual workloads. Because it's important to expose you to as many variations as possible, our use case is going to include a lot of extra requirements that might not come up when and if you need to use iSCSI. It's perfectly okay if you don't end up implementing some of the features we use here, such as CHAP, because it's ultimately your specific use case that determines what is implemented.

Without further ado, let's get cracking.

iSCSI Design

All great implementations stem from much time spent thinking about the overall design. And all poor implementations skip the design step and go straight into clicking buttons. We hate poor implementations, so we start with the design for our scenario to kick things off.

Use Case

The use case scenario plays out as follows:

> Your boss at Initech Corp is looking to add storage to the virtual environment using a new storage array. In order to keep costs down, he wants you to use the existing Ethernet network to attach the array instead of purchasing the infrastructure required to implement a new fiber channel SAN. Additionally, many of your critical virtual workloads require block-based storage—meaning they must be able to directly manipulate the blocks inside of a volume or LUN—to meet software support requirements. Reviewing the options with various storage array vendor specification sheets, you realize that the only option you have is to implement the iSCSI protocol.

> The iSCSI storage design needs to be able to handle a large quantity of storage traffic during peak times. It also needs to be as secure as possible to meet the security requirements set by your audit team.

There are a few nuggets of information that help feed a design based on the scenario:

- "Critical virtual workloads" are being supported, which most likely drive the need for low latency and multiple paths to storage for redundancy.

- You must use the "Ethernet network" to reduce cost and support "block-based storage" for workload software support—this is a constraint that limits the design to iSCSI or Fiber Channel over Ethernet (FCoE). However, because your storage array vendor supports only iSCSI, you are constrained to iSCSI.

- "Large quantity of storage traffic" might tip you in favor of using a large Maximum Transmission Unit (MTU) value to be able to further saturate the Ethernet network with iSCSI data.

- "Be as secure as possible" feeds many different requirements, such as the need for an isolated iSCSI VLAN, not routing the iSCSI VLAN, and potentially using CHAP for the initiator and target.

Not everyone will read the use case and come to the same conclusions, but it is important to at least call out the requirements and constraints to determine what choices are available. For example, you might determine that having 10 Gb Ethernet is enough to meet the "large quantity of storage traffic" requirement without using jumbo frames.

REAL WORLD

It's hard to design in a bubble. When given a use case that is open ended, as this one is, it's best to talk out your thoughts on the design with your team and with other stakeholders in the design. This ensures that you have buy-in from all parties who have an investment in the success of your architecture, as well as other pairs of eyes to pick out any requirements or constraints you might have missed. Lack of communication is often the root cause of many design flaws.

Naming Conventions

We're going to build upon the work completed in Chapter 13, "Distributed vSwitch Design." It doesn't matter that we're using a Distributed vSwitch, as the design is almost identical for a Standard vSwitch: a Standard vSwitch requires building a VMkernel Network Adapter directly on the vSwitch, where a Distributed vSwitch requires first building a distributed port group and then a VMkernel port.

While much of the work has already been completed in the Distributed vSwitch chapter, there are some changes that we're going to make. This will modify the original design from one that is not optimal into one that is superb.

First off, our vSphere hosts have only two network adapters—vmnic0 (Uplink 1) and vmnic1 (Uplink 2). So we need two distributed port groups, one for each network adapter, in order to use network port binding. We've decided to use vmnic0 for the "A" side of iSCSI, and vmnic1 for the "B" side of iSCSI.

Thus, the names and failover order will look like:

- **Distributed port group #1**: iSCSI_A, Uplink 1 Active, Uplink 2 Unused
- **Distributed port group #2**: iSCSI_B, Uplink 2 Active, Uplink 1 Unused

Notice the naming structure? We've denoted that both distributed port groups will handle iSCSI traffic and are using a common SAN-naming structure of "A" and "B" fabrics.

The next items we need to call out are the VMkernel ports. There's an existing VMkernel port, vmk3, on each host. However, we need two of them, one for each network port binding. Let's verify and create the following:

- **VMkernel Port #1**: vmk3 for the "A" iSCSI network
- **VMkernel Port #2**: vmk4 for the "B" iSCSI network

Putting it all together, the end result is a topology that looks like that shown in Figure 15.1.

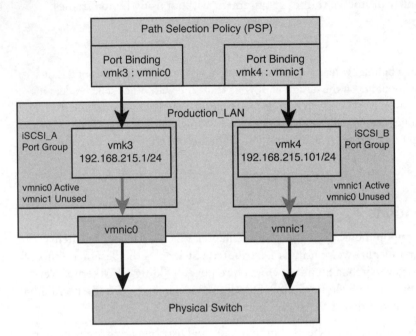

Figure 15.1   Topology of the iSCSI design

Network Addresses

Since we're using network port binding, it's important that we carve up the Ethernet network to support all the hosts for the future. The iSCSI network uses VLAN 215 on the 192.168.215.0 /24 network which is on the same subnet as the iSCSI targets, hence eliminating any need for routing the traffic to another network. The proposed network address scheme is as shown in Table 15.1.

Table 15.1   iSCSI Network Addresses

iSCSI Network	Network Range	Example
A Network	192.168.215.1-100 /24	192.168.215.1
B Network	192.168.215.101-200 /24	192.168.215.101

Based on this range, the first host named esx1 will use the first IP addresses in the range, 192.168.215.1 and 192.168.215.101. The next host named esx2 will use the next two IP addresses from the range, which are 192.168.215.2 and 192.168.215.102.

We've drawn up a table containing the IP addresses for the first five hosts to help you visualize how this works (see Table 15.2). The network address structure allows for 100 hosts, which is okay because the storage array we're using would wither under the IO stress long before we exhausted the IP address list. If you need more addresses for your environment, you could use a larger subnet or a unique subnet for each vSphere cluster.

Table 15.2   iSCSi IP Addresses for Initech Corp Hosts

Host	iSCSI A Network Address	iSCSI B Network Address
ESX1	192.168.215.1	192.168.215.101
ESX2	192.168.215.2	192.168.215.102
ESX3	192.168.215.3	192.168.215.103
ESX4	192.168.215.4	192.168.215.104
ESX5	192.168.215.5	192.168.215.105

This has an added bonus of making it easy to eyeball the IP address and know which host is using it, because the last octet in the IP address is equal to the host name's number. If you have the ability to make the numbering scheme simple like this, go for it. But don't sweat it if the numbers don't jibe, it's not that terribly important.

The iSCSI Server address will be 192.168.215.254, which is the last IP address in the range.

vSwitch Configuration

It's time to build out our iSCSI network. We start by ensuring that all the needed distributed port groups have been created, followed by the VMkernel ports, and then we bind them together using network port binding.

iSCSI Distributed Port Groups

Based on the design, we need two distributed port groups:

- Distributed port group #1: iSCSI_A
- Distributed port group #2: iSCSI_B

We already have one created named "iSCSI_Storage" that can be reconfigured. From the vSphere Web Client, navigate to the Networking pane, select the **iSCSI_Storage** distributed port group, open the **Actions** menu, and choose **Edit Settings**. Change the name to **iSCSI_A** like that shown in Figure 15.2.

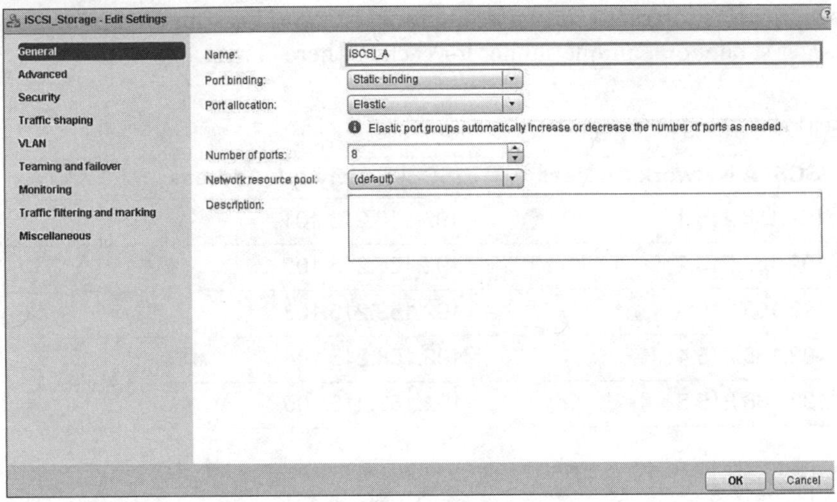

Figure 15.2 Renaming the iSCSI_A distributed port group

Next, click on **Teaming and failover.** The current configuration is to have Uplink 1 as active and Uplink 2 as standby. This is not a supported configuration for network port binding. We need to change Uplink 2 to Unused. Select **Uplink 2** and click the down arrow to move it into the Unused uplinks section, as shown in Figure 15.3, then click **OK**.

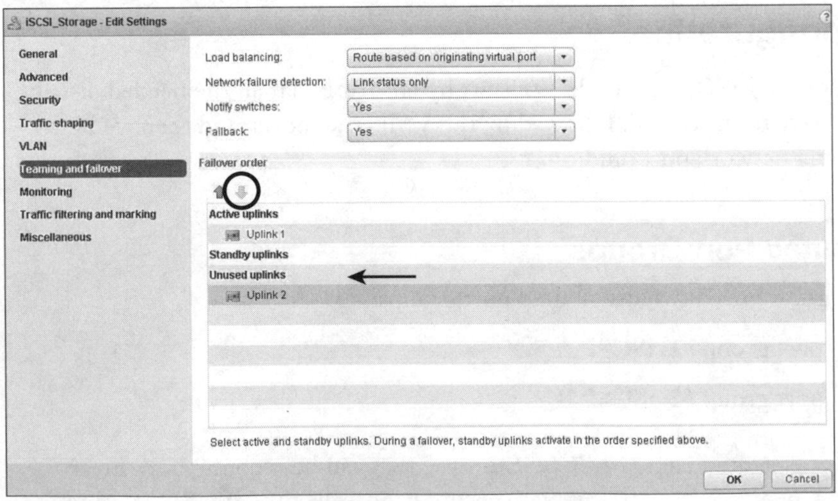

Figure 15.3 Setting Uplink 2 as Unused

There, iSCSI_A is now named and configured properly. It's time to build the iSCSI_B distributed port group. Start by clicking on the **Production_LAN** Distributed vSwitch, open the **Actions** menu, and choose **New Distributed Port Group**. When the wizard opens, enter the name **iSCSI_B** as shown in Figure 15.4.

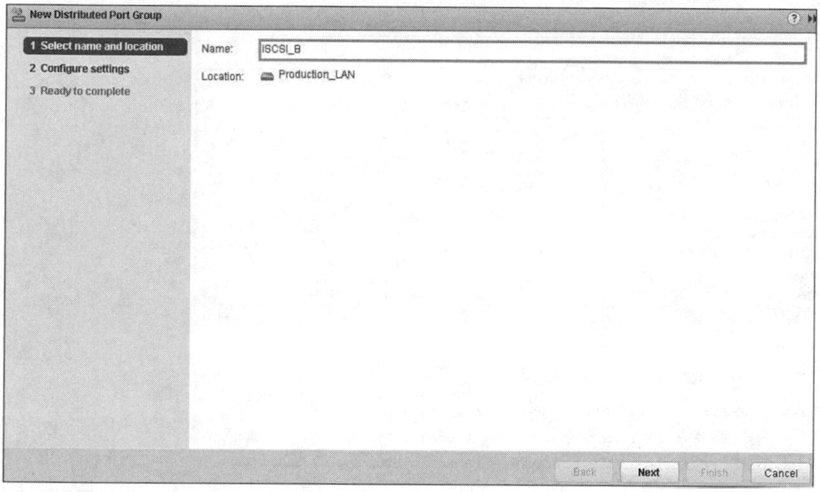

Figure 15.4 Creating the iSCSI_B distributed port group

In the configure settings screen, make sure to set the VLAN type to **VLAN** and enter the VLAN being used for iSCSI—215. Also, check the box for **Customize default policies configuration**, as shown in Figure 15.5, so that we can set the teaming and failover policy in the wizard.

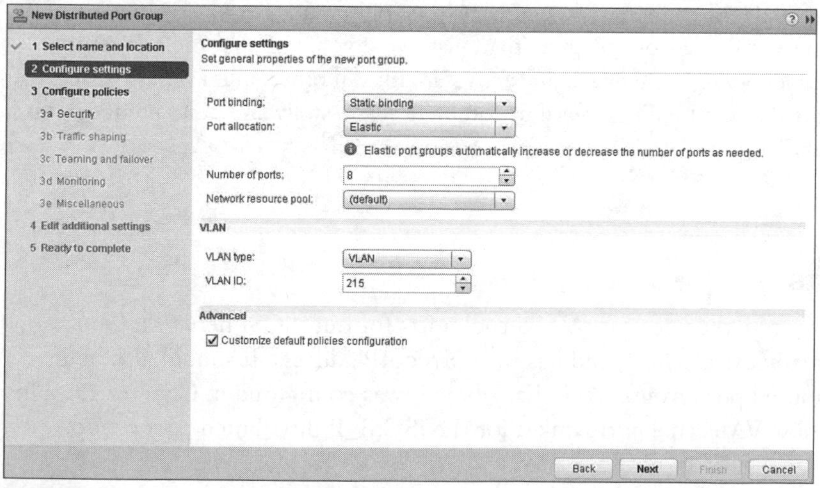

Figure 15.5 Configure settings for the iSCSI_B distributed port group

Keep clicking **Next** until you arrive at the Teaming and Failover screen in the wizard. Select **Uplink 1** and click the blue down arrow until it is in the Unused uplinks group. Make sure that Uplink 2 remains in the Active uplinks group, as shown in Figure 15.6.

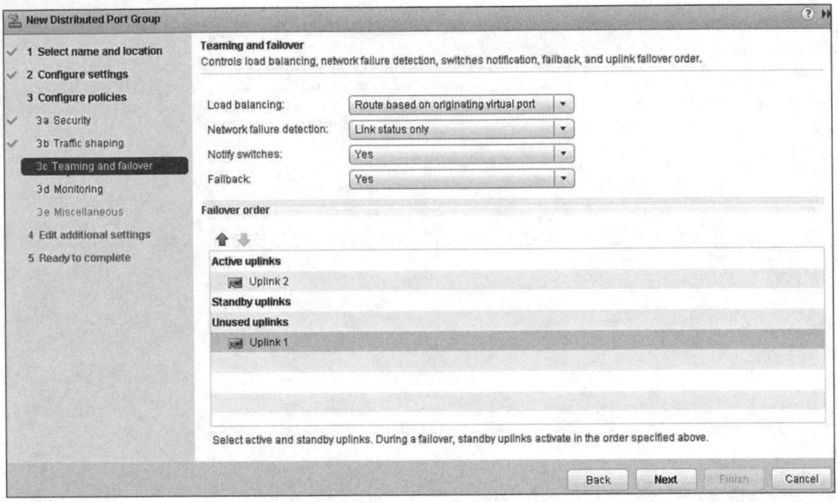

Figure 15.6   Failover order for the iSCSI_B distributed port group

Complete the wizard with default values and click **Finish**. There should now be both an iSCSI_A and iSCSI_B distributed port group.

> **NOTE**
>
> We've only made two distributed port groups because we only want to use two network adapters. You can use more network adapters than just two if you wish, but the rules still apply: Each VMkernel port can only have one active uplink. All other uplinks must be set to Unused in order for the port binding wizard to complete successfully and build unique paths to the iSCSI target.

VMkernel Ports

The next step is to create the necessary VMkernel ports for our iSCSI network. One VMkernel port already exists, vmk3, and has the correct IP address. It should also be in the iSCSI_A distributed port group, since that's how it was configured in Chapter 13. This leaves us with the new VMkernel port, vmk4, for the iSCSI_B distributed port group.

NOTE

There is nothing significant about the vmk number. It's just a way we can track the VMkernel port number for this walkthrough. Yours will most likely be a different number from ours, and that's perfectly fine. It's wise to try and use the same vmk numbers on each host to enforce consistency, improve identification, and assist troubleshooting, but not required.

Let's go ahead and create vmk4. Start by visiting the vSphere Web Client, navigate to the Host and Clusters pane, and select host **esx1**. From there, click the **Manage** tab, choose the **Networking** sub-tab, and click on the **VMkernel adapters** menu item. The list looks like that shown in Figure 15.7.

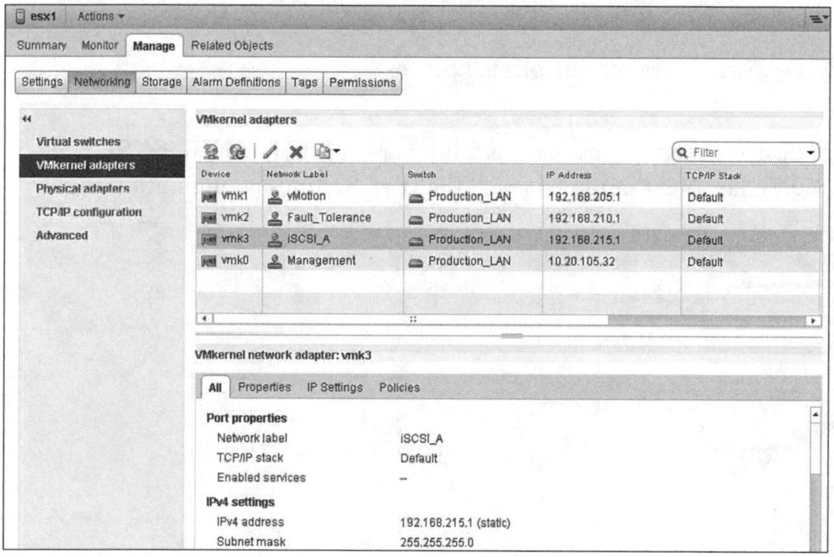

Figure 15.7 A list of VMkernel adapters on host esx1

Click on the **Add host networking** icon, which looks like a small globe with a green plus sign, and choose the **VMkernel Network Adapter** radio button, as shown in Figure 15.8. Click **Next**.

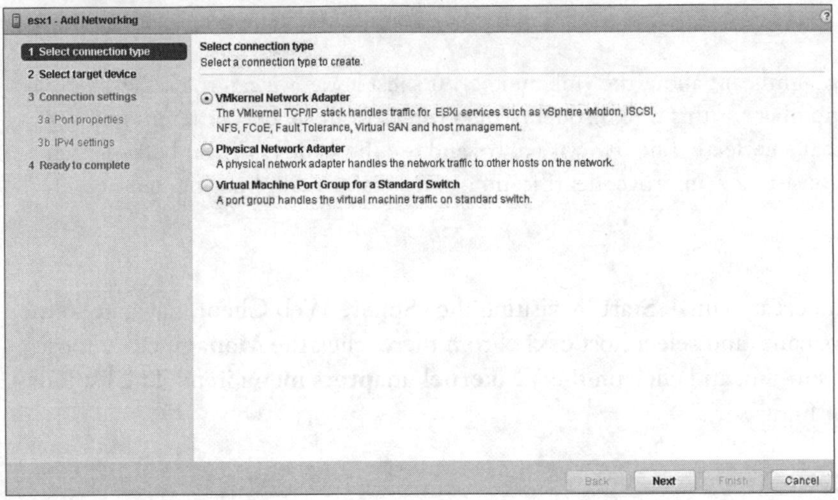

Figure 15.8   Adding a VMkernel network adapter to host esx1

In the select target device screen, choose the distributed port group named **iSCSI_B**, as shown in Figure 15.9. Click **Next** until you reach the IPv4 Settings configuration page.

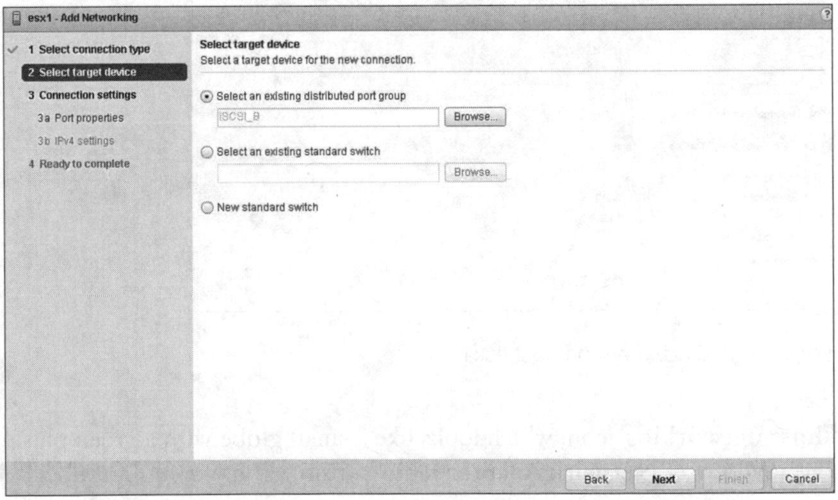

Figure 15.9   Put the new VMkernel network adapter on the iSCSI_B distributed port group

Enter the IPv4 address and subnet mask for the iSCSI_B network on host esx1. Refer to Table 15.2 for the values, which we have put into Figure 15.10.

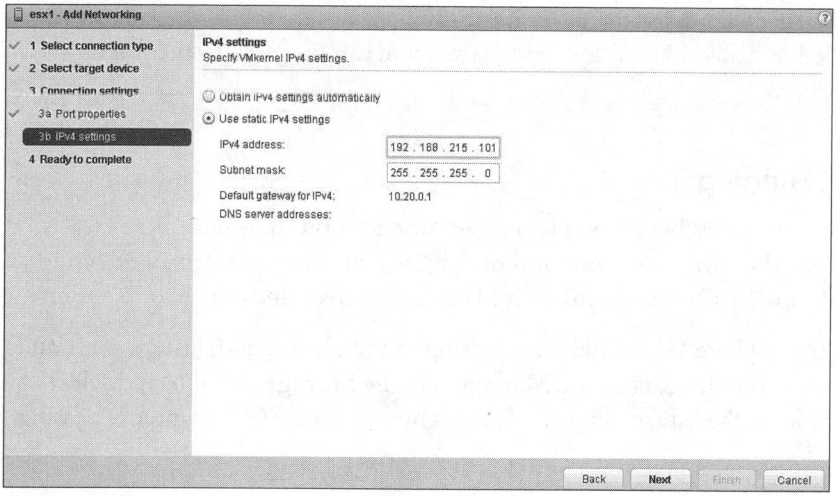

Figure 15.10 Configuring the new VMkernel network adapter on the iSCSI_B distributed port group

Complete the wizard with default values and click **Finish**. The end result should be a new VMkernel port, which is vmk4 for our environment, as shown in Figure 15.11.

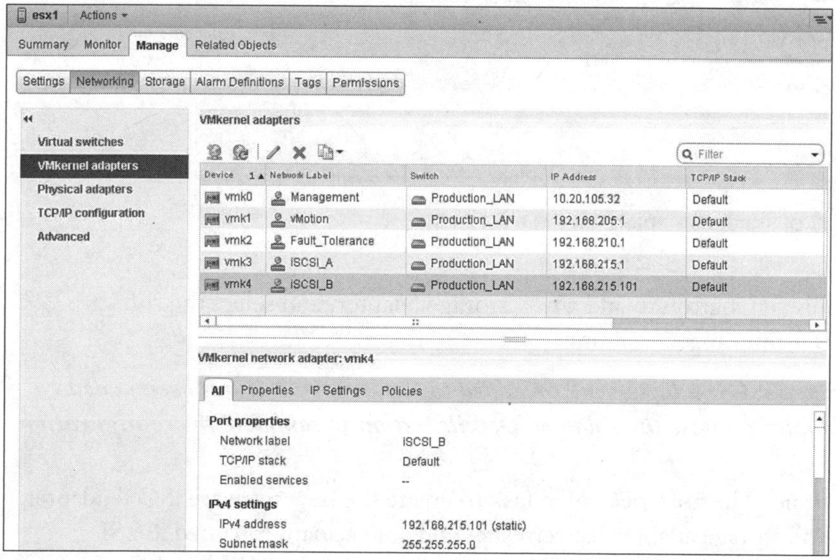

Figure 15.11 Host esx1 now has both the iSCSI_A and iSCSI_B VMkernel ports added and configured

You need to repeat this section for the other host, esx2. Make sure to use the correct IP address as described in Table 15.2. When completed, you can move on to the fun bit—network port binding.

Network Port Binding

It's now time to blur the lines between network and storage a bit. In order to create a relationship between the VMkernel ports and the physical network adapters, we need to enable the software iSCSI adapter. Think of it like the glue that binds the two together.

Start by opening the vSphere Web Client, navigating to the Hosts and Clusters pane, and choosing host **esx1**. From there, click the **Manage** tab, the **Storage** sub-tab, and select **Storage Adapters** from the list (see Figure 15.12). The software iSCSI adapter is missing from the list.

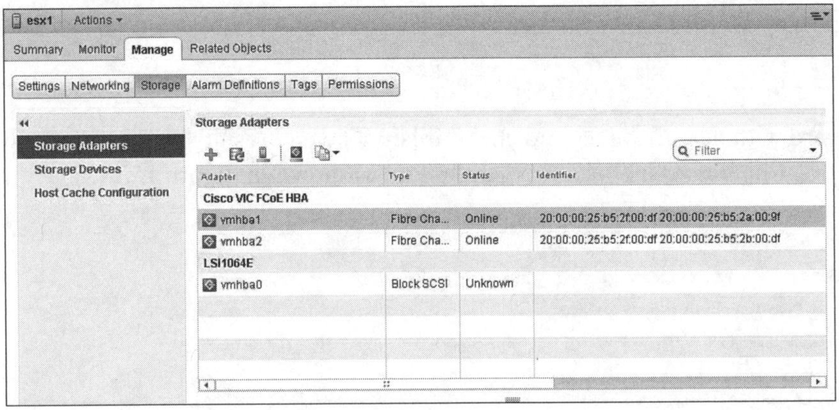

Figure 15.12   A list of storage adapters on the esx1 host

Click the green plus sign button to add a new storage adapter, and select the software iSCSI adapter. A warning appears stating:

> *A new software iSCSI adapter will be added to the list. After it has been added, select the adapter and use the Adapter Details section to complete the configuration.*

Click **OK** to continue. The host kicks off a task to create the new software iSCSI adapter. When complete, the storage adapter list refreshes and a new adapter named iSCSI Software Adapter appears. The adapter is automatically assigned an IQN and given a vmhba value—this is an assignment provided by the vSphere host for any Host Bus

Adapters (HBAs). Click on the iSCSI software adapter to view the properties, as shown in Figure 15.13.

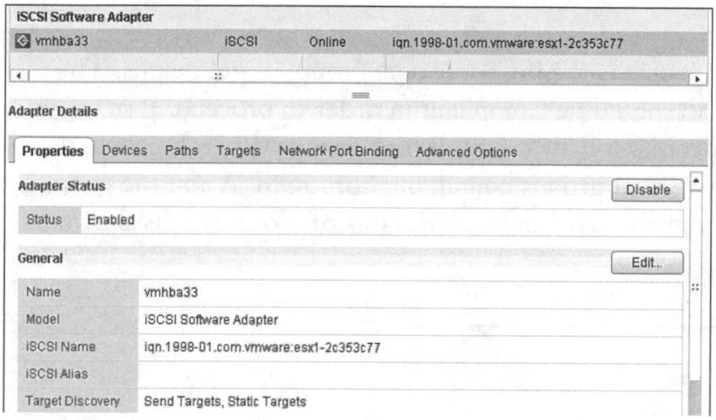

Figure 15.13   The new software iSCSI adapter on host esx1

Now, click on the **Network Port Binding** tab in the Adapter Details section. Because this is a brand new adapter, the list is empty with a "No VMkernel network adapters are bound to this iSCSI host bus adapter" statement. Let's fix that. Start by clicking the green plus sign to add a new binding, which begins a binding wizard, as shown in Figure 15.14.

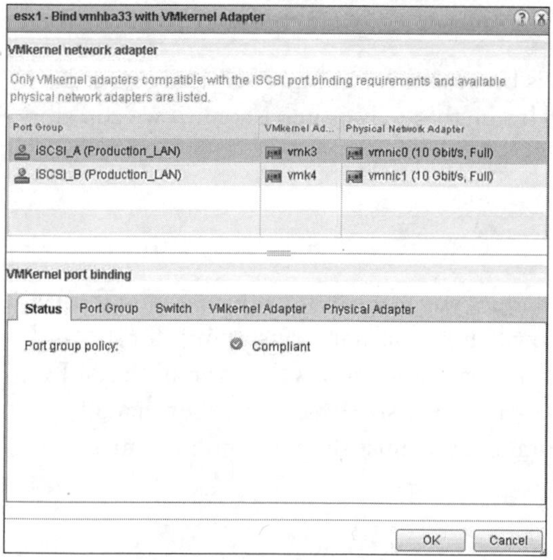

Figure 15.14   Creating new bindings on the iSCSI software adapter

This is a great figure to help pull all of the concepts of network port binding together. Here, you can see the relationship between a distributed port group, the VMkernel port, and the physical network adapter. Creating a port binding formally recognizes this relationship.

Click on the first item on the list, which is the **iSCSI_A** port group, to get details. The Port group policy on the Status tab should be Compliant in order to proceed. If so, click the **OK** button, then repeat the process for the iSCSI_B port group. When finished, the network port binding list shows two port groups bound, one for iSCSI_A and the other for iSCSI_B, with a policy status of compliant and a path status of Not Used, as shown in Figure 15.15.

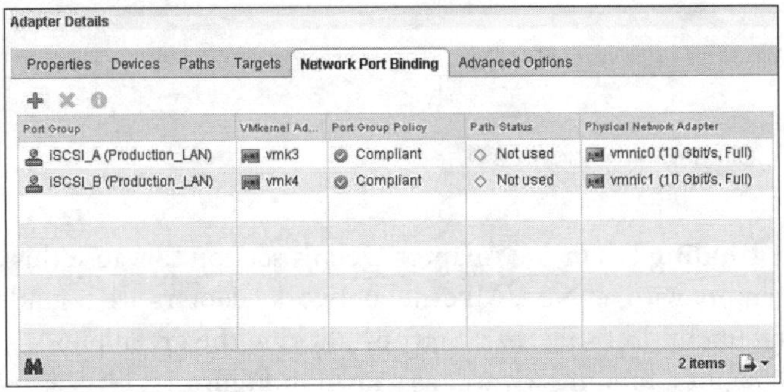

Figure 15.15   A list of network port bindings on the software iSCSI adapter

The reason we see a path status of Not Used is because there are no iSCSI targets connected. The paths are literally not being used by anything. This persists until we add storage in the next section.

Jumbo Frames

This is a good point to take a breather and decide if you want to introduce jumbo frames to the mix. It's good to make up your mind now before you start consuming storage, as it can be risky to change later when workloads are in production. We cover all the MTU changes that need to be made on the virtual environment size, but remember that all the devices between your ESXi server and the storage array must support jumbo frames in order for this to work optimally.

In our use case, we have decided that the requirements justify the use of jumbo frames. We have verified with our network team that jumbo frames have been enabled on all physical devices between the hosts and the storage array. So, we need to edit the MTU size on the following objects in the vSphere environment: the Production_LAN Distributed vSwitch and both VMkernel ports. Navigate to the Networking pane in the vSphere Web Client and click on the **Production_LAN** Distributed vSwitch. From there, open the Actions menu and choose **Edit Settings**. Select the **Advanced** menu and change the MTU value to 9,**000**, as shown in Figure 15.16, then click **OK**.

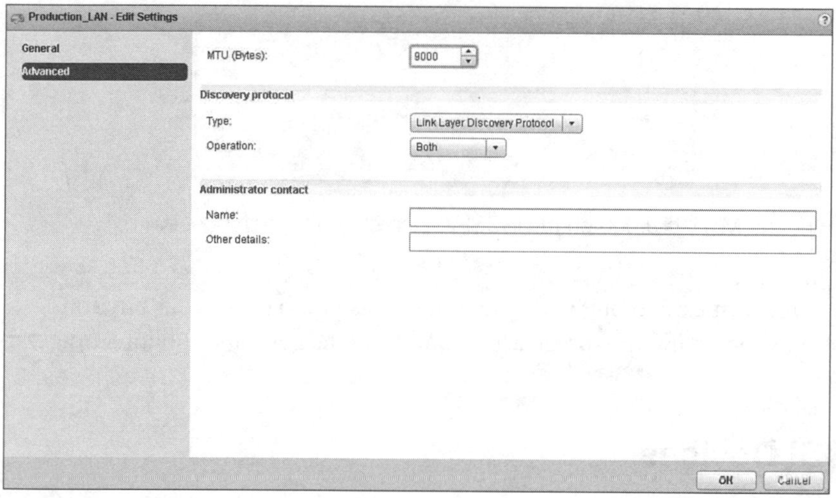

Figure 15.16 Setting the MTU to 9,000 on the Production_LAN Distributed vSwitch

The Distributed vSwitch should quickly configure itself to the new MTU value. You can now navigate to the Hosts and Clusters pane in the vSphere Web Client, click on host **esx1**, then find the Manage tab, Networking sub-tab, and the VMkernel adapters menu item to view a list of all the VMkernel ports on the host.

Edit both the iSCSI VMkernel ports, which are vmk3 and vmk4 in this environment, by changing the MTU value in the NIC settings menu as shown in Figure 15.17.

Figure 15.17   Setting the MTU to 9,000 on the iSCSI VMkernel ports within host esx1

Repeat this process for host esx2, along with any other hosts you have in your environment. It's now time to add an iSCSI storage array, find some targets, and mount storage.

Adding iSCSI Devices

Now that the entire iSCSI network is properly configured and operational, we can point our iSCSI initiators toward some iSCSI targets and begin mounting storage. The Initech Corp storage admin has already carved up several LUNs on the storage array and presented them to three different iSCSI targets: production, development, and engineering.

iSCSI Server and Targets

We're going to connect to the array using dynamic discovery (send targets) to show you how to map three different targets using a single iSCSI server IP. If you recall from earlier, the storage array is located at 192.168.215.254 /24.

From the vSphere Web Client, navigate to the Hosts and Clusters pane, select host **esx1**, click on the **Manage** tab, the **Storage** sub-tab, and the **Storage Adapters** menu item. From there, click on the iSCSI Software Adapter, which is **vmhba33** for Initech Corp, and then click on the **Targets** menu in the adapter details bottom pane, as shown in Figure 15.18.

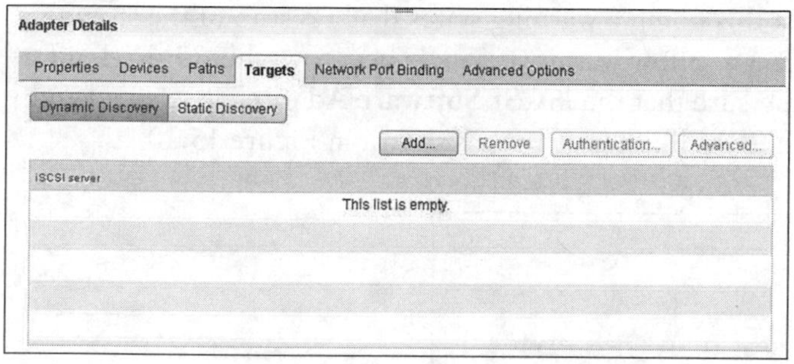

Figure 15.18 An empty list of targets for our iSCSI software adapter on host esx1

Click the **Dynamic Discovery** button, and then click **Add**. Enter the storage array's IP address into the iSCSI server field, and leave the port set to the default of 3260, as shown in Figure 15.19. We'll leave the "Inherit settings from parent" check box checked for now, but we come back to the authentication settings later.

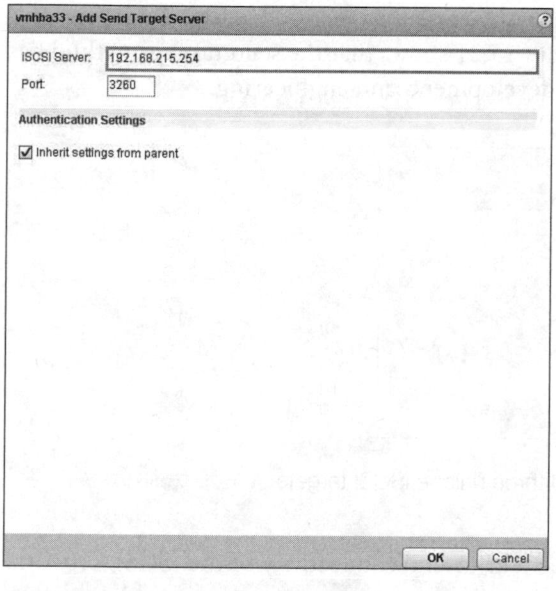

Figure 15.19 Configuring the iSCSI Server address

Click **OK** to finish the wizard. At this point, a warning states that a rescan of the storage adapter is recommended, including a yellow warning triangle next to vmhba33. Kick off a rescan for the adapter by making sure that the **iSCSI Software Adapter** is selected and clicking the rescan button, which looks like a grey box, as shown in Figure 15.20.

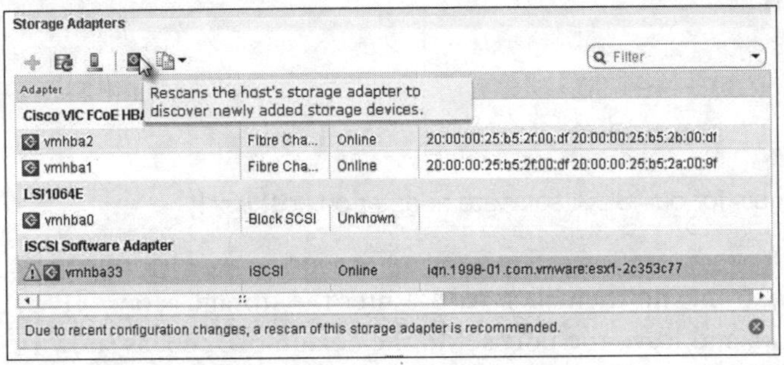

Figure 15.20   Rescanning the iSCSI Software Adapter for new storage devices

When the rescan is completed, check the list of targets for the iSCSI software adapter by clicking the **Static Discovery** button. Figure 15.21 shows that the send targets method has found three iSCSI targets for production, development, and engineering.

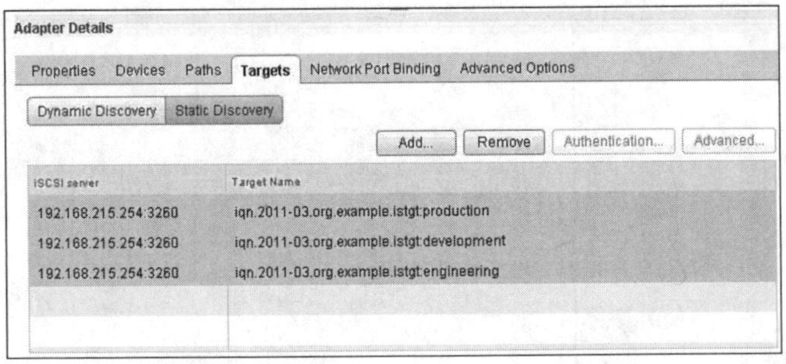

Figure 15.21   The iSCSI Server has revealed three unique iSCSI targets

Congratulations, we've successfully verified end-to-end connectivity of the iSCSI network. Go ahead and do a celebration dance, unless you're at work—your coworkers might not appreciate your magnificent triumph to the same degree. In that case, find someone for a high five.

REAL WORLD

Why not just configure CHAP first? It's often best to slowly walk your way into a new configuration, and we prefer to save authentication for after we know that the network is operational. Otherwise, if the connection were unsuccessful, you would not know whether it was the network connectivity or the authentication causing problems. By making small configuration changes that lead up to a final configuration, we ensure that each step was successful.

Authentication with CHAP

It's time to add a bit of security to the mix using CHAP. There are two ways that CHAP is typically employed for an environment:

- **Discovery Authentication**: CHAP can be used by the iSCSI Server to protect the discovery of targets via dynamic discovery (send targets).

- **Target Authentication**: CHAP can also be used to protect the iSCSI target, preventing the initiator from being able to view the devices associated with a target. In this case, you can discover the target itself but cannot view the devices without authentication.

The security manager at Initech Corp has mandated that CHAP is only required on the Production iSCSI target. This opens up a variety of options for CHAP configuration since the authentication credentials can be configured in a variety of locations:

- Configure CHAP on the iSCSI Software Adapter (vmbha33) and let the server and target inherit the settings.

- Configure CHAP on the iSCSI Server entry and let the target inherit the settings.

- Configure CHAP on the iSCSI Target directly.

If you have different secret passwords for each target, you have to configure them directly on the target. In this case, we configure the authentication credentials on the iSCSI server object and let the target inherit the configuration.

To begin, open the vSphere Web Client and navigate to the Hosts and Clusters pane; then select host **esx1**, click the **Manage** tab, the **Storage** sub-tab, and select **Storage Adapters** from the menu. From there, click on the iSCSI Software Adapter **vmhba33** and choose **Targets** in the adapter details pane. Make sure the iSCSI Server **192.168.215.254:3260** is selected and click **Authentication**, as shown in Figure 15.22.

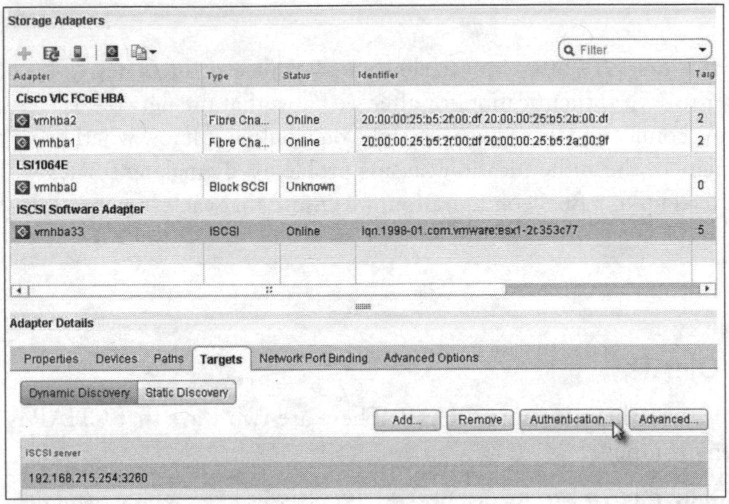

Figure 15.22   Configuring authentication on the iSCSI Server entry

In the Authentication Settings screen, change the authentication method from None to **Use Unidirectional CHAP if Required by Target** and enter the name and secret (see Figure 15.23). In our case, the name is **swingline** and the password is **1weLoveREDStapl3rs!**—this is a strong password. In a production environment, it's best to use a lengthy password that includes greater complexity to weed out brute force attacks. When entered, click **OK**.

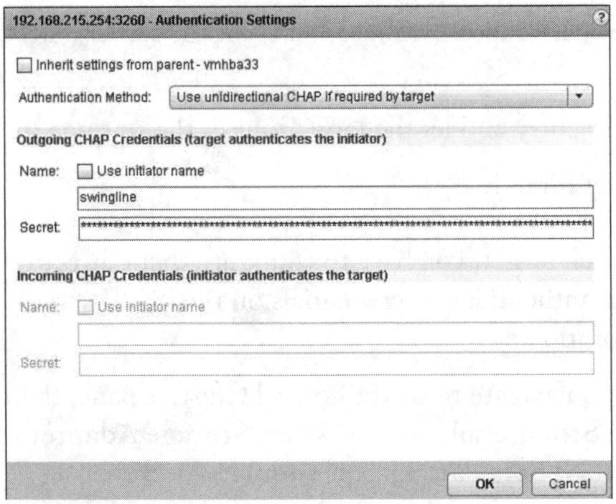

Figure 15.23   Entering the CHAP credentials

Make sure to rescan your iSCSI Software Adapter and ensure that the new CHAP credentials are working properly. If the configuration was successful, you should be able to see all the devices associated with the target that required CHAP.

Click on the **Devices** tab to view all the LUNs available. In our case, each iSCSI target is associated with a single LUN, which are outlined in Table 15.3.

Table 15.3   iSCSI Target and LUN Associations

iSCSI Target	CHAP Required?	Size
Production	Yes	10 GB
Development	No	9 GB
Engineering	No	8 GB

Figure 15.24 shows a view of the devices (LUNs) from the vSphere Web Client.

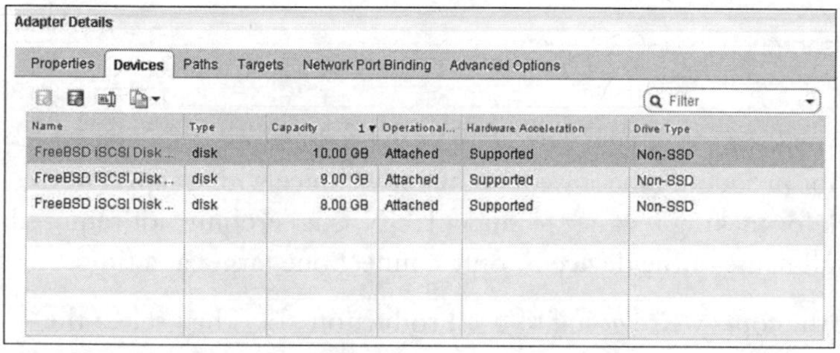

Figure 15.24   Available LUNs through the iSCSI targets

Make sure to visit host esx2 and repeat the steps necessary to configure CHAP authentication. When completed, we'll put the LUNs to good use and start creating datastores for the VMs.

Creating VMFS Datastores

Because the devices, or LUNs, are now available to the hosts, they can be used as VMFS datastores. The process for consuming iSCSI LUNs is identical to a local disk, fiber channel LUN, or any other block device.

From the vSphere Web Client, navigate to the **Hosts and Clusters** pane and select host **esx1**. Open the **Actions** menu and choose **New Datastore**. Work through the first two screens in the wizard, making sure that the host is esx1 and the type is VMFS, before you get to the name and device selection screen. You should see the three available LUNs as potential choices, as shown in Figure 15.25.

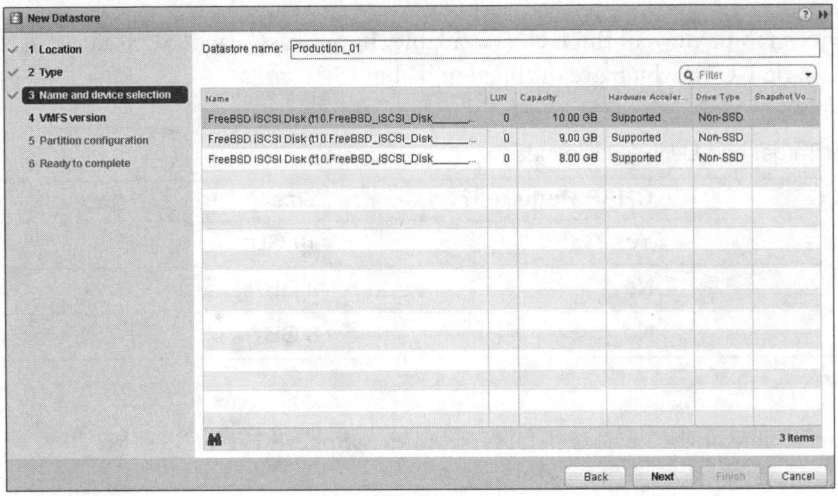

Figure 15.25   Available LUNs through the iSCSI targets

We made it easy for you by making sure that no two LUNs were the same size. The 10 GB LUN must be the one for production because it is the only choice with a capacity of 10 GB. This is a handy trick for making it easier to find a LUN, but certainly not required. You could also record the full name of the device or only connect one target at a time.

Enter a Datastore Name at the top—we're going to use Production_01. Then select the **10 GB LUN** from the device selection area. Continue through the wizard and accept the remaining defaults. A task will begin to format the VMFS datastore. When completed, click on the **Related Objects** tab followed by the **Datastores** sub-tab to see the new datastore. You should be able to see the newly created Production_01 datastore, as shown in Figure 15.26.

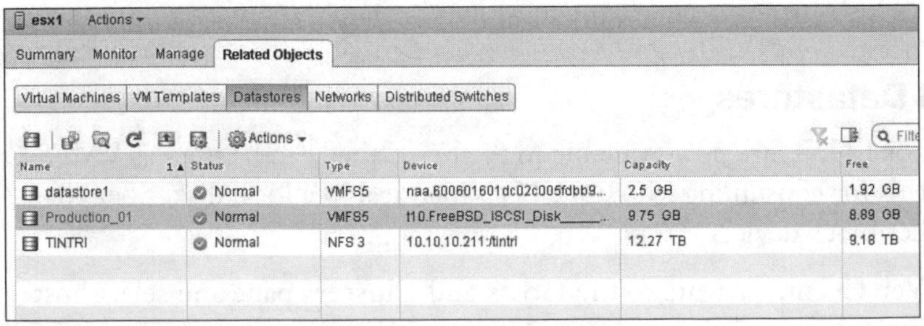

Figure 15.26   The datastores available on host esx1

Congratulations, you now have an operational datastore mounted over the iSCSI protocol. It's slightly smaller than 10 GB due to some formatting and overhead data, but that is to be expected. Continue adding datastores for the Development and Engineering departments, naming their datastores Development_01 and Engineering_01. The end result should look like that shown in Figure 15.27.

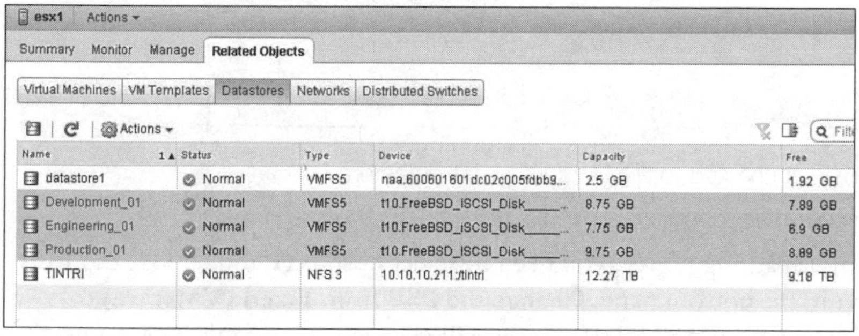

Figure 15.27   All the iSCSI-presented LUNs are now formatted as VMFS datastores

There's no need to repeat these steps for any of the other hosts. Rescan the iSCSI software adapter on host esx2 and it will realize that it now has access to the new VMFS datastores.

If you recall from earlier, one of our requirements is to ensure that we allow for a large quantity of throughput on the network adapters. One way to do this—assuming it is supported by your workload and storage array—is to use Round Robin for your Path Selection Policy (PSP).

Path Selection Policy

We're going to change the PSP for the Production_01 datastore from Fixed, the default for our particular storage array type, to Round Robin. To do this, we need to drill into the multipathing policy configured on the datastore.

Open the vSphere Web Client and navigate to the Storage pane. Select the datastore named **Production_01** from the list; then click the **Manage** tab and the **Settings** sub-tab. From there, pick the **Connectivity and Multipathing** menu item. You should see both hosts, esx1 and esx2, in the list connections, as shown in Figure 15.28.

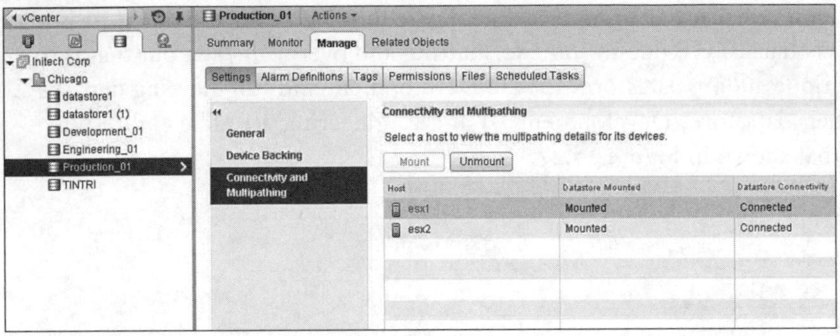

Figure 15.28   The hosts connected to the Production_01 datastore

In order to edit the multipathing policy, you need to select host **esx1** and choose the **Edit Multipathing** option in the bottom pane. Change the PSP from **Fixed (VMware)** to **Round Robin (VMware)**. At this point, the paths will grey out because there is no need to select a path (see Figure 15.29) —they will both be used in a Round Robin fashion. By default, 1,000 IO will be sent down one path, then 1,000 IO down the next path, in an alternating fashion.

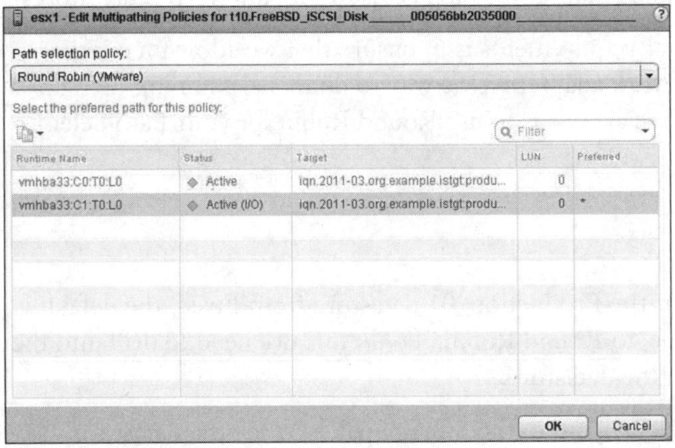

Figure 15.29   Changing the default PSP from Fixed to Round Robin

Repeat the process for the other host, esx2. Now both hosts will use the Round Robin PSP to send data to the storage array, which will use both network adapters. Keep in mind that anytime you change the PSP for a LUN on a host, you must repeat that change for all other hosts that access that same LUN. Otherwise, weird (and often bad) things might happen.

REAL WORLD

Exercise caution before you just go wildly changing the PSP for a datastore. Carefully verify that all the VMs using the datastore support the new policy. For example, until vSphere 5.5 was released, Round Robin was not supported for LUNs mapped by raw device mappings (RDMs) used with shared storage clustering (such as Microsoft SQL) failover clusters, also referred to as MSCS or Microsoft Clustering Services). Additionally, make sure your storage array vendor supports Round Robin. Failure to do so can result in an outage or data loss—or an "oopsie" to use the technical term.

Summary

You should now feel confident about the process required to design and configure your iSCSI SAN to include the virtual network. Using Ethernet to send and receive storage traffic is not that labor-intensive to implement, but requires a lot of thought behind the architecture. Data traffic is very sensitive to latency and lost packets, and requires that you treat it with a very high priority on the network. By respecting this fact, you can successfully deploy iSCSI or any other IP-based storage protocol, as many others can attest.

Chapter 16

NFS General Use Cases

Key Concepts

- Network File System (NFS) Protocol
- NFS Exports and Daemons
- Access Control Lists (ACLs)

Introduction

Another IP based storage protocol that is supported by VMware vSphere is Network File System (NFS). For long periods of time, it was shuffled off into a dark corner, being branded as a protocol good for nothing more than mounting ISO files to virtual guests. For the past several years, however, NFS has gained a lot of traction as a valid tool in enterprise architecture for presenting storage to a VMware virtual infrastructure. It is a protocol that is difficult to properly design for but very simple to operate and consume. In this chapter, we go deep into the weeds on how to be successful with NFS from a networking perspective.

Understanding NFS

The name "Network File System" tends to cause a lot of confusion, so let's address that first. NFS is a file system protocol, not a file system itself, and is only responsible for getting data to and from a storage array. The storage array can run whatever file system it wishes. There is no such thing as formatting a partition with "NFS" because, again, it's just a protocol. Furthering the confusion, the disk type field in vSphere shows "NFS" when connected via the NFS protocol. Just think of it as an abstraction of the storage array's underlying file system.

KEY TAKEAWAY

NFS is a file system protocol, not a file system.

NFS has traditionally been much more flexible than VMFS. For example, there is no vSphere-imposed limitation on the size of a datastore—it's up to the storage array to provide the limit. Additionally, NFS does not have LUN locking issues, as with block storage, because locking occurs at the individual file level. Since a VM can only run on a single host at any given time, having a lock on a file (such as a VM Disk [VMDK]) is acceptable.

Due to its incredible flexibility and access to large quantities of capacity, NFS became a popular method for providing storage for things like ISO files, log files, and other non-VM workload objects that have no serious performance needs. An administrator could whip up an NFS configuration in a short period of time and easily share out very large datastores to all the hosts in multiple clusters with ease. As lower-latency, priority-based Ethernet networking technology became more affordable and powerful, NFS began to gain some fame. The fact that the NFS client in ESX/ESXi has matured over the years has also promoted NFS to an active role supporting more intense workloads.

REAL WORLD

To be clear, we've seen entire corporations run hundreds and thousands of production VMs on NFS. In each case, NFS met the design use case and was architected to fulfill the requirements and constraints. There is nothing inherently better or worse about NFS. We just want you to know that it's a perfectly valid design option for many environments.

Lossless Versus Best Effort Protocols

In Chapter 14, "iSCSI General Use Cases," we talk about ensuring priority for iSCSI storage traffic. The same rules apply here. Both are forms of IP storage that use an Ethernet network to pass along data. And Ethernet is a best effort protocol that is expected to drop traffic from time to time. You can use methods like Priority-based Flow Control (PFC) to configure Classes of Service (CoS) that avoid dropping NFS traffic during times of congestion.

VLAN Isolation

The same idea for VLAN isolation, which we also cover heavily in Chapter 14, is relevant for NFS. If you plan to run both protocols to run VMs, it's best to create unique VLANs for each. This enhances security because no one breach will result in both networks being compromised.

Additionally, having a unique VLAN for each traffic type aids in troubleshooting and any environment changes. For example, if you need to do maintenance on the NFS VLAN, it would most likely not affect the iSCSI VLAN, meaning you would only need to issue a change control request for the NFS network. There are very few valid reasons to avoid creating a dedicated VLAN for NFS, so it's best to assume that you'll need one.

NFS with Jumbo Frames

Jumbo frames, which allow frames with a payload size configured beyond 1,500 bytes, are about as sticky of a subject with NFS as they are with iSCSI. Some people absolutely swear by the idea of using jumbo frames, and others have been horribly scarred by the process or see little to no benefit. It's important to note that it can be an operational nightmare to try and configure the end-to-end networking stack to support a Maximum Transmission Unit (MTU) beyond the 1,500 byte default, as shown in Figure 16.1 with a value of 9,000.

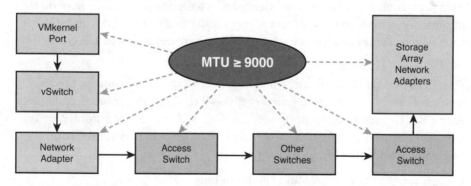

Figure 16.1   A complex network topology using jumbo frames

If you are working with a brand new environment and can easily make changes to the networking components, both physical and virtual, the stress is significantly reduced. Having an issue with a mismatched MTU value prior to going into production just means making a few tweaks during the day. It is entirely different to try and get an outage or maintenance window for a large quantity of production switching gear and arrange for the appropriate staff to be on hand during a night or weekend.

NFS Components

Before we get into the bits and pieces that make up NFS, we should clear up a few terms. Connecting to storage via NFS is often referred to as consuming network-attached storage (NAS). Connecting to storage via iSCSI is referred to as accessing a storage area network (SAN). What's the difference between NAS and SAN? NAS is file-based storage; SAN is block-based storage. With NAS, something else is doing the heavy lifting of providing a file system to the storage consumer, and the host manipulates files on that remote file system. With SAN, the host is consuming raw chunks of disk and must build a file system on top of them.

VMware supports NFS version 3. This is a rather old implementation that was solidified back in 1995. It has aged gracefully, though, and supports the ability to provide a large quantity of addressable storage. Let's start by defining the various components of NFS.

Exports

A storage array that wishes to share out storage over NFS must create an export. Think of it like sharing a folder or directory with the network in that you are making a container available for others to consume storage space. In fact, the storage array (which often runs a variant of Linux or UNIX) literally has a file called "exports" that lists out all the various directories that are shared out, who can read them, and what permissions they have on the directory. In some ways, the idea of an export is very similar to a target in the iSCSI world. We're defining which clients can connect, what the client can see, and what the client can do.

Data in a file system lives inside a volume, which is similar to the LUN concept used with block storage. A volume is a logical abstraction of disk—it could be the entire disk device, such as an entire RAID-5 set, or just a portion of the disk. Volumes allow a storage array to abstract physical disk configurations from the file system, granting additional control over how files are isolated by the file system.

Adding it all together, the entire stack looks similar to Figure 16.2.

Daemons

In order to share, retrieve, and write data to the network, the storage array requires the help of a daemon. Daemons are background services that do work for a Linux system without requiring a person to activate or interact with them. If you've ever worked with a Service in Windows, you already have a good idea of what a daemon is.

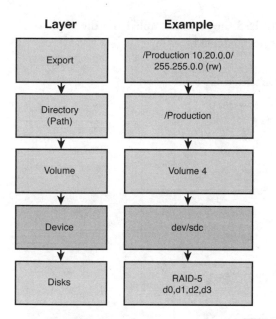

Figure 16.2   The various layers in sharing storage via an export

A storage array that implements NFS employs several different daemons to share out the file system data over NFS. These are commonly:

- **Rpc.nfsd**: The main NFS daemon

- **Rpc.lockd**: A legacy daemon that handled file locking

- **Rpc.statd**: Used by rpc.lockd to implement lock recovery when the NFS server machine crashes and reboots

- **Rpc.mountd**: Handles requests from a host to mount storage

- **Rpc.rquotad**: Provides quota information on the volume

While each storage array will add their own twist to NFS, the basic components do not change—there is always an export for you to mount storage and daemons that are providing the storage.

Mount Points

Now that we've covered much of the storage array side of the equation, let's focus on the vSphere host. Every vSphere host has an NFS Client used to mount storage on an NFS export. The NFS Client is visible in the Security Profile of each host and should be enabled if you plan to use NFS storage. Figure 16.3 shows an example from the vSphere Web Client showing that the NFS Client has been enabled.

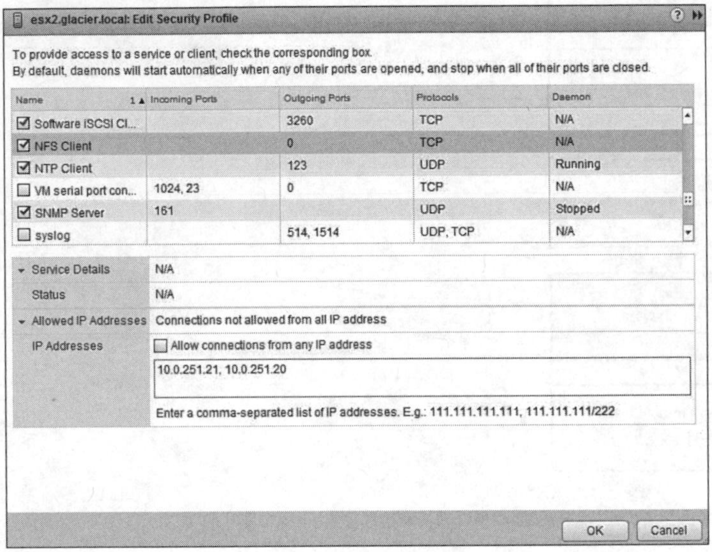

Figure 16.3   Enabling the NFS Client is required to use NFS storage

Very little information is required to mount an NFS datastore. The host just needs to know:

- What to call the datastore within vSphere
- The IP address or fully qualified domain name (FQDN) of the storage array
- The folder path (export) on the storage array
- Whether the NFS datastore should be mounted in read-only mode (optional)

All the remaining work is done by the underlying network configuration. As storage is added to a host, some additional fun commands are available via the ESXi Shell:

- Examining the state of various NFS processes using the ps command, such as ps -tgs | egrep -I '(wid|nfs)' to see the nfsRemountHandler and nfsLockFileUpdate processes. This can be handy if troubleshooting running processes with VMware Support.

- Examining the status of various NFS mounts using the esxcfg-nas -l command. We use this from time to time to see the status of various mounted storage exports.

Figure 16.4 shows both these commands in use.

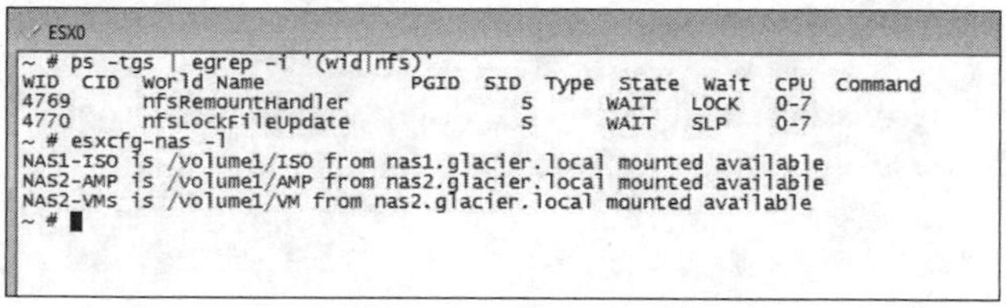

```
/ ESX0
~ # ps -tgs | egrep -i '(wid|nfs)'
WID  CID  World Name          PGID  SID  Type  State  wait   CPU  Command
4769      nfsRemountHandler          5          WAIT   LOCK   0-7
4770      nfsLockFileUpdate          5          WAIT   SLP    0-7
~ # esxcfg-nas -l
NAS1-ISO is /volume1/ISO from nas1.glacier.local mounted available
NAS2-AMP is /volume1/AMP from nas2.glacier.local mounted available
NAS2-VMS is /volume1/VM from nas2.glacier.local mounted available
~ # ∎
```

Figure 16.4   Examining NFS processes and mounts using ESXi Shell

Security with ACLs

Let's imagine you had two exports: Production and Development. Production is needed to be available for hosts in the 10.20.0.0/16 subnet, while Development is used by hosts in the 10.30.0.0/16 subnet. Both sets of hosts need to read and write to the NFS storage array. In order to control access to the two exports, an Access Control List (ACL) is employed.

The exports file would look something like this:

- /Production   10.20.0.0/255.255.0.0 (rw)

- /Development   10.30.0.0/255.255.0.0 (rw)

Notice that we're creating a relationship between a path on the file system and the hosts that can use that path. The (rw) indicates that hosts are allowed to issue both reads and writes, whereas (ro) would allow only reads (read-only). If you ever mount an NFS export and cannot issue writes, one common point of troubleshooting is to check the permissions of the export to ensure it is (rw).

Additionally, the type of user account accessing the export can also come into consideration. The two major users are:

- **Nobody or "NFSnobody"**: This is very similar to a guest account and should be avoided for vSphere hosts. You are typically allowed to mount NFS storage as "Nobody" but unable to write files or perform any useful activities.

- **Root**: By using the no_root_squash parameter on an NFS export, we prevent the export from assigning a host the Nobody level of access.

While it's important to verify the proper way to configure NFS storage for VMware vSphere with your storage array vendor, it almost always boils down to making sure of the following:

1. The export is properly assigned read-write (rw) permission.

2. The export is set to no_root_squash.

NOTE

vSphere likes to mount NFS with full permissions, and defaults to doing so using the "root" user. NFS, by default, will "squash" root access to the exports unless the no_root_squash parameter is included.

Network Adapters

There are no specific network adapters designed for NFS storage. This is different from the concepts of dependent and independent hardware network adapters described in Chapter 14 on iSCSI. As long as your network adapter is supported by VMware via the Hardware Compatibility List (HCL), it will work with NFS.

With that said, there are definitely some advantages to using a network adapter that supports TCP Offload Engine (TOE). These cards allow the TCP/IP stack to be offloaded from the hypervisor and onto the network adapter, thus freeing up some valuable CPU cycles. Keep in mind, however, that CPU is often the one resource that most VMware environments have in abundance. Unless you're worried about being CPU-constrained, such as with a virtual business critical application (VBCA) or end user computing (EUC) workloads, it's often best to spend your budget on something other than a network adapter with TOE.

REAL WORLD

TOE is included in many of the latest generation enterprise-grade network adapters, so you might have little choice in deciding if you want it or not. Typically, the choice comes up for those deciding on adapters in the midrange market. Most consumer grade network adapters do not have TOE capabilities.

NFS Design

NFS is one of the harder protocols to design around if your goal is resiliency and performance. This mainly stems from the fact that VMware only supports NFS version 3, which has absolutely no ability to perform multipathing. This means that each NFS export you mount storage to will always have just one active path to use for IO—period! This doesn't mean that you have a single point of failure—there can be many other passive paths set aside in the event of failure, such as a dead switch or failed network adapter. But only one path will ever be active. Parallel NFS, often just shortened to pNFS, is only available in NFS version 4.1 or later.

Let's dive into three different configurations for NFS, many of which offer options that allow you to configure multiple exports to help create additional active paths for IO.

Single Network

The single network design is quite common, simple, and popular for networks that can take advantage of 10 Gb network adapters. In this design, a single network is set aside specifically for NFS traffic. This network should also use a unique VLAN to help isolate and secure the NFS network.

To start with, we use the 10.0.251.0/24 network and VLAN 251 for NFS storage traffic. VLAN 251 will be entirely dedicated to NFS traffic without any routable gateway for ingress or egress from the network. Additionally, a single VMkernel port will be created and placed onto a standard vSwitch with a pair of 10 Gb uplinks. The failover policy has been configured so that both uplinks are active. The host has decided to place the VMkernel port on vmnic0.

Let's look at the design (see Figure 16.5) and then review the various configuration points.

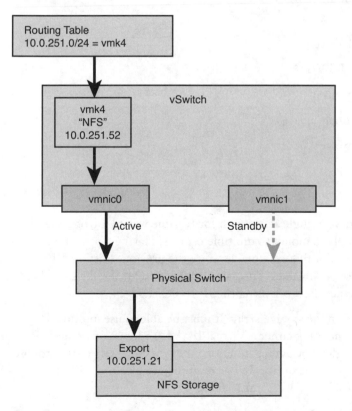

Figure 16.5   Single network design for NFS storage

The NFS VMkernel port, vmk4, was configured with the IP 10.0.251.52/24, and the NFS storage array has been configured with the IP 10.0.251.21/24. Whenever the host needs to communicate with the NFS export, it first does a routing table lookup to see how to reach the target array. Because vmk4 is on the 10.0.251.0/24 network, and is the first (and only) VMkernel port on that network, it is selected as the VMkernel port used to transfer traffic.

In the event of a vmnic0 failure, the VMkernel port (vmk4) is migrated over to vmnic1 by the host. Because both uplinks are marked active, there is no failback—vmnic1 will continue to be used by vmk4 until an administrator manually moves it back or until vmnic1 fails. This helps avoid the VMkernel port from being rapidly shifted around, which is called *flapping*.

> **NOTE**
>
> Implementing load balancing by way of a Link Aggregation Group (LAG) on this pair of NICs does not typically help since there is just one source IP and one target IP. Most LAG-hashing algorithms would always put the traffic onto the same uplink anyway. No point in increasing complexity for minimal return.

Let's review the single network design:

- One NFS network and NFS VLAN
- One export on the storage array
- One IP address on the storage array
- One active path to the storage

Multiple Networks

Because each export can only have a single active path for IO, one way to introduce additional paths for active IO is simply to mount to multiple exports. Having a pair of unique networks can make this possible. For this example, let's use the previous existing NFS network, 10.0.251.0/24, but also add in a new one using 10.0.252.0/24. We'll also add on another VMkernel port for the new network using the IP 10.0.252.52/24.

This will require a few changes on the storage array. It must be able to use multiple IP addresses. This is commonly done using either a Virtual IP (VIP) address or Logical IP (LIP) address, but could also be done by adding additional network adapters to the storage array and assigning an IP address to the device. In our example, we give the NFS storage array an IP for each network: 10.0.251.21/24 and 10.0.252.21/24.

Figure 16.6 shows the network.

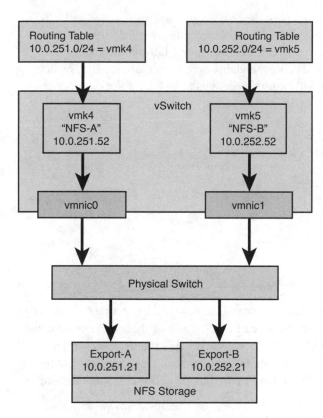

Figure 16.6 Multiple network design for NFS storage

In this configuration, you'll want to specify one vmnic as the Active uplink, and the other vmnic as the Standby uplink. Otherwise both VMkernel ports might end up using the same uplink. We've assigned them as follows:

- **VMkernel "NFS-A" (vmk4)**: vmnic0 Active, vmnic1 Standby
- **VMkernel "NFS-B" (vmk5)**: vmnic1 Active, vmnic0 Standby

The downside to this design is that it requires mounting two exports, one for each network. This adds some administrative overhead when deciding where to place a new VM's virtual disk(s). However, it does allow you to create additional active paths to the storage array, which is especially handy in environments that do not have access to 10 Gb networks.

> **REAL WORLD**
>
> The multiple network design is still rather popular for hosts that use many different 1 Gb connections to the network, as a single 1 Gb link has a reasonable potential for saturation with storage traffic. Many designs we've seen call for using four 1 Gb connections with two networks, which allows for full bandwidth availability even in a failure scenario of an adapter, switch, or port. It's often overkill to use this design for 10 Gb networks.

Let's review the multiple network design:

- Two NFS networks and NFS VLANs
- Two exports on the storage array
- Two IP addresses on the storage array
- Two active storage paths

Link Aggregation Group

The final design allows for the use of a LAG. From a load distribution perspective, since they use the same IP-hashing algorithm, the type of LAG, static or dynamic, can be considered irrelevant. However, in link failure situations, static LAG requires administrator intervention where dynamic lag does not. And unless you're running a vSphere version prior to 5.1, which doesn't support dynamic LAG, you'll likely choose dynamic instead.

In the LAG design, the two uplinks are placed in a LAG on the upstream switch. The VMkernel port is also set to a teaming policy of **Route based on IP hash** as shown in Figure 16.7.

Only a single VMkernel port is required on the vSphere host, but the storage array must have two IP addresses on the NFS network. This is due to the requirement of using an IP hash. If the source and destination IP address are always the same, the hash results will also always be the same. The vSphere routing table will always use a single VMkernel port for a single network, so it's not possible to use different source IP addresses. Therefore, you must introduce different destination IP addresses to the storage array for the hash results to differ—we're going to use 10.0.251.20 and 10.0.251.21. It's also critical that the two storage array IP addresses have unique least significant bits.

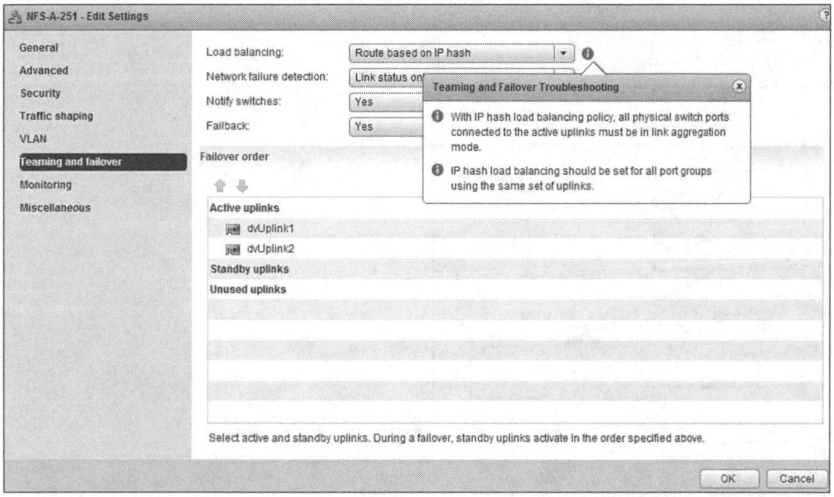

Figure 16.7   The Route Based on IP Hash teaming policy is used for a LAG

UNDERSTANDING THE LEAST SIGNIFICANT BIT

The last bit in an IP address is known as the Least Significant Bit or LSB. When doing an IP hash, the LSB is used to determine which uplink is used for traffic. If two IP addresses have identical LSBs, the hash results are the same—and therefore the same uplink will be chosen.

In our example, we have used 10.0.251.20 and 10.0.251.21. Look at the binary values of each:

10.0.251.20: 00001010 00000000 11111011 0001010**0**

10.0.251.21: 00001010 00000000 11111011 0001010**1**

Notice how the first binary address ends with a 0, and the second address ends with a 1. These are different, and thus the IP hash results will be different.

The LAG design also requires using multiple mount points—one mount for each of the storage array's unique IP addresses. Figure 16.8 shows the overall design.

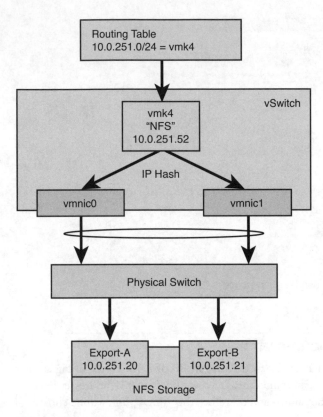

Figure 16.8   LAG design for NFS storage

The LAG design can scale with additional uplinks, but each uplink that you wish to use requires an additional IP address and export on the storage array. Also, each additional IP address needs to use an LSB, which expands as more uplinks are brought into the LAG, like so:

- 2 uplinks = the last bit

- 3 to 4 uplinks = the last 2 bits

- 5 to 8 uplinks = the last 3 bits

Another consideration to keep in mind is how the virtual switch will be used. If the uplinks are being shared with other types of traffic, then they will also need to be placed into the "Route based on IP hash" teaming policy. Mixing routing policies on uplinks configured in a LAG is not supported.

Let's review the LAG network design:

- One NFS network and NFS VLAN

- Two exports on the storage array

- Two IP addresses on the storage array

- Two active storage paths

Summary

In this chapter, we walked through the various design considerations of NFS, including the components necessary to make NFS operational. Although the NFS architecture does not allow for true multipathing, we reviewed many ways to introduce additional active paths to the design. The design that fits your environment will be highly dependent on your use case and your array, and is often not applicable to another company's environment. Over the course of the next chapter, we get some actual exposure to a real environment that is using NFS storage for running VMs.

Chapter 17

NFS Design and Configuration

Key Concepts

- NFS Network Address Scheme
- Naming a Standard vSwitch
- Mounting an NFS Datastore

Introduction

Now that the concepts of attaching NFS storage have been explored, we're ready to begin applying that shiny new knowledge into a working design and configuration. This chapter focuses on implementing NFS storage in a new environment to meet a specific use case. Because there are so many different ways to go about the configuration, we also hit on the various decision points and alternative methods.

NFS Design

Every design should be crafted in order to meet a specific use case, working to satisfy requirements, work within constraints, and mitigate risks. Creating a network for NFS traffic is no different. Let's begin by examining the use case.

Use Case

The use case scenario will play out as follows:

> Initech Corp has decided to open a new branch office in Portland, Oregon, for the handful of sales staff that cover the western US territories. The company has provided three vSphere hosts running ESXi 5.5 Enterprise that were already gently used at another location. The hosts will use four different 10 Gb network adapters across two physical cards as uplinks to the physical network. All hosts and components are listed in the VMware hardware compatibility list (HCL) for ESXi 5.5.

> The IT manager at Initech Corp has mandated that the storage solution must be cost-effective and re-use the existing Ethernet network. She has purchased a small storage array capable of providing storage via the NFS protocol and provided a network and VLAN for storage traffic. You've been tasked with making sure that all the vSphere hosts have been properly configured to participate in the NFS network.

Let's take a look at the use case to identify some key decision points:

- This is a new branch office. The design work completed in Chapter 12, "Standard vSwitch Design," which provided NFS storage at the Chicago data center, is no longer a constraint.

- We're using the Enterprise license, which does not allow for the creation of a distributed vSwitch.

- There are four 10 Gb network adapters across two physical cards in each host. It will make a great bit of sense to split up the adapters by function. We're going to take two network adapters for NFS storage and leave the remaining two for all other functions: Management, vMotion, and Virtual Machine traffic.

The requirements seem straightforward, so let's move on to providing naming conventions.

Naming Conventions

Even though this is an entirely new office and vSphere cluster, there's no need to start from scratch on the naming conventions. In fact, using standardized names across geographically dispersed locations is a great thing—it makes the environments uniform and easier to troubleshoot.

Let's start by focusing on virtual network components. We're going to need a new standard vSwitch for our NFS network, which will give itself the default name of vSwitch# (with # being the first available number). There's really no need to use such a boring name for a new switch, so let's make the name Storage_Switch.

Additionally, we need a name for the VMkernel port. This particular design only requires a single network for NFS traffic, and as such, we only need one VMkernel port. We could easily call the VMkernel port "NFS"—but what about future growth? There might come a day that more VMkernel ports and NFS networks are required. So, let's make sure we name the VMkernel port in a way that can be added to later and call the VMkernel port "NFS_1."

Network Addresses

The IT manager has already assigned an NFS network and VLAN:

- **NFS Network**: 10.0.251.0 /24.

- **NFS VLAN**: 251.

- The VLAN is nonroutable.

Knowing that the VLAN is nonroutable gives us a clue that there are no other IPs on the network that have been taken for a default gateway, although it's often best to confirm. We'll use the IP addresses shown in Table 17.1.

Table 17.1   NFS Network Addresses

Name	Type	IP Address
ESX0	vSphere Host	10.0.251.10
ESX1	vSphere Host	10.0.251.11
ESX2	vSphere Host	10.0.251.12
NFS-Storage	Storage Array	10.0.251.20

The final topology will look like that shown in Figure 17.1.

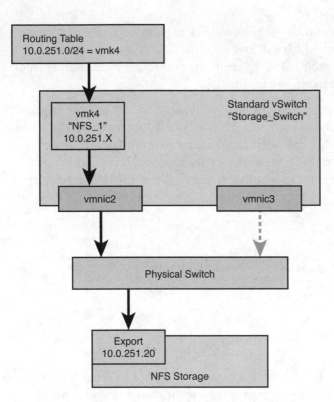

Figure 17.1   The single network NFS storage topology

vSwitch Configuration

Let's dive right into creating the virtual network necessary to mount NFS storage.

NFS vSwitch

The first item on our list is to create a standard vSwitch specifically for NFS storage named "Storage_Switch." There's no way to do this via the vSphere Web Client, so we'll have to resort to a little command line interface (CLI) action. In this example, we use SSH to connect to the host and run the necessary commands, although you can most certainly use other methods, such as PowerCLI, as you see fit.

To begin, we need to ensure that the SSH daemon is running. Open the vSphere Web Client and navigate to the Hosts and Clusters pane. Select one of your vSphere hosts (we're going to use host **ESX2**), click the **Manage** tab, the **Settings** sub-tab, and then find the **Security Profile** menu item. From there, scroll down to the Services area and click the **Edit** button.

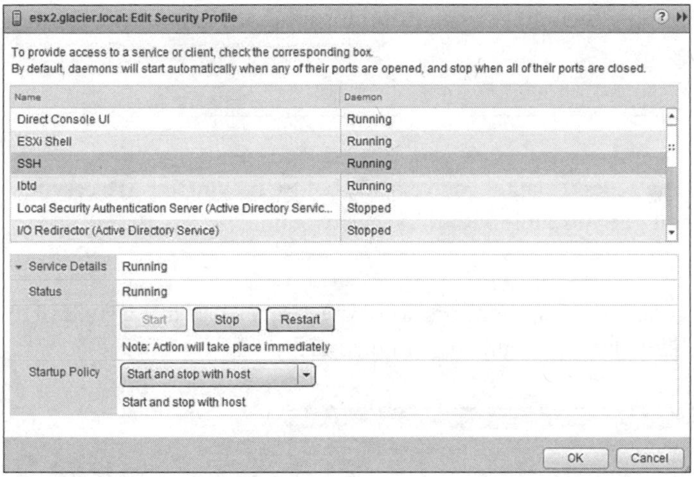

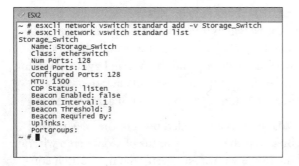

Figure 17.2 Starting the SSH daemon on the first vSphere host

Find the SSH service and, if the daemon shows Stopped, make sure to select **SSH** and click the **Start** button. It might take up to a minute for the SSH service to start and become available.

You can now use an SSH client of your choice (such as PuTTY) to open a session to the vSphere host. When connected, issue the following two commands:

- **To create the new vSwitch**: `esxcli network vswitch standard add -v Storage_Switch`

- **To verify the new vSwitch is created**: `esxcli network vswitch standard list`

The results will look similar to the output shown in Figure 17.3.

```
ESX2
~ # esxcli network vswitch standard add -v Storage_Switch
~ # esxcli network vswitch standard list
Storage_Switch
    Name: Storage_Switch
    Class: etherswitch
    Num Ports: 128
    Used Ports: 1
    Configured Ports: 128
    MTU: 1500
    CDP Status: listen
    Beacon Enabled: false
    Beacon Interval: 1
    Beacon Threshold: 3
    Beacon Required By:
    Uplinks:
    Portgroups:
~ #
```

Figure 17.3 Creating a new vSwitch named Storage_Switch

Assuming you see your new Storage_Switch, you can now close the SSH connection and stop the SSH service.

REAL WORLD

Get in the habit of tidying up any access changes you've made before moving on. It's easy to forget that you enabled SSH and get in trouble with the security team.

The new Storage_Switch is in need of your configuration expertise, as it is just a shell of a vSwitch in its current state, naked and vulnerable (see Figure 17.4).

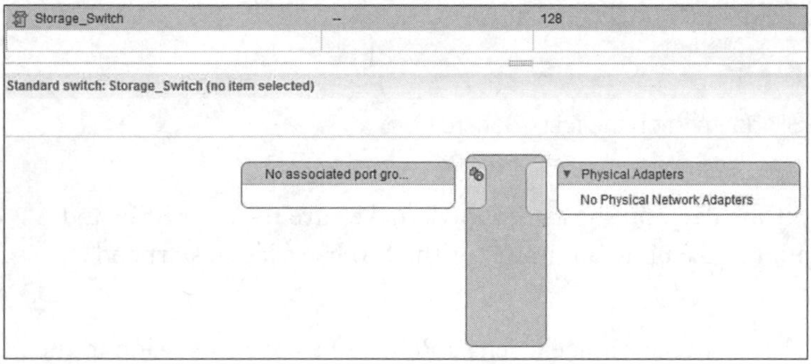

Figure 17.4   The new Storage_Switch is an empty shell

Repeat the steps in this section for the other hosts. Let's get some network adapters added and make the new vSwitch feel a little more useful.

Network Adapters

The design calls for using two uplinks, vmnic2 and vmnic3, on this new vSwitch. These network adapters are on different physical cards, which prevent a single point of failure. To add them, open the vSphere Web Client and navigate to the Hosts and Clusters pane. Then, click on the **Manage** tab, the **Networking** sub-tab, and the **Virtual switches** menu item. Find the Storage_Switch vSwitch in the virtual switches list and click the **Manage Physical Network Adapters** button, which looks like a green card with a grey wrench.

Click the green plus sign to add network adapters. We've added both in the previous figure, vmnic2 and vmnic3, and have verified that they show a status of Connected without any warnings or errors. Click **OK** to complete the wizard and verify the new switch configuration. The vSwitch should now look more like that shown in Figure 17.6.

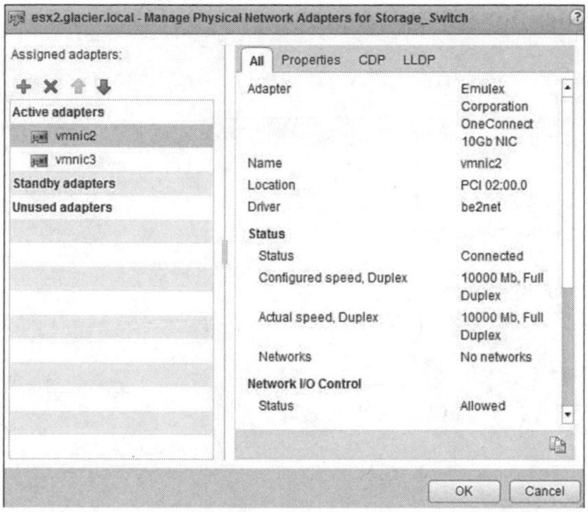

Figure 17.5   Adding network adapters to the Storage_Switch

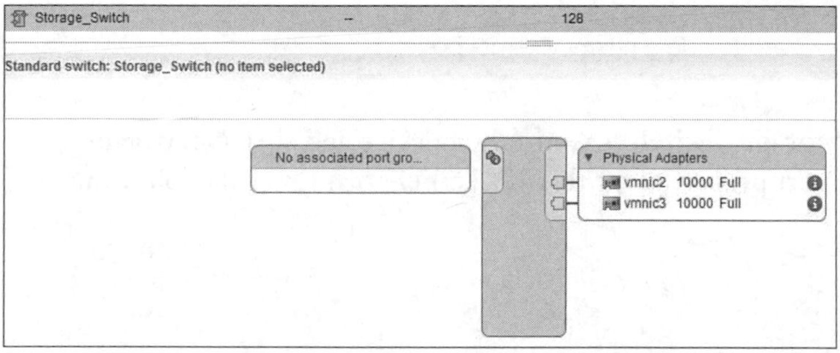

Figure 17.6   Storage_Switch now has a pair of 10 Gb network adapters

Repeat the steps in this section for the other hosts. It's now time to build out a new VMkernel port for the NFS traffic network.

VMkernel Ports

It's now necessary to create a VMkernel port on the same network and VLAN as the NFS storage array. Open the vSphere Web Client and navigate to the Hosts and Clusters pane. Then, click on the **Manage** tab, the **Networking** sub-tab, and the **Virtual switches** menu item. Find the Storage_Switch vSwitch in the virtual switches list and click the **Add host networking** icon with the little globe and green plus sign.

When the wizard begins, select the **VMkernel Network Adapter** type and click **Next** as shown in Figure 17.7.

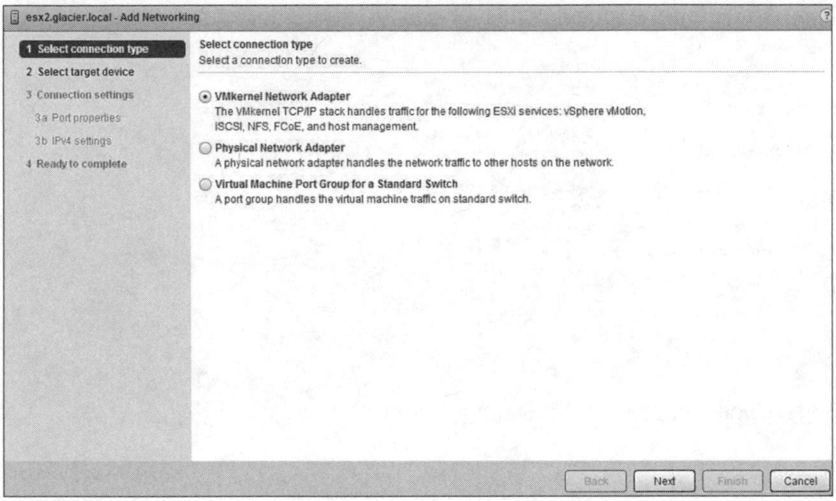

Figure 17.7   Beginning the wizard to add a new VMkernel port

Make sure to choose the **Storage_Switch** as your target device and click **Next** again. It's now time to enter the port properties for this VMkernel port. Enter the following information:

- **Network label**: NFS_1
- **VLAN ID**: 251

Leave the remaining items as the defaults shown in Figure 17.8.

Click **Next** to reach the IPv4 Settings page of the wizard. Enter the following:

- Use static IPv4 settings
- **IPv4 address**: 10.0.251.12 (because this is host ESX2)
- **Subnet mask**: 255.255.255.0

You can now click **Next** and **Finish** the wizard. Repeat the steps in this section for the other hosts.

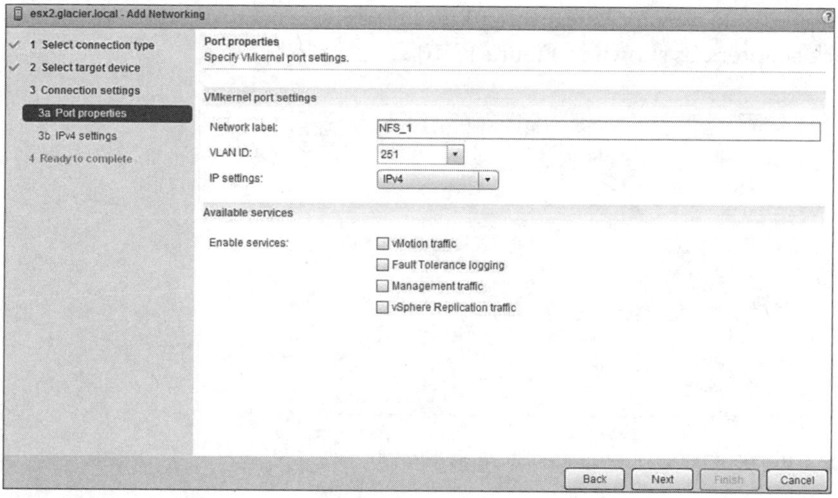

Figure 17.8   Entering the port policy information for NFS_1

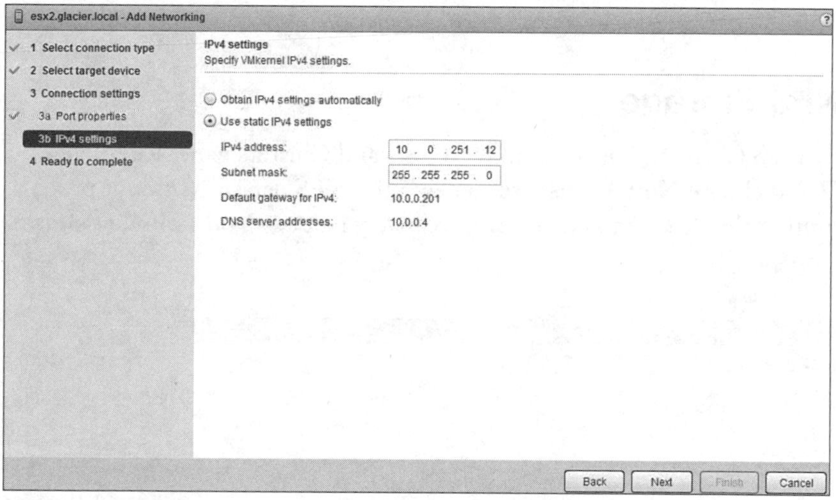

Figure 17.9   Assigning IPv4 address information for NFS_1

REAL WORLD

Why not DHCP for the VMkernel port address? It's rarely a good idea to create dependencies for your storage network. If something were to happen to your DHCP server, your host would be unable to receive an IPv4 address. Additionally, should the IP address assigned by the DHCP server change, the NFS mount might fail due to a new IP outside of the access control list (ACL) range. Stick to static IP addresses.

The Storage_Switch should now look healthy and useful with a valid VMkernel port and two active network adapters, as shown in Figure 17.10.

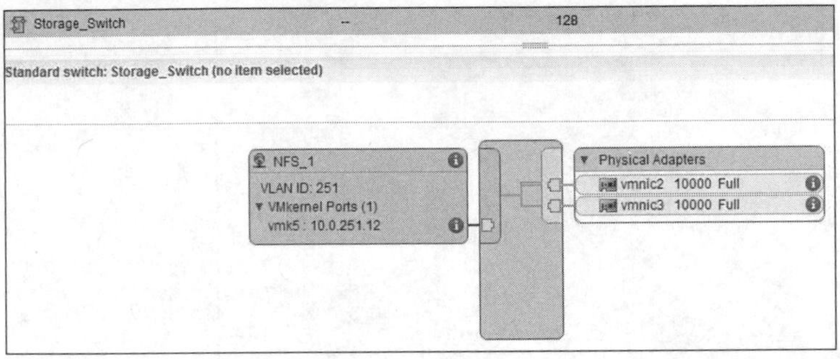

Figure 17.10   The completed and operational Storage_Switch

To celebrate this newfound success, let's mount some NFS storage. This will ultimately validate that the configuration is operational and also allow you to begin using the hosts.

Mounting NFS Storage

Open the vSphere Web Client and navigate to the Hosts and Clusters pane. Right click on the host **ESX2** and choose **New Datastore** to begin the NFS datastore mount process. We begin by mounting the Production datastore, creatively named **Production**, as shown in Figure 17.11.

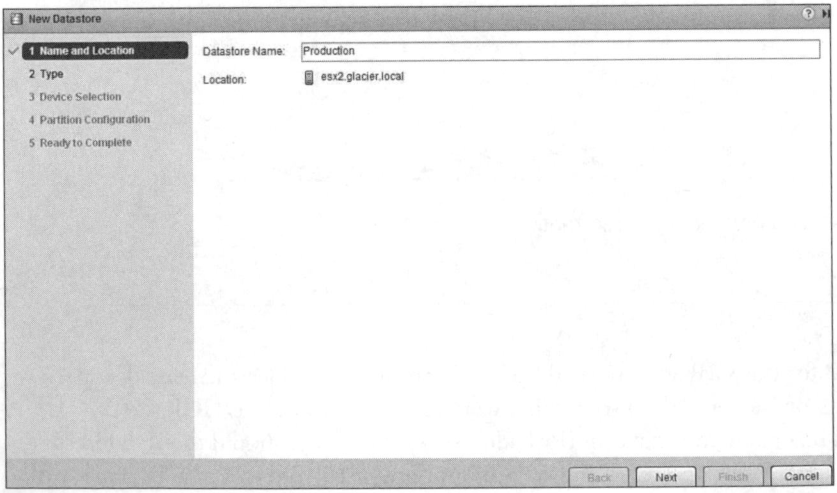

Figure 17.11   Creating a new datastore over NFS

Enter the name **Production** and click **Next**. Choose **NFS** as your storage type and click **Next**. Then enter the following configuration details (see Figure 17.12):

- **Server**: 10.0.251.20

- **Folder**: /volume1/Production

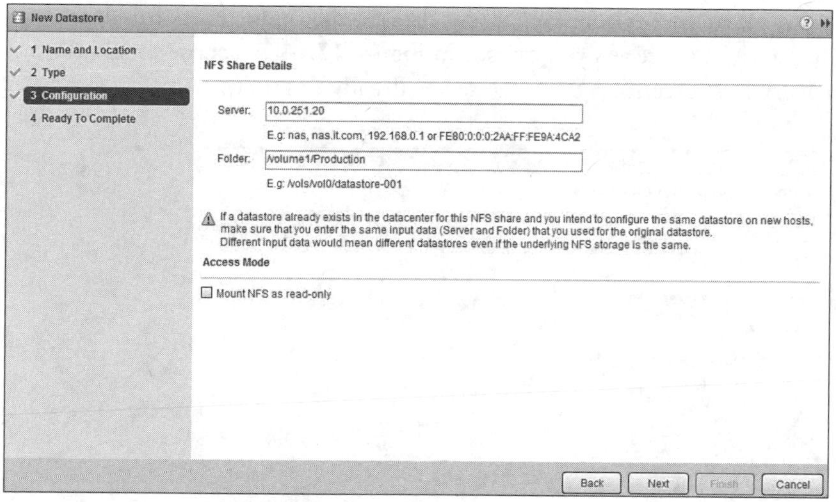

Figure 17.12   The Production NFS configuration details

Click **Next** and then **Finish** to complete the wizard. If all was successful, you should now have a new datastore named Production added to host ESX2. To verify this, select host **ESX2** and then click on the **Related Objects** tab and **Datastores** sub-tab. You can see the new Production datastore in Figure 17.13, along with some other NFS and VMFS datastores there were previously configured.

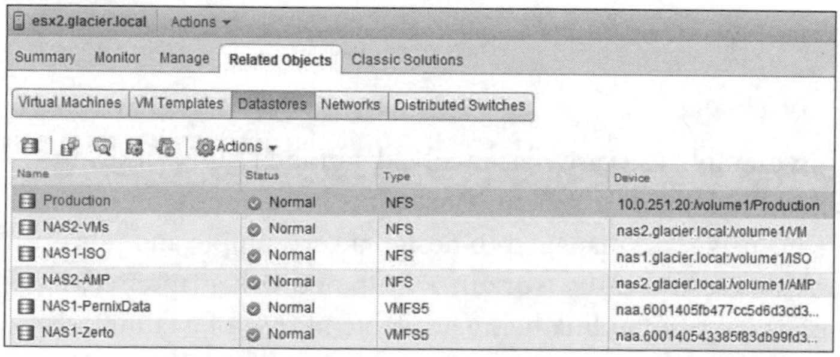

Figure 17.13   The Production NFS datastore is available for use

At this point, you can repeat the steps performed in this section for the remaining hosts, or use a very handy feature found in the vSphere Web Client to add the NFS datastore to all your hosts.

Adding NFS datastores to each host individually was a painful truth of the past. It's super easy to globally create or add an NFS datastore with the vSphere Web Client (version 5.1 or better). Just right click on your **vSphere Cluster** and choose **New Datastore**. The steps are almost identical to this section, except you also get the opportunity to select which hosts should see the storage. As you can see in Figure 17.14, we chose to add the NFS datastore to every host except ESX2 (because we already did that).

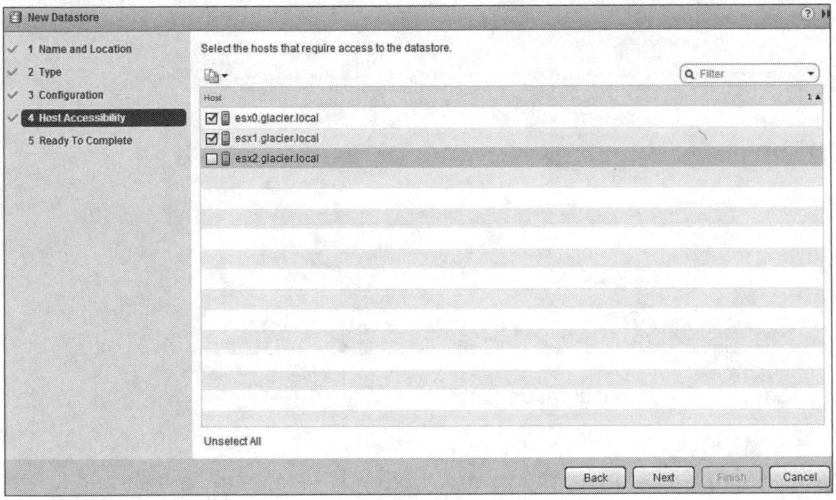

Figure 17.14   Mounting an NFS datastore to many hosts in a cluster

That's it—you're now ready to start creating VMs on the fancy new NFS datastore.

Summary

In this chapter, we went over an example use case that involved a branch office desiring to consume storage via NFS. Although many different constraints were imposed upon us, such as a lower tier of vSphere licensing, we managed to design a very simple and powerful network for NFS traffic. The design would easily work in a 1 Gb network adapter environment without any changes, with the second uplink being available in case of a failure.

Chapter 18

Additional vSwitch Design Scenarios

Key Concepts

- Gather Requirements
- Design Options
- Use Case
- Hardware Redundancy
- Fault Isolation

Introduction

Back in Chapters 12, "Standard vSwitch Design," and 13, "Distributed vSwitch Design," we walked you through a virtual network design exercise for a server with two 10-Gigabit Ethernet (Gb) NICs. This is the most common configuration we run into, but we recognize that there are many other adapter combinations that are out there, and some might be more relevant to you. In this chapter, we go through options for configuring virtual networks with 2, 4, 6, and 8 network adapters, including options for use cases with and without Ethernet-based storage. Here, we focus on the logical configuration. The detailed step-by-step instruction offered in Chapters 12 and 13 can be referenced when it comes time to actually build the vSwitches.

Use Case

As we did earlier, we start with a snappy company overview, for color. Vandelay Industries is embarking upon a virtualization project. They are considering two possible hardware configurations: blade servers with two converged networking adapters or rack mount servers with four built-in 1 Gb adapters. The former would involve an investment in 10 Gb infrastructure; the latter would allow them to use existing switch ports. The rack-mount option also gives them the option of adding additional NICs for more capacity and redundancy. Vandelay has not ruled out a hybrid approach—they might have 10 Gb ports become available as part of another project and would like to see options for using them. If they do add extra NICs, they expect to add two dual-port adapters for up to four additional 1 Gb or 10 Gb ports. They have stressed "up to," as they might only cable one uplink per adapter to reduce overall port consumption.

In short, they haven't made any real decisions on the hosts' network configuration. They want to see every option available, and then make a decision. Sound familiar?

The virtual networking requirements are a little closer to ironed-out. The Vandelay design must support a Management network, a vMotion network, and virtual machine (VM) traffic for the three VM workloads we've come to know and love: Web servers on VLAN 100, Application servers on VLAN 110, and Database servers on VLAN 120.

Storage connectivity is still up in the air. Their new array will support access via either NFS or FiberChannel. If they go with the former, the hosts must support two additional networks for NFS. If they go with the latter, the hosts will have a pair of FiberChannel HBAs for storage connectivity, allowing us to avoid provisioning virtual storage networks.

Naming Standards

As before, we start with defining names for these networks:

- **Management Traffic on VLAN 20**: Management Network

- **vMotion Traffic on VLAN 205**: vMotion

- **NFS Network #1 on VLAN 220**: NFS_V220

- **NFS Network #2 on VLAN 221**: NFS_V221

- **Web Servers on VLAN 100**: Web_192.168.100.x_V100

- **Application Servers on VLAN 110**: App_192.168.110.x_V110

- **Database Servers on VLAN 120**: DB_192.168.120.x_V120

Two Network Adapters

The two 10 Gb network adapter scenario should look familiar—it's the same configuration used as the example for Chapters 12 and 13. We use it again here with minor adjustments to fit our new use case.

With only two uplinks, we're going to have to forgo physical separation of functions—which is fine, because Vandelay had no explicit requirement for that. All port groups created will use both uplinks.

> **NOTE**
>
> You could follow this same model on a host with only two 1 Gb adapters, too, though we wouldn't recommend it for production. That's squeezing a lot of traffic into very small pipes.

With Ethernet-based Storage

The Management and vMotion port groups will be pinned as active on vmnic0 and vmnic1, respectively, with the complementary vmnics configured as standby. We will do the same with the two NFS storage port groups, distributing traffic across both physical uplinks. VM traffic will be active on both physical uplinks, with each port group configured for either "Route based on originating virtual port" if we're using a standard switch, or "Route based on physical NIC load" if we're using a distributed switch. This configuration is shown in Figure 18.1.

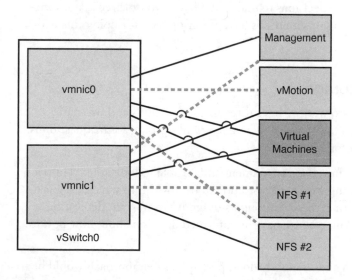

Figure 18.1   A two-uplink vSwitch, with Ethernet-based storage

Without Ethernet-based Storage

If Vandelay elects to use FiberChannel storage, we simply forgo the NFS port groups, as shown in Figure 18.2.

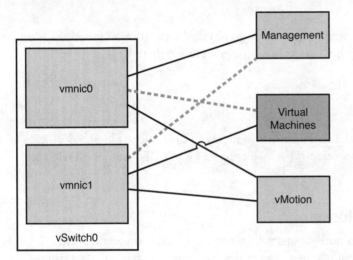

Figure 18.2   A two-uplink vSwitch, without Ethernet-based storage

Four Network Ports

With two extra ports, now we have decisions to make. We have two or three major functions and two pairs of adapters to play with. Let's look at our options for doing this with Ethernet-based storage first.

With Ethernet-based Storage

Accounting for Ethernet-based storage, we have three major functions and two pairs of uplinks. Two functions will need to coexist on the same uplinks group, so the question is: which two will play most nicely together?

Ideally, you'd have some insight into the environment and be able to look at current performance statistics to see if existing workloads use enough bandwidth to warrant dedicating NICs to just VM networks, or if there is enough storage IO to warrant dedicating NICs to storage networks, allowing you to make an informed decision about how best to allocate resources.

If you lack that information, as Vandelay surely does, perhaps a safer approach would be to combine all four uplinks into a single vSwitch. Management and vMotion can be pinned to vmnic0 and vmnic1, and the NFS networks can be pinned to vmnic2 and 3. VM traffic can be active on all four. This configuration is shown in Figure 18.3.

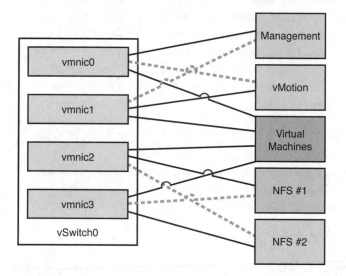

Figure 18.3 A four-uplink vSwitch, with Ethernet-based storage

Without Ethernet-based Storage

If Ethernet-based storage is not required, the configuration becomes much simpler. We can create two separate vSwitches, one for Management and vMotion, and one for VM traffic. Our older-school readers will recognize this as the classic vSwitch design, widely considered to be a best practice prior to the arrival of 10 Gb networking. This is shown in Figure 18.4.

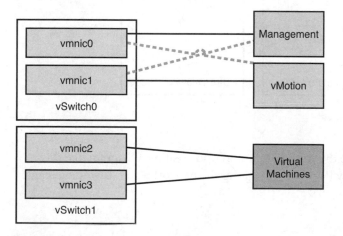

Figure 18.4 Two two-uplink vSwitches

Six Network Ports

Adding more network adapters gives us even more options. In the two- and four-uplink scenarios, we used a single network controller, either a mezzanine card in the two-uplink blade scenario, or an on-board network controller in the four-uplink rack-mount scenario. These represent single points of failure. By this point in the book, we hope that we have sufficiently beaten into you the idea that single points of failure should be avoided wherever possible. Adding additional network adapters for this use case allows us to protect some functions from these single points of failure.

SORT OF

In the rack-mount scenarios, the quad-port network controller is embedded into the system board. Adding NICs can protect us from the effects of that particular bit of silicon failing, but if a larger problem takes out the system board entirely, no number of extra NICs will save you.

Figure 18.5 provides a logical depiction of how our vmnics will be distributed between physical network adapters.

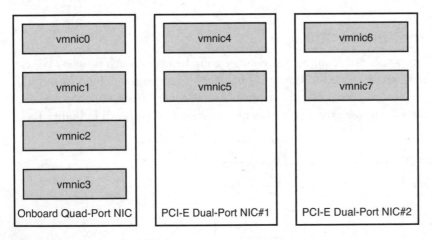

Figure 18.5   Sample vmnic placement

Your hardware might enumerate the vmnics differently, so creating a diagram like this for your environment can be very helpful in designing the networking and avoiding single points of failure.

In six 1 Gb scenarios, we assume that two ports per adapter are cabled—vmnic0 and vmnic1 on the onboard controller, vmnic4 and vmcni5 on NIC #1, and vmnic6 and vnic7 on NIC #2. In the four 1 Gb + 2 10 Gb scenarios, we assume all four on-board ports are cabled, plus vmnic4 on NIC #1 and vmnic6 on NIC #2.

With Ethernet-based Storage—Six 1 Gb

With six available uplink ports spread across three discrete network adapters, we have breathing room to allow each of our three major functions to get its own pair of ports. Management and vMotion will share one pair, the two NFS networks will share another pair, and VM connectivity will share a third. We will create a separate vSwitch for each pair of uplinks, and ensure that the uplinks assigned to each vSwitch are not on the same physical adapter, as shown in Figure 18.6.

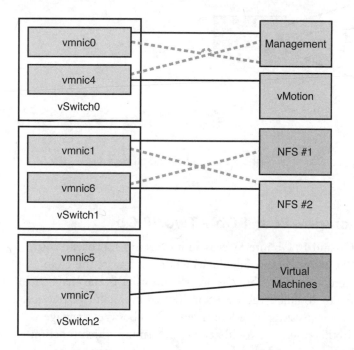

Figure 18.6   A six-uplink vSwitch configuration, with Ethernet-based storage

Without Ethernet-based Storage—Six 1 Gb

If Ethernet-based storage is not required, we can dedicate four uplinks to VM traffic. Again, we will distribute vSwitch uplinks across physical adapters, as shown in Figure 18.7.

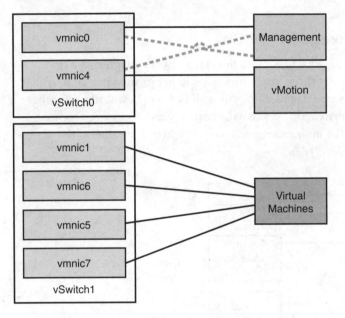

Figure 18.7   A six-uplink vSwitch, configuration, without Ethernet-based storage

With Ethernet-based Storage—Four 1 Gb + Two 10 Gb

A split configuration mixing 1 Gb and 10 Gb interfaces is an interesting approach. You might be asking, if I have two 10 Gb interfaces available, why not just ignore the 1 Gb interfaces, and configure everything to just use those as described earlier in the chapter? In most cases, that would be the way to go unless there are specific requirements for physical separation. Let's pretend Vandelay is insisting on physical separation between management, storage, and VM traffic. In this case, you would need to determine which function would benefit most from the 10 Gb ports. In Vandelay's case, let's say storage activity is expected to be fairly low, but network access to VMs is expected to be fairly high. In such a case, we would give the 10 Gb adapters to VM traffic, and carve up the on-board ports into a pair for management and vMotion, and a pair for NFS. This is shown in Figure 18.8.

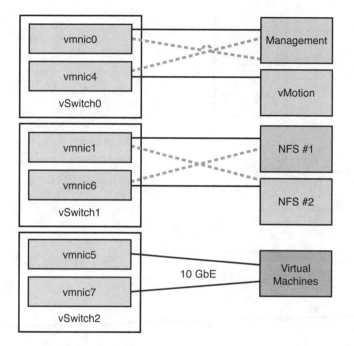

Figure 18.8   A six-uplink vSwitch, configuration, with Ethernet-based storage

Without Ethernet-based Storage — Four 1 Gb + Two 10 Gb

Removing the Ethernet-based storage requirement leaves us with two available ports, and no obvious place to re-allocate them. We already have two 10 Gb interfaces allocated to VM traffic, two more 1 Gb connections aren't going to help a ton there, and mixing NICs of different speeds in the same port group is frowned upon. If Vandelay had a requirement to support VMs with differing connectivity requirements, such as DMZ VMs that needed uplinks connected to another set of switches, those two available ports could be used for that. That would look something like Figure 18.9.

DMZ NETWORK

A DMZ network is one isolated from the main network, usually for security or compliance reasons. DMZ networks are typically run on separate physical switching infrastructures, so trunking them with other internal VLANs is usually not possible. If VMs need to be connected to these networks, the underlying ESXi hosts will need additional physical NICs connected to the DMZ infrastructure.

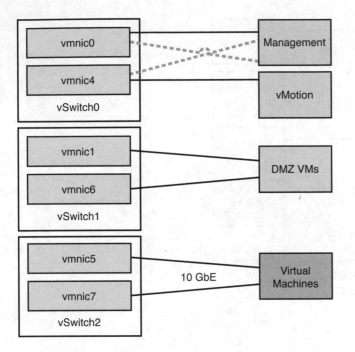

Figure 18.9   A six-uplink vSwitch configuration, with DMZ connectivity

Eight Network Adapters

Eight available uplink ports give us a good bit of breathing room. We should be able to provide physical separation for every major function, but we're contributing quite a bit of cable sprawl in the process. We're also reaching a point where we need to consider whether the complexity of the solution might outweigh any benefits derived.

With Ethernet-based Storage—Eight 1 Gb

With eight uplinks, we can dedicate a pair of uplinks to Management/vMotion and a pair of uplinks to IP storage, and the remaining four uplinks to VM guest traffic. All functions can be spread across more than one physical adapter, ensuring no single points of failure. Feels good, right? Just don't look behind the rack. This configuration is shown in Figure 18.10.

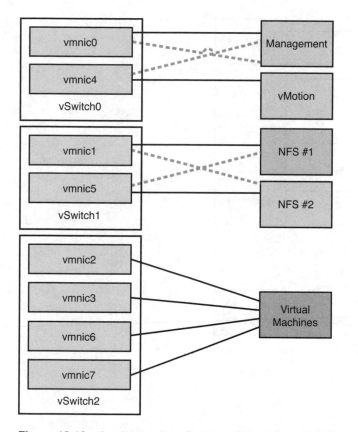

Figure 18.10   An eight-uplink vSwitch configuration, with Ethernet-based storage

Without Ethernet-based Storage—Eight 1 Gb

If we don't need the storage networks, we can either fold vmnic1 and vmnic5 into the VM traffic vSwitch, or find some other use for them. We could use them for DMZ connectivity, as shown in the previous section. Another option would be to configure them for multi-NIC vMotion, as shown in Figure 18.11. Multi-NIC vMotion is discussed in detail in Chapter 19, "Multi-NIC vMotion Architecture."

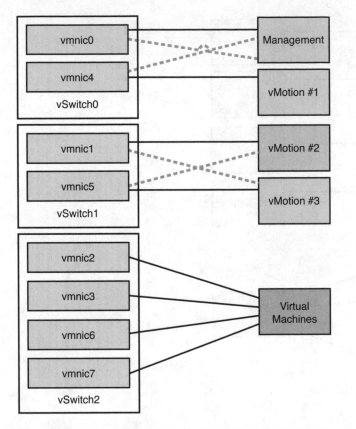

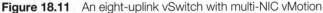

Figure 18.11   An eight-uplink vSwitch with multi-NIC vMotion

With Ethernet-based Storage—Four 1 Gb + Four 10 Gb

As before, if we have four 10 Gb interfaces available, you really need to consider whether you need to bother with the 1 Gb ports. Absent a requirement to physically separate functions, we would recommend using the two or four network adapter approaches, whichever best fits the situation. But, if you really need the management network segregated, Figure 18.12 shows one way to do it. In this approach, we have used the on-board 1 Gb ports for management and multi-NIC vMotion, and used the 10 Gb ports for storage and VM networks. The storage and VM vSwitches have their uplinks split between the two dual-port 10 Gb adapters.

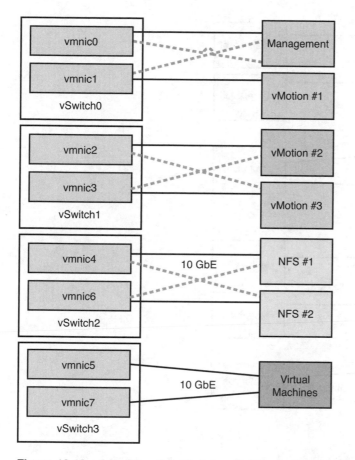

Figure 18.12   An eight-uplink vSwitch, with Ethernet-based storage

Without Ethernet-based Storage—Four 1 Gb + Four 10 Gb

If storage networks are not needed, that frees up two 10 Gb ports that can either be added to the VM traffic vSwitch or repurposed. Here, we've elected to use the 10 Gb ports for blistering-fast multi-NIC vMotion, and re-use the 1 Gb ports for DMZ connectivity, as shown in Figure 18.13.

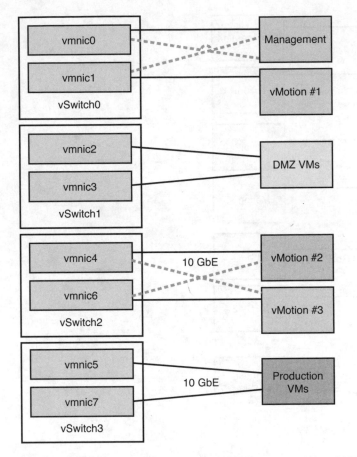

Figure 18.13 An eight-uplink vSwitch configuration with multi-NIC vMotion and DMZ connectivity

Summary

In this chapter, we worked through a number of design options for building vSwitches with varying numbers and types of uplinks. While we couldn't possibly cover every combination of requirements and options, we hope we've covered a representative sample, allowing you to apply the guidance here to the unique sets of circumstances you encounter in your environments.

Chapter 19

Multi-NIC vMotion Architecture

Key Concepts

- Is Multi-NIC vMotion Right for You?
- Verifying Available Bandwidth
- Controlling Bandwidth Usage

Introduction

It would be difficult to overstate how big a deal vMotion is, and how important it was in revolutionizing the world of x86 server virtualization. The ability to migrate the working state of a virtual machine (VM) from one physical server to another, without downtime, was a game changer. We remember our first vMotions as something like a religious experience.

It has been interesting to watch the acceptance of vMotion over time, as it has gained the trust of various user communities—typically starting with development and test servers, then less-critical production workloads, and all the way up to mission-critical applications. In some cases, though, vMotion can begin to saturate its underlying network when used with very large, critical workloads. To combat this, VMware introduced the ability to use multiple network adapters for vMotion in vSphere 5.0.

Multi-NIC vMotion Use Cases

The best designs are tailored to a use case with a set of requirements, constraints, and risks to work against. Deciding to use multi-NIC vMotion is no different. Because it does add an additional level of complexity to your environment, it's best to know why you would design and configure multi-NIC vMotion for your workloads.

In our experience, it really boils down to two different use cases:

- **Large or High-Performance Workloads**: Your critical workloads are large enough that a single 1 Gb or 10 Gb link does not satisfy your requirements for vMotion. Either the vMotion would take too long, affecting performance, or it would have difficulty keeping up with your workload's memory write rate (an application that issues a high volume of writes to memory).

- **Host Maintenance**: The VMs on your vSphere hosts are evacuated for maintenance activities on a regular basis. A reduction in time waiting on vMotions would directly benefit the operations staff handling maintenance such as firmware upgrades, kernel patching, and hardware upkeep.

While we certainly won't stop you from implementing multi-NIC vMotion for whatever reason strikes your fancy, do know that there will be little if any benefit in doing so unless either of those use cases applies. Just cranking up the juice on vMotion speed won't make much of a difference if your workloads are all relatively small, and if your hosts are rarely taken offline for maintenance. We want to continue to stress our belief that simple designs are better, and you can always come back and add this feature later if you truly need it. That said, we move on from here assuming that you're doing this for a good reason.

Design

Compared to some of the previous configuration chapters on iSCSI and NFS (see Part 3, "You Got Your Storage in My Networking: IP Storage"), where we spent a large quantity of time focusing on design, there's considerably less to worry about with vMotion design. This is mostly due to the nature of how VMware engineered vMotion, allowing it to function with complete awareness of the topology, and giving the vSphere host complete control over the traffic. A host is never surprised by vMotion traffic—it's an expected event.

The first portion of the design revolves around the need to ensure there is enough bandwidth available for vMotion to play nicely with other traffic types—Management, VMs, or any IP Storage. If the virtual environment is saturated with network traffic, adding more vMotion traffic will only cause problems. In most environments, however, the network is largely idle, which allows for much of the unused bandwidth to be put to good use toward vMotion.

Verifying Available Bandwidth

Answering the available bandwidth question is straightforward for an existing environment—you can examine the average and peak network usage by looking at the relevant counters on the vCenter Server, VMware's vCenter Operations Manager software, or some other third-party tool. In brand new environments, this can get a little tricky—it is best to work with your application teams to understand the required network performance to gain insight and develop an educated guess on network requirements.

To view network traffic in the vSphere Web Client, follow these steps:

1. Select a host.

2. Click on the **Monitor** tab.

3. Click on the **Performance** sub-tab.

4. Select **Advanced** from the menu.

Change the View dropdown to Network and click on the **Chart Options** link to adjust the time span. We've set it to one week for the example show in Figure 19.1.

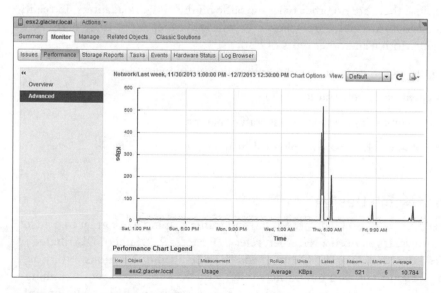

Figure 19.1   Network traffic on host esx2

This particular host, esx2.glacier.local, looks relatively idle (because it has been) and would easily be able to handle increased vMotion traffic. You would then want to repeat this exercise for any other hosts that would participate in multi-NIC vMotion.

> **NOTE**
>
> Although we show a week of time in this example, you might need to stretch your timeline out to multiple weeks or months to get a good feel for your traffic patterns. Or, check around to see if any of your colleagues are running a corporate network traffic monitor.

Controlling vMotion Traffic

Even though we've verified that there is unused bandwidth for vMotion to consume, we still don't want vMotion to go nuts and crush the host's network adapters. Although vMotion doesn't typically take that long to complete, it does try to squeeze every last drop of bandwidth it can from a network adapter. Without proper controls in place, this could adversely affect VM performance—and remember, VMs are first-class citizens in a virtual infrastructure.

In a best-case scenario, you have dedicated 1 GbE or 10 GbE network adapters that are used only for vMotion. In this scenario, there is no harm in letting vMotion run without any controls because there are no other types of traffic on the network adapters. In reality though, this scenario is extremely rare—most everyone we've met has to share network adapters between vMotion and other types of traffic.

This leads us to the idea of using one of the following control methods:

- **Standard vSwitch**: Ingress traffic shaping only
- **Distributed vSwitch**: Ingress and egress traffic shaping
- **Either type of vSwitch**: Upstream physical switch control

Distributed vSwitch Design

When combined, Network IO Control (NIOC) and traffic shaping work great to control vMotion traffic flows. If you need a refresher, refer to Chapter 9, "vSphere Distributed Switch," and read the "Network I/O Control" and "Traffic Shaping" sections. NIOC is used to control the source of vMotion traffic, meaning the host that is currently running the VM, while traffic shaping can be used to protect the destination for the vMotion traffic, meaning the host where the VM is moving toward.

With NIOC enabled on a distributed vSwitch, any host looking to send a VM to another host will be constrained by the configured network resource pool share values in times of congestion or an admin defined limit.

Let's use an example where an administrator has turned on NIOC and has kicked off a vMotion task over a 10 Gb network adapter. The host has decided that due to current traffic flow congestion and defined share values, it will only use 5 Gbps of bandwidth for the vMotion. The destination host will receive traffic equal to about 5 Gbps. This example could be equally valid if the administrator had defined a hard limit of 5 Gbps in NIOC. Figure 19.2 shows this example scenario in detail.

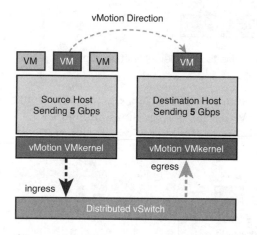

Figure 19.2   vMotion traffic flowing from a source host to a destination host

For most environments, the flow we've described is typical. It could be that the Distributed Resource Scheduler (DRS) has decided to move a VM, or an administrator has manually executed the task. In some cases, it might be that an administrator has toggled the host into maintenance mode, triggering DRS to evacuate the VMs to other hosts. But what if we had a scenario where two source hosts were both sending VMs to a single destination host as shown in Figure 19.3?

Because NIOC is only able to control ingress traffic—that is, traffic entering the Distributed vSwitch from a VMkernel that is destined for another host—the destination host is being hammered with two vMotion traffic flows that consume nearly all of the 10 Gb network adapter's bandwidth. While this is definitely an edge case, it does illustrate a possible congestion issue on the vMotion network.

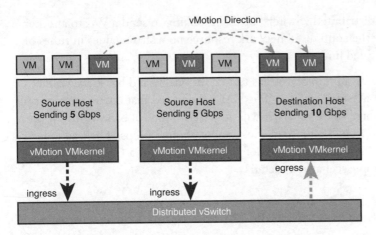

Figure 19.3   Multiple source hosts sending vMotion traffic to a single destination host

Egress traffic shaping can be used to combat this scenario. In this case, egress is a flow out of the Distributed vSwitch and into the vMotion VMkernel port, as shown in Figure 19.4.

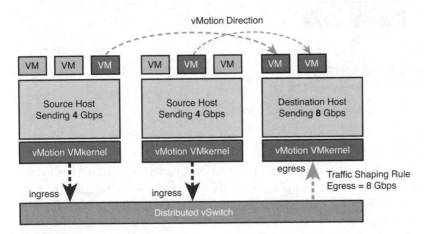

Figure 19.4   The traffic shaping egress rule limits vMotion to 8 Gbps

By creating an egress limitation of 8 Gbps on the vMotion port group (8 Gbps being an arbitrary number that we chose for this example), we've effectively told vMotion that it's not allowed to use more than 8 Gbps on a single network adapter. An example of the configuration is shown in Figure 19.5.

This is still much faster than having a single network adapter for vMotion, since two adapters at 8 Gbps is a total of 16 Gbps of available vMotion bandwidth, or 60% more than what a single network adapter could provide. You could also choose to raise the egress traffic shaping limitation to a higher value for increased vMotion performance, such as 9 Gbps or 9.5 Gbps. The point is that it is a good idea to impose some kind of limit to ensure that other traffic is not starved during times when there might be many vMotions going on.

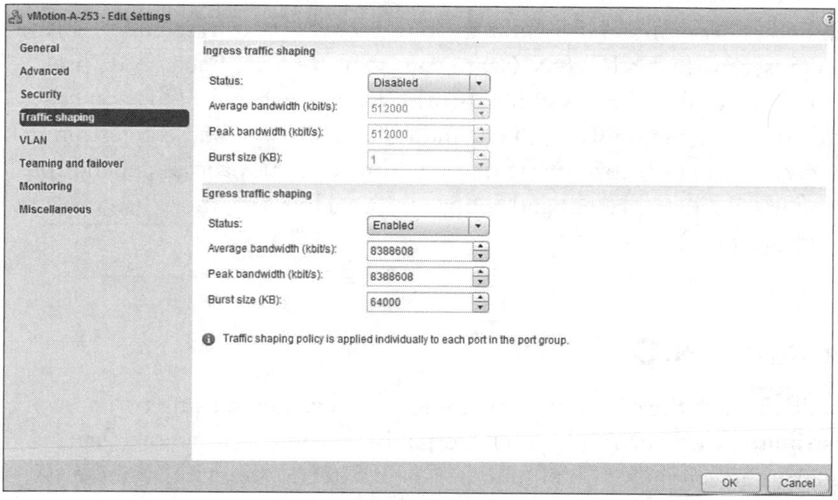

Figure 19.5   An example traffic shaping rule for a vMotion port group

Standard vSwitch Design

A Standard vSwitch is limited to controlling traffic via ingress traffic shaping. This allows setting a hard limit on how much bandwidth a source host can send to a destination host. There is no way to configure network resource pools to throttle vMotion traffic during congestion, nor is there a way to use egress traffic shaping.

For these reasons, it's a bit more tricky—but not impossible—to have solid control over multi-NIC vMotion traffic with a Standard vSwitch. You could, for example, use either dedicated network adapters and completely eliminate the issue, or in some cases, rely on your upstream physical switches to properly throttle your vMotion traffic.

Upstream Physical Switch Design

In some scenarios, there's a desire to completely remove bandwidth control from the vSphere environment and stick it in the upstream switch. This can be beneficial if you already have policies configured at this layer and it avoids the need to configure traffic shaping in two places—the physical switch and the virtual switch.

REAL WORLD

Control your vMotion traffic from either the physical switch or virtual switch, but not from both. Having two control points to manage is complex and difficult to troubleshoot.

One common method of executing on this strategy in the converged infrastructure (blade server) world is to present virtual NICs (vNICs) to your vSphere host. Each vNIC pretends to have bandwidth equal to the physical network adapter, such as 10 Gb. You can then apply control policies to the vNIC, such as bandwidth limitations and congestion rules, so that it knows how to prioritize traffic flows. Ultimately, this process depends on your hardware vendor's ability to present and control traffic. However, those specifics are beyond the scope of this book.

Configuring Multi-NIC vMotion

We're going to walk through the configuration of multi-NIC vMotion using two network adapters on a Distributed vSwitch. While you're certainly welcome to use more than that—up to the maximum configuration of four 10 Gb or sixteen 1 Gb with vSphere 5.1 and later—the process is the same for any number of adapters.

We're going to assume that you have an operational Distributed vSwitch with two uplinks on each vSphere host:

- dvUplink1 is mapped to vmnic0.
- dvUplink2 is mapped to vmnic1.

We're also going to magically declare that vMotion will use VLAN 253 on the subnet 10.0.253.0 /24, which is not routable on our physical network—this prevents vMotion traffic from trying to crossover to another network, and prevents other networks from entering the vMotion network.

Let's review the various components necessary to get multi-NIC vMotion operational.

Distributed Port Groups

To begin with, we need two port groups specifically crafted for vMotion traffic. For simplicity's sake, let's call the port groups vMotion-A and vMotion-B. Each vMotion port group needs to be assigned to VLAN ID 253.

The port group failover policies should be configured as follows:

- **vMotion-A**: vmnic1 is Active; vmnic6 is Standby.
- **vMotion-B**: vmnic6 is Active; vmnic1 is Standby.

NOTE

Why did we choose to mark the second vmnic as Standby instead of Unused? All vMotion VMkernel ports will attempt to communicate with the destination host VMkernel ports. If one of the network adapters fails, the VMkernel port must be allowed to move over to a Standby adapter. Otherwise, the VMkernel port will be unable to communicate on the vMotion network and your vMotions will fail.

All other policies can remain at default value for now. Create the distributed port groups using the same steps found in Chapter 13, "Distributed vSwitch Design."

The end result is a port group that looks like Figure 19.6.

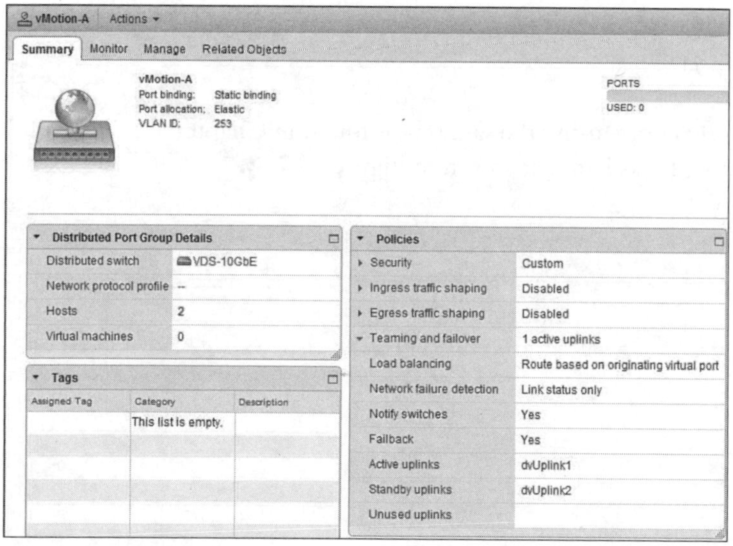

Figure 19.6   The vMotion-A port group configuration summary

Now we need to build out the vMotion VMkernel ports.

VMkernel Ports

You need a unique vMotion VMkernel port for each network adapter you want vMotion to utilize. Because we're using two network adapters for multi-NIC vMotion, we need two VMkernel ports and two unique IP addresses.

Both of the VMkernel ports need to use the vMotion network—which is 10.0.253.0 /24—without conflicting with another IP on the network. We also strongly advise using a single Layer 2 network for all vMotion VMkernel ports because you have no control over which VMkernel port on the source host talks to any particular VMkernel port on the destination host. One easy way to avoid IP conflicts is to slice up the subnet into vMotion A and B addresses; for example:

- The vMotion-A portion of the subnet will be 10.0.253.50 through 10.0.253.99.

- The vMotion-B portion of the subnet will be 10.0.253.150 through 10.0.253.199.

You are free to slice up your network however you wish, but we find it pleasing to have IP addresses that end with similar digits (such as 50 and 150). For the first host we're going to configure, called esx1, we'll use:

- **vMotion-A**: 10.0.253.51

- **vMotion-B**: 10.0.253.151

Create the vMotion VMkernel ports using the same steps found in Chapter 13. The end result is a VMkernel port that looks like that shown in Figure 19.7.

```
Virtual network adapter: vmk1

 All   Properties   IP Settings   Policies

 Port properties
   Network label                 vMotion-A
   Enabled services              vMotion traffic
 IPv4 settings
   IPv4 address                  10.0.253.51 (static)
   Subnet mask                   255.255.255.0
   Default gateway for IPv4      10.0.0.201
   DNS server addresses          10.0.0.4
 IPv6 settings
   IPv6 addresses                fe80::250:56ff:fe64:5f92/64
   Default gateway for IPv6:     --
 NIC settings
   MAC address                   00:50:56:64:5f:92
```

Figure 19.7   The vMotion-A VMkernel port configuration summary

Repeat this section for all other hosts that need to participate in multi-NIC vMotion. Congratulations, you now have an environment configured to use multiple network adapters during a vMotion. If absolutely necessary, you can mix hosts configured for multi-NIC vMotion with hosts that only have a single vMotion NIC—and it will work—but it sort of defeats the purpose. We'd only really suggest doing this if you're migrating to a new environment or have some corner case that requires it.

To verify that both network adapters are participating in vMotion, migrate a VM from one host to another and then check the "Maximum" network performance statistics on either the source or destination host for both vmnics, as shown in Figure 19.8.

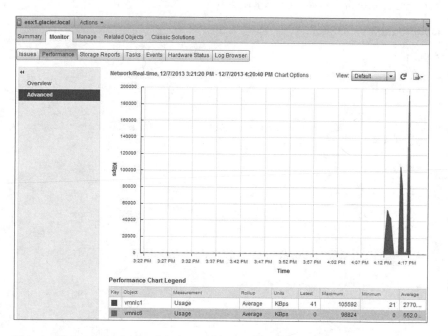

Figure 19.8   A stacked network statistics graph showing both vmnic1 and vmnic6 sending traffic

Both vmnic1 and vmni6, the two dvUplinks we chose to use for vMotion, show the correct amount of maximum network activity simultaneously in the third network spike, which peaks at 20 Gbps. It's a bit easy to see this in a controlled environment with no other significant workloads using the adapters and is mainly here to demonstrate a point and give you the warm and fuzzies.

Traffic Shaping

As a final, optional step, we'll configure traffic shaping for the two vMotion port groups. Because earlier examples focused on using an 8 Gbps limit, we'll configure that here. But again, this is an optional step to help solve a corner case where multiple vSphere hosts are sending vMotion traffic to a single destination host. If your environment has little risk of encountering this scenario, you can skip this configuration item.

On each of the two vMotion port groups, edit the policy settings and configure egress traffic shaping as follows:

- **Status**: Enabled
- **Average bandwidth (kbit/s)**: 8388608 (multiply 8 Gbit/s by 1024 to convert to Mbit/s, then by 1024 again to convert to Kbit/s))
- **Peak bandwidth (kbit/s)**: 8388608
- **Burst size (KB)**: 1

The results are shown in Figure 19.9.

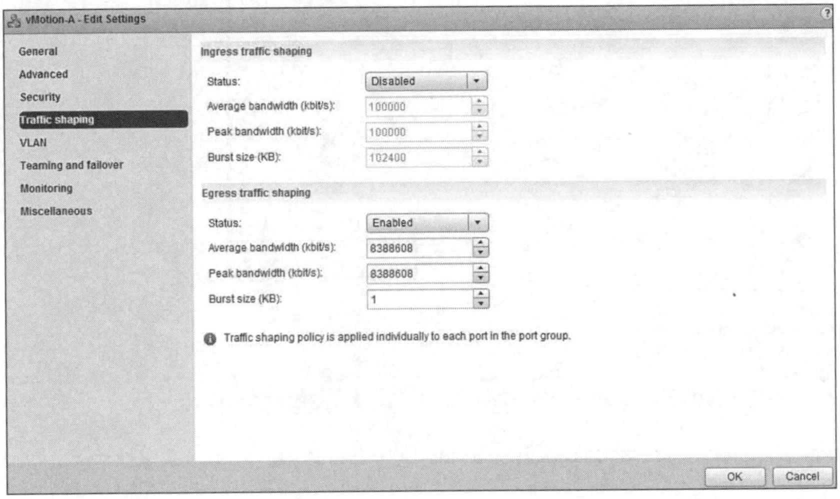

Figure 19.9   Egress traffic shaping configuration for the vMotion port group

Summary

vMotion is a superb technology that many businesses rely on for meeting workload resource needs, maintenance activities, and data center migrations. Occasionally, a single uplink no longer satisfies the requirements for a design, which evolved into the necessity to use multiple uplinks. In this chapter, we explored the use cases for multi-NIC vMotion and offered some considerations that should be made before implementing this feature. We then walked through an example configuration and verification.

Networking for VMware Administrators: The VMware User Group

The VMware User Group

We wanted to leave you with one last plug, and we're suckers for a good pun. After the wide array of quality titles from VMware Press, the next best way to learn more and stay on top of new VMware-related developments is to engage with the VMware community. The VMware User Group (VMUG) is a great way to get involved. Consisting of a global steering committee and local chapters, VMUG offers local groups, user conferences, special interest groups, and eLearning opportunities, all built on the idea of getting VMware users together and allowing them to trade experiences and learn from each other. It's free to join and worth every penny. You can get more information (and join) at www.vmug.com.

Index

host design, 137-138
iSCSI, 233-239. *See also* iSCSI; network
  design
lab scenario, 139-143
network design, 136-137
NFS, 276-283. *See also* NFS; network
  design
ARP (Address Resolution Protocol), 13, 51
ARPANET, 8
attenuation, 24
authentication, CHAP, 227-229, 261-263
available bandwidth, verifying, 313-314
average bandwidth, 80

B

backup ports (RSTP), 36
bandwidth, verifying availability, 313-314
beacon probing, 84-85
best effort protocols, 220, 270
BladeSystem, 57-59
BLK (Blocked Port) switch ports, 34
blocking state (ports), 34
booting from iSCSI, 239-241
BPDUs (Bridge Protocol Data Units), 33
bridge IDs, 33
Bridge Protocol Data Units (BPDUs), 33
broadcast addresses, 23
broadcast domains, 25
broadcast storms, 32
burst size, 80

C

cables, Ethernet, 19-21
CAM (Content Addressable Memory), 25
Carrier Sense Multiple Access with Collision
  Detection (CSMA/CD), 19
CDP (Cisco Discovery Protocol), 79, 97
  changing to Both mode, 214-215
CHAP (Challenge Handshake Authentication
  Protocol), 227-229, 261-263
CIDR (Classless Inter-Domain Routing), 48-49
Cisco Discovery Protocol (CDP), 79, 97
  changing to Both mode, 214-215
Cisco Nexus 1000V, 121-122
  architecture, 123
    advantages, 132

VEM (virtual Ethernet module), 128-132
VSM (virtual supervisor module), 124-126
licensing, 132-134
port profiles, 126-128
vSphere integration, 122-123
Cisco UCS (Unified Computing System), 55-57
classful addressing, 48
Classless Inter-Domain Routing (CIDR), 48-49
clusters, comparison with distributed vSwitches,
  94
CNAs (Converged Network Adapters), 233
collision domains, 24
collisions, 18-19
  avoiding with switches, 25
  on hubs, 24
communication, importance of, 245
community VLANs, 107-108
configuring
  distributed port groups for VMkernel ports,
    190-197
  distributed vSwitches
    discovery protocol settings, 214-215
    Health Check feature, 212-214
    LBT (load based teaming), 188-190
    network adapters, 185
    port groups, 186-188
  multi-NIC vMotion, 318
    distributed port groups, 318-319
    traffic shaping, 321-322
    VMkernel ports, 320-321
  network adapters, NFS, 290-291
  standard vSwitches
    failover order, 156-157
    iSCSI distributed port groups, 247-250
    iSCSI jumbo frames, 256-258
    iSCSI network port binding, 254-256
    iSCSI VMkernel ports, 250-253
    multiple hosts, 173
    network adapters, 151-152
    NFS, 288-290
    port groups, 153-156
    security settings, 172
  VMkernel ports, 158
    failover order, 170-171
    Fault Tolerance port, 166-167
    Management port, 158-161
    NFS, 291-294
    NFS Storage port, 168-169
    vMotion port, 161-165